HOSEA BALLOU

The Challenge
to Orthodoxy

Ernest Cassara

UNIVERSITY
PRESS OF
AMERICA

He went through the land proclaiming this great truth, and he has wrought a revolution in the thoughts and minds of men more mighty than any which has been accomplished during the same time by all the politicians of the nation.

—*Theodore Parker*

To Beverly

PREFACE

Hosea Ballou (1771-1852) was one of the most influential figures in American religious life of the nineteenth century. A convert from the Calvinistic Baptists, he was to become an outstanding leader of the forces which strove to overturn the orthodox theories of the atonement of Christ and to humanize man's thought of God. His conception of the Deity as a loving Father Who will save all His children did much to undermine the Calvinistic theory of the salvation of an elect few and to mitigate the harsher features of the religion of Americans of the early nineteenth century. He was himself a man of the common people, of meager formal education; and his pungent, argumentative writings and vigorous preaching were responsible for a great upsurge of liberalism among the lower classes, which were mostly untouched by the more literate liberalism of the day.

Outside the Universalist denomination, Hosea Ballou today is practically unknown. No biography of him has been published since 1889. Instead, historians of this period of American life have focused attention on William Ellery Channing, Ralph Waldo Emerson, Theodore Parker and the other Boston Unitarians among the literati who made such a remarkable contribution to what Van Wyck Brooks has called "the flowering of New England." As a result, the great liberal stirring among the humbler people which manifested itself in the rise of Universalism has been ignored.

The present work is designed to fill this very serious gap in our understanding of the religious and intellectual history of the early years of the United States. The biography and thought of Hosea Ballou are treated genetically and set in the context of the denominational and intellectual history of the day. I have attempted to put in perspective those events and experiences which played an important part in shaping Ballou's character and (what has never been done before) to discover the sources of his religious thought. The major facets of his thought as found in his many writings are examined, with emphasis on the significance of his theology in the life of his own denomination and in the rise of American religious liberalism.

ERNEST CASSARA

CONTENTS

CHAPTER I

RICHMOND, 1770

Nestled among the hills of the little town of Richmond, New Hampshire, near the Massachusetts border, is the beautiful valley still known to some as Ballou's Dell. Here, within sound of the gushing of several refreshing springs, Elder Maturin Ballou built the log cabin which was to be the home of his large family. With his young sons at his side, he struggled to make the stony soil produce enough to insure, at best, a bare existence.

Maturin and his wife, Lydia, who was big with her tenth child, had come to Richmond probably in the spring of 1768. The preceding October, Maturin had purchased eighty acres of un-cleared land for fifteen pounds.[1] It was an abrupt change—from the civilization of Rhode Island to the wilderness of Cheshire County, New Hampshire. But the new life was well worth the price paid in toil, for Maturin was doing the Lord's work. A Baptist preacher, he had come to minister to a growing community of fellow believers.

Maturin Ballou had been born in Providence on October 30, 1722.[2] His great-great-grandfather, the first Ballou in America, was among the co-proprietors with Roger Williams in Rhode Island in 1646.[3] This Mathurin Bellow (for so he spelled his name) was apparently descended from the Normans who crossed over to Eng-land with William the Conqueror.[4] Thus the blood was originally French.

Maturin Ballou was a turner by trade, and, according to tradi-tion, he for a time manufactured spinning wheels.[5] He began his preaching in Smithfield (later Lincoln), Rhode Island, in 1752. Like most Baptist ministers of the day, he probably had no theologi-cal education.[6] Such education was considered unnecessary; the important thing was to have the Spirit speak to you through the Scriptures. Nor did Maturin ever accept money for his ministra-tions.[7] The Baptist preachers of the day earned their daily bread with their hands.

Maturin and Lydia were married in Smithfield in 1744.[8] She

was born on February 6, 1725,[9] in Providence, the daughter of
Richard Harris, a Quaker whose forebears had come to the colonies
seeking asylum in the time of Charles and Laud.[10] Aside from
these details, little is known of Lydia Harris Ballou.

Maturin and Lydia lived the first twenty-four years of their
married life in various towns in Rhode Island, laboring, ministering
and raising a large family. Nine of their eleven children were
born to them in these years, and at least one of them died. Amey
lived just six years, dying in 1756.[11]

When the Ballous moved to Richmond in 1768, they brought
with them Mary, Lydia, Maturin Junior, David, Nathan, Sarah
and their sickly three-year-old Phebe. Stephen was born to them
that September. Benjamin, now a young man of twenty-one, stayed
behind in Scituate, Rhode Island,[12] anxious to strike out on his own.
So the burden of clearing land, building the cabin and tilling the
soil fell on the shoulders of Maturin, Senior, with the help of young
Maturin, who was thirteen; David, ten; and Nathan, eight. No
wonder that it was at best a meager existence that the farmer-
preacher could wring from the uncooperative soil.

But the Ballous were not without friends in their new wilderness home. Lydia had two brothers there, Anthony and Uriah
Harris, and two sisters, Mrs. Sweet and Mrs. Phillips.[13] They probably were the determining factor in bringing the Ballous to Richmond. The Harris, Phillips and Sweet families were among the first
settlers of the town. The township's charter had been granted in
1752, but not till ten years later did the real movement of population to the area begin.[14] When the first town meeting was held in
1765, Uriah and Anthony Harris, Israel Phillips and Jonathan
Sweet were among the qualified voters.[15]

It was a promising area that these families had come to. When
the first census was taken in 1773, Richmond was found to be
second in population in the county, with 745 residents.[16] By the
late eighteenth century its population had risen to almost fourteen
hundred.[17] It was probably with great expectation that Maturin and
Lydia Ballou threw in their lot with these pioneers.

The people of Richmond were no doubt happy to have this
preacher as their own. For they were of a very serious type: Baptists
and Quakers. (These two sects were to predominate for the first
seventy years of the town's history.[18]) With their new preacher

among them, the Baptists were able to form their church in 1768. Not for twelve more years were they strong enough to put up a meetinghouse,[19] but meetinghouses were not important to these simple people. They met in the homes of their leaders: when not at Maturin's place, they would gather at the homesteads of Elder Artemus Aldrich and Deacon Simon Thayer.[20]

Maturin Ballou was their kind of man. He was plain-spoken, like themselves. His sermons were earnest and only occasionally eloquent.[21] But it was as a man that they probably liked him best: his unostentatious manner, which bordered on meekness, and above all his forgiving spirit earned him high respect and influence.[22] Maturin took his Calvinism seriously. He was, on occasion, light-hearted and would tell a good story or a joke—but he would soon sigh and repent his indulgence of this part of his nature.[23]

Despite the poverty and trials of this pioneer existence, life held much happiness for Maturin and Lydia. The autumn of 1770 was especially joyful, for Lydia could tell her husband that again the Lord had smiled on them and that she was with child.

September held another happiness for the Ballous. The Baptist community now officially set aside Elder Maturin Ballou as its minister. On September 27, in one of the most solemn moments of his life, Maturin was ordained a preacher of the gospel of Christ and a minister to his people.[24] It was a proud and happy father who was thus enabled, the following month, to perform the marriage ceremony of his daughter Mary, the first to marry and the first to make him a grandfather.

Mary was the Ballous' oldest child, born in the first year of their marriage. Now, at what was no doubt considered the "advanced" age of twenty-five, she was to leave her parents' home. Her spouse was David Bullock of Rehoboth, Massachusetts, whom she had met and loved before her family made its trek to the wilderness. David had purchased a farm in Richmond and planned to settle there. So Maturin, in his own home, on October 20, gave the couple the blessing of church and state.[25]

CHAPTER II

THE EARLY YEARS

In the spring, a son was born to Lydia Ballou. She and Maturin turned to the pages of God's Word for a name, and their choice was prophetic.

Hosea Ballou was born on April 30, 1771,[1] the last of eleven children. The home into which he came had little wealth. In his first three years in Richmond, the lot of Maturin Ballou had not much improved. Since he spent much of his time in the duties of his ministry—without pay—and since he had nothing but the land, his family was in great need. His children went without the most common necessities; it is said that little Hosea often was without underclothes, shoes and stockings, even in the coldest of winters.[2] But the Ballou children probably were unaware of their plight, for it was a home of love.

Hosea was not to remember his mother's tender affection, for when he was twenty months old, Lydia Ballou died.[3] There is no record of what took her life just short of her forty-sixth year. Hosea was too young to appreciate his family's sorrow as the body of his mother was laid to rest in the hillside cemetery not far from their home. On the newly covered grave was placed a small, crude stone, engraved with the letters L. B. In later years he was to say: "The Treasure was gone before I could realize its value." [4]

It is not good for man to be alone; and within a year Maturin took to himself another Lydia. Little is known of Lydia Bliss of Attleboro, Massachusetts, except that she was married to Maturin Ballou on September 15, 1774.[5] It is believed that she died in 1790 or 1791.[6] Maturin needed this helpmate, for his daughter Lydia, now twenty, had married Samuel Moses a short time after her mother's death[7] and had gone off to Warwick, Massachusetts,[8] to live near the new home of her sister Mary.[9] Nine-year-old Sarah and seven-year-old Phebe were the only girls now at home to cook and keep house.

Although Hosea did have a stepmother, Maturin Ballou acted

as father and mother to the young child. Hosea himself never referred to the influence of his stepmother. The boy formed a deep attachment for his father; and it is probable that his later thought of God as a heavenly Father, capable of both love and chastisement because He truly loves His children, was not a little influenced by his earthly father.

How I used to cherish a kind word from my father, when I was a boy! He was in some respects an austere man; and when I was born, being the youngest of our large family, he had got to be advanced in years, and looked with a more serious and practical eye on the events of life and all things about us. He was Puritanic, strictly religious, as he interpreted the meaning of that word, and his mind was ever engrossed upon serious matters. But when he put his hand sometimes upon my head, and told me I had done well, that the labor I had performed might have been more poorly done by older hands, or that I was a good and faithful boy, my heart was electrified beyond measure; and I remember his words and smile, even now, with delight.[10]

Hosea's earliest years were lived in unsettled times, both in state and church. He was barely five when the Revolution broke out. Being distant from the seacoast, Richmond was never really in danger from British troops, but the men of his town still did their part. Several joined the regiment recruited among the Massachusetts towns of Worcester County and fought in the battle of Bunker Hill.[11]

Agitation did not cease with the end of the war. In the late '70s and early '80s, sentiment in the Cheshire County area was very strong in favor of seceding from New Hampshire and becoming a part of the newly formed state of Vermont.[12] Richmond went so far as to vote such action in the March town meeting of 1781.[13] Long after the plans for secession had been frustrated, feeling ran high in the area.[14] It was probably in these years that young Hosea first heard the name and exploits of a Green Mountain warrior by the name of Ethan Allen. Hosea did not then know how greatly his life was to be changed by the thoughts of "Gen'r'l" Allen.

Of more immediacy to the Ballous was the agitation in 1776 among Baptists in Richmond over their minister's legal rights. The royal charter of the town had called for the setting aside of certain tracts of land to be used to support ecclesiastical activities. One section of this glebe land was reserved for the Episcopal church, one for the Society to Propagate the Gospel in Foreign Parts and one for the first settled minister of the town. Maturin Ballou was that

first settled minister, and, by right, the land belonged to him. But
the opposition of the non-Baptist residents was vigorous, and self-
effacing Maturin deeded his share of glebe land to the town of
Richmond.[15] During the course of this controversy, the Baptists in
town were split asunder. Some, less meek than their minister, held
out for his right to the land; others appear to have sided with the
opposition. The practical result of this division of feeling was a
division in the church. A number followed the lead of Elder
Artemus Aldrich and formed a second society of Baptists.[16] This
schism lasted for about thirteen years.

Maturin Ballou's thoughts regarding this break in Baptist ranks
are not known, but his position was surely not a happy one. Three
years later, after a ministry of eleven years, he asked to be dismissed
as pastor of his flock.[17] He was then only fifty-seven years old, so
that age could not have been the determining factor. His resignation was accepted, but he did not give up preaching. It is said that
he spent the remainder of his life preaching in the neighboring
towns.[18]

The effect of this schism on young Hosea can only be surmised,
but he very likely had the disillusionment of this event in mind
when he later wrote:

I have often seen, in the same churches, persons at such variance,
about matters of their religion, that truth seemed not to be regarded, in
the least, on either side; each would strive to *crush his brother,* until
two parties were formed, and a whole town set in an uproar.[19]

Hosea had his first conscious experience with death when the
news came, in January 1778, that his sister Mary had died in
Warwick.[20] In January 1781, his brother David took a wife, their
cousin Mercy Harris.[21] And he was again in his Sabbath best when
his father married Sarah Ballou to Moses Wheaton the following
October.[22]

Hosea's "formal" education proceeded along the usual lines of
a pioneer community. The learning he gained was with his father's
help, for there was no school. The family library was not large; it
consisted of only three volumes. Of course, the Bible was the
family's prize possession. Hosea pored over its pages, teaching
himself new words and thrilling to its tales of adventure. Also useful was an old dictionary of pre-Johnsonian vintage. The library

was completed by "a well-thumbed pamphlet of the scriptural story
of the tower of Babel." [23]

Paper, pen and ink were luxuries not to be afforded. Instead,
Hosea stripped pieces of birch bark to serve as paper; coals from the
fire served as pencils. With these implements he would lie before
the fire at night, laboriously learning to write. By the time he was
sixteen, he had taught himself to read and write with a fair amount
of ease.[24]

There were chores to do, but Hosea had much time to roam
the surrounding hills. Ballou's Dell is a place of natural beauty;
beholding it today, it is easy to see how Hosea Ballou came by the
love of nature which is mirrored in many of his writings.
Fortunately the Ballou farm stands, with the exception of the
original house, much as it did in Hosea's day. It is one of the comparatively few farms in the area which were not abandoned as the
tide of migration swept many Richmondites west. One can still see
the green dell and the sudden rise of the surrounding hills as they
looked to the youth's eyes; and the cool, clear springs still run,
which were the source of much of his joy.

Hosea was over six feet tall when he reached his full growth.
He stood straight and had a ruddy face, dark hair and sparkling
blue eyes.[25] The work he did on the farm no doubt helped maintain his good health. He lived the outdoor life; and in later days,
when circumstances demanded that he spend much time in the
study, he still insisted that physical exertion out of doors is absolutely
necessary for physical well-being.

Among the boys of the neighborhood, Hosea demonstrated
early his natural talent for leadership. He excelled in the sports of
the country town of that day. He was a good runner and a skilled
wrestler, and he showed his brawn in the popular sport of "pitching
the bar" (that is, hurling a crowbar javelin style).[26] His friends
soon learned to trust his leadership in other ways. By nature
straightforward and completely open, he was often called upon to
fill the role of umpire in disputes on the field of sport.[27]

Important as these things are to a boy, Hosea's mind was often
on more weighty matters: sin and salvation. Maturin was deeply
concerned for the spiritual well-being of his children. He prayed
often for their conversion to the ways of God, calling them by name
in the family prayers.[28] His children were guilty of no particular

evil, but, according to his Calvinistic outlook, this did not guarantee them a place on God's roll of the elect.[29] For this election he prayed mightily. Furthermore, he was careful that they learn well the religious tenets of his denomination.

Hosea was well instructed in the doctrines of Calvinism at an early age.[30] He was taught that he, like all men, had inherited the sin of the first parents of the race and had thus come into the world totally depraved. Because of this inheritance, the greater part of men were doomed to eternal misery after death. For an elect portion of mankind, however, things would be different, for God had provided a way in which they would be saved. These fortunate ones, sometime during their lives, would feel the working of the Holy Spirit upon them: it would manifest itself in the ecstatic experience of conversion. But this experience would come to very few; it was the belief of the Baptists who surrounded Hosea that "not more than one in a thousand" would be chosen.[31]

Along with this central belief, he learned all the theological jargon of the day, for theology was then the concern of the average layman.

. . . I was well acquainted with the most common arguments which were used in support of predestination, election, reprobation, the fall of man, the penal sufferings of Christ for the elect, the justice of reprobation, and many other particulars, such as regard the moral agency of man and his inability to regenerate himself, the sovereignty and irresistability of regenerating grace, &c., &c.[32]

Yet Hosea had a very inquisitive mind; he did not accept these beliefs without question. He was particularly absorbed by the problem of free will and necessity.

This trait of independence, which was to predominate in his intellectual development, was seen early in his youth—perhaps most clearly in the radical questionings which made his father somewhat uncomfortable. One day his theological precocity caught his father completely off guard. He asked Maturin: "Suppose I had the skill and power out of an inanimate substance to make an animate, and should make one, at the same time knowing that this creature of mine would suffer everlasting misery,—would my act of creating this creature be an act of goodness?"

Maturin was visibly shaken by his young boy's question. He did not reply.[33] Hosea would have to find his own answer.

CHAPTER III

THE GREAT REFORMATION

To the south of Richmond, over the boundary line between New Hampshire and Massachusetts, is the town of Warwick. To Warwick in 1771 came Caleb Rich, a dreamer of dreams and a seer of visions. He had been born in Sutton, Massachusetts, in 1750, the son of Congregationalist parents. When Caleb was a boy, however, his father had been converted by the Baptists. The fact that his mother remained Congregationalist appears to have started him thinking about religion. He turned the pages of the Bible, hoping to find the truth.[1]

Caleb Rich appears to have been a mystic capable of great emotion. Although he affiliated with the Baptists when he moved to his farm in Warwick, through a series of dreams and visions he came to a belief in universal salvation.[2]

The idea of universalism—that all men will be saved, and not only the elect—was not new in the history of Christianity. It had emerged briefly here and there in the church from the earliest times, the most notable exponent being Origen of Alexandria, the great third-century scholar and teacher. On the whole, however, universalism was rejected as contrary to the established belief in ever-lasting punishment for some of the human race. It was, in short, heretical.

In the eighteenth century, however, with the coming of the Enlightenment, the way was prepared for an amelioration of the harsher doctrines of Christianity. A more optimistic view of the nature of the Deity and of the possibilities for man, both in this world and in the next, emerged in various parts of the church. The climate was now favorable for a reappearance of universalism.

Universalist ideas were first brought to the American colonies by various pietistic and mystical groups, such as the German Dunkers and the Schwenkfelders who settled in the liberal atmosphere of Pennsylvania. With these people universalism was incidental to other religious beliefs. Living among them, however, was Dr. George De Benneville, a physician and Universalist preacher, who came to America in 1741. Although De Benneville organized no churches, his preaching and publishing activities were credited with converting many persons to universalist views.

Universalism as a movement is dated from the landing of the Englishman John Murray on the New Jersey shore in 1770. A restless, active spirit, he traveled widely through the colonies preaching the message that all men will be saved. The orthodox clergy and many of their followers were convinced that Murray's doctrine was of the devil. Opposition to his activities arose wherever he went, and it often took violent forms.

Caleb Rich, however, apparently came to his belief in universal salvation independently of Murray's activities. Universalism was "in the air." With the rise of the democratic spirit in the era of the Revolution, it is not surprising that the Calvinistic belief in the election of some men to everlasting life and the condemnation of others to everlasting hell-fire for no apparent reason should be challenged. Universalist sentiments arose naturally among men who could not accept an aristocracy of the spirit any more than they could accept a political aristocracy.

In the spring of 1778, Rich began to preach in Warwick, and he soon extended his activities across the border into Richmond and Jaffrey.[3] As he won adherents to the cause, he found himself minister to a new church—the "General Society"—consisting of believers in Warwick, Richmond and Jaffrey.[4] A few years after its formation, the group decided that Rich should be ordained. The ordination took place at Richmond and was a big occasion for the town, with over three hundred persons attending.[5] The date of the ordination is not certain, but it was probably in the early 1780s, when Hosea was ten or twelve years old. He may have been present on that gala occasion; if not, he was certainly aware of it.

Universalism did not come to Richmond without opposition. The new doctrine was despised wherever it was introduced, for it seemed to undercut the very basis of religion and morality. To preach that all men would be saved was to deny the core of Calvinism, its tenets of election and reprobation. Furthermore, what was to keep people on the straight and narrow path if the fear of hell were taken away? It was certain—and Hosea heard this repeated with authority many times—that a person who believed in universal salvation would be guilty of the lowest sort of vileness.

He would lie, cheat, indulge in dissipation and commit every possible sin. He would not hesitate to steal—and even to murder! The lives of everyone around him, including his own family, would be in peril.[6]

Hosea heard and believed these charges made against Universalists.[7] It must have been a very great shock when he learned that Caleb Rich had found friends in a Ballou household. One of Maturin's distant cousins, James Ballou, and his sons, James, Jr., and Silas, had been converted to the new heresy! [8] Worse, they were outspoken in their advocacy of Universalism. James Ballou and Caleb Rich would often attend the Baptist meeting and, when the meeting was over, debate their new-found doctrines. Now that relatives had accepted the new doctrine, it was more difficult than ever for Hosea, driven by intellectual curiosity, to resist contact with it.

In his middle teens, Hosea spent several summers away from home, working on his relatives' farms.[9] His oldest brother, Benjamin, for example, was now living in Guilford, Vermont, farming and preaching the Baptist faith. Hosea enjoyed his visits to Guilford, for he and Benjamin's son Asahel (who was, of course, actually Hosea's nephew) got along like brothers. They were the same age and, Hosea said later, could not have been closer had they been twins.[10]

Another summer was spent at Putney, Vermont, where Maturin, Junior, was farming and preaching. Maturin was a very devout Baptist. He never married and was probably very happy to have company during the summer.

Things changed at home in these years. Hosea's sister Phebe, who had never been well, died in young womanhood. His brother Nathan married Mary Holbrook[11] but stayed on the farm to take care of Maturin, Senior, in his declining years.

The year 1789 was one of the most important years in Hosea's life. For some time, probably under the influence of the new universalist ideas, he had been troubled by the Calvinistic doctrine of eternal reprobation. How could God be good if He consigned most of His children to everlasting misery? Hosea's thoughts along this line had not yet led him to renounce the faith of his childhood, but Caleb Rich and James Ballou and his sons were giving him little rest. Hosea had a knack for debating and spent many hours in trying to meet their arguments. His own arguments, however, led him to either of two conclusions: either God will save all men, or else He is partial. This dilemma gave Hosea no rest, for he was not satisfied to hold a position he could not defend.[12]

In January 1789, two Baptist evangelists named Blaisdell and Marshall came to Richmond.[13] Under the heat of their preaching, the Baptists of the town, who had been split for thirteen years, were welded together. The revival, which became known in Richmond history as the Great Reformation, was responsible for the conversion of over one hundred persons,[14] including nineteen-year-old Hosea Ballou.[15] He and his young friends were swept by the excitement right into church membership.[16] In mid-winter they were immersed in ice-cold water[17] and so became professing Baptists.

If Hosea thought that his baptism and profession of faith would quiet his troubled mind, he was wrong. He continued to be pressed by doubts:

> I was much troubled in my mind because I thought I did not stand in such fear of the divine wrath as I ought to do, or as others had done before they found acceptance with God. I well remember that as I was returning home from a conference meeting, one evening, when about a quarter of a mile from home, being alone, I stopped under a large tree, and, falling on my knees, prayed as well as I could for the favor I sought.[18]

But peace of mind was not to be his until he could reconcile his faith in the goodness of God with the doctrine of eternal reprobation. He could not believe that God would place in his heart the desire that all men be saved if such a thing were not possible.[19]

The six months after Hosea's "conversion" were apparently the determining period in the development of his thought. He applied himself to reading the Bible, grasping every text which might possibly favor the universalist position. It is doubtful whether any universalist literature was then available to him, but the story is told that his father once found him reading a book tainted with the heresy. Maturin informed his son that he would not tolerate such stuff in his house. Hosea bowed to his father's authority. A few days later, however, Maturin found Hosea reading beside the woodpile.

"What book are you reading there?" asked the old man.

"A universalist book," was the answer, given in a respectful tone.

Maturin grumbled his discontent and headed back to the house. From there he watched his son place the book on the woodpile and leave. When the lad was out of sight, he headed straight for the woodpile, probably with the intention of destroying the dangerous book. When he picked it up, he found it was the Bible.[20]

That spring Hosea traveled to New York with his brother Stephen to spend the summer working on a farm at Westfield (later Hartford).[21] After each long day's work was done, Hosea spent the evening studying the Bible, seeking the answer to his problem: could the Universalists be right? Turning the pages, he would now and again run across a text which might be used to substantiate their claims. A passage such as Romans 5:18 was particularly striking: "Therefore as by the offence of one judgment came upon all men to condemnation; even so by the righteousness of one the free gift came upon all men unto justification of life." The "free gift" of justification was given not to just a few, an elect, but to all men —or so this passage seemed to say. How could this be explained by the orthodox?

Stephen and Hosea attended the Baptist meetings in Westfield and sat under the preaching of one Elder Brown. Apprehensive that Hosea was being misled into the errors of universalism, Stephen arranged for a discussion with the good elder after a Sabbath meeting, hoping that Brown could show Hosea that the Universalists were preaching false doctrine. Hosea, he hoped, would then settle down in his newly professed faith.

With a very confident air Elder Brown seated himself and asked Hosea to produce from the Bible just one text which seemed to him to favor the dangerous error of universal salvation, so that he could demonstrate that the young man was misinterpreting the Sacred Writ. Hosea directed the elder to Romans 5:18 and confessed that he found it impossible to reconcile Paul's words with the Calvinistic doctrine of eternal reprobation. If Paul said all men would be justified as a free gift, how could the endless misery of any human being be true?

Elder Brown immediately began to speak in a very loud voice, but he was not answering the question. When he stopped, Hosea observed that what he had said had nothing to do with the question. He pointed out that the "all men" who were condemned in the first part of the text were the same "all men" who were given justification as a free gift in the second part. Elder Brown became confused and flustered, obviously angered by the young man's correction. He showed so much heat that those present found it discreet to end the "conference."

Stephen was very upset by this incident. He was sorry he had even suggested such a meeting and told Hosea, "As he could by no means answer you, and as he manifested anger, you will think you had the best of the argument, and will feel encouraged to indulge favorable thoughts of Universalism." [22]

Hosea continued to read his Bible and continued to ask questions of those who opposed the heretical doctrine;[23] by thus defending Universalism against its opponents, he probably hastened his own conversion. By the time he returned home in the fall, he was thoroughly convinced of the truth of universal salvation.[24] The year which had begun with his baptism and acceptance of the Baptist faith ended with his departure from that faith and his acceptance of the despised gospel of Universalism.[25]

If Hosea expected an unfriendly reaction from his family, he must have been pleasantly surprised. The edge had been taken off his announcement, for during the summer his older brother David had also seen the light, most likely under the influence of Caleb Rich. By the time Hosea returned home, David was already preaching the new gospel. But the unity of the Ballou family was not broken by these conversions. Whatever Maturin Ballou thought of Universalism, he loved his sons nonetheless. The brothers and sisters were as close as they had ever been.[26]

The attitude of Hosea's neighbors was somewhat different. His fellow church members strove mightily to save him from the terrible abyss. But the debates, as might be expected, only helped to further his acceptance of the dangerous doctrine.[27] Having failed to persuade, the church then took stern action. Fearing that Hosea, with his great influence among the youth of the town, would lead many of them astray, the Baptist church of Richmond officially excommunicated him. It served him with a copy of its action, which stated that no fault was to be found with him except that he believed that God would save all men.[28] Thus the heretic was cut off from the body of the elect.[29]

The previous spring, Mercy Ballou had died,[30] leaving David with three young children to care for. Hosea, therefore, on his return from New York, left his father's home and settled in with David on his farm. This sojourn, which lasted two years, helped confirm both men in their new-found faith. Hosea no doubt learned much from his brother, who was thirteen years older than himself.

David, like Hosea, was a meditative, philosophical person,[31] not prone to accept an idea without thorough examination. He was particularly adept at the Socratic method, though he probably had never heard the term.

Alas for the opposer who once began to answer the simple and easy questions; while he yet could discover no dilemma towards which they were carrying him, he suddenly found himself fast enclosed, helpless, bound tight with his own chain.[32]

CHAPTER IV

THE WRITTEN JEHOVAH

It is readily understandable that Hosea decided to devote his life to preaching the gospel. His father had spent most of his life expounding Holy Writ, and three brothers, one by one, had taken up the cause. Benjamin, the oldest, although primarily a farmer, was preaching the Baptist faith. (Hosea eventually converted him.[1]) The pious Maturin, Junior, preached Baptism until late in 1790, when Hosea was just beginning his preaching career. (He died on November 28, 1790, at the age of only thirty-five.[2]) And David was now preaching the gospel of universal salvation. Add to these the probable influence of Caleb Rich and James Ballou, and it is not difficult to see that Hosea had incentive for his choice. He also had ability: if his later writings are a fair criterion, he was adept at the art of debate—so necessary in that day of theological combat—and was gifted with powerful logic.

However, he had had no schooling. With his father's help, Hosea had learned to read and write, but he still had little understanding of English grammar. He must have recognized the handicap, for he soon took measures to overcome it. The Friends of Richmond had for some time been conducting a private school at various places in the town. In 1790 they built a meetinghouse[3] and moved the school there.[4] Hosea, now in his nineteenth or twentieth year, attended the school with several of his young friends. With great determination he began to make up for lost time. He studied night and day, taking little food and getting little sleep.[5]

Yet he was not satisfied with this, at best, elementary education. With the money he had earned working away from home during the past few summers, he enrolled at the academy then being conducted in Chesterfield, on the Connecticut River boundary between New Hampshire and Vermont. Here he received what he considered excellent instruction. He again found it necessary to study night and day to keep up with those who had the educational background he lacked.[6]

This experience was invaluable. For the first time in his life,

Hosea was in an atmosphere of culture, with an opportunity to gain a real appreciation of the power of education.[7] Professor Logan, principal of the academy, took a particular interest in the rough-appearing but obviously intelligent and eager young man. He was pleased to watch the progress Hosea made despite his lack of educational background. When Hosea left the academy, Principal Logan awarded him a certificate which enabled him, a little later, to set himself up as a schoolmaster.[8]

This was the end of Hosea's formal education. Though rich in native intelligence, he was always to suffer from the lack of a good, thorough educational background. His accomplishments were to be made in spite of this deficiency.

Hosea's immediate concern was to preach, but his first attempt was painful and discouraging. In the fall of 1791[9] he made his first appearance in his new role at the home of old Baptist Deacon Simon Thayer, who was now professing the new faith. Both David Ballou and Caleb Rich were present, but this only added to Hosea's discomfort. As he stood before his friends and prepared to begin his discourse, his face was flushed, his throat dry and his knees unsteady. He could feel the perspiration covering his brow and beginning to roll down his cheeks. With difficulty he announced his text, I Corinthians 1:30, and began to read: "But of him are ye in Christ Jesus, who of God is made unto us wisdom, and righteousness, and sanctification, and redemption." Then he looked up to begin the sermon—but nothing else came. He could not get the words out.

Hosea's failure was so terrible that his brother David and Caleb Rich began to doubt that he would ever make the grade.[10] But he was determined not to end his preaching career on such an ignominious note. He must give himself another chance.

A short time later he accompanied David to Brattleboro, Vermont, where his brother had a Sabbath engagement.[11] David preached in the morning and, probably against his better judgment, allowed his brother to hold forth in the evening. This second appearance was little better than his first. Sebastian Streeter, later a prominent Universalist preacher, who was present on this occasion, described the event:

The exordium went off very well; but, as he proceeded with the discussion, he often hesitated, now and then came to a pause, and was finally obliged to sit down before he had reached the original design of the discourse.

He was deeply mortified. He was discouraged.[12]

But such is often the experience of the fledgling preacher.

Discouraged as he was, Hosea's friends would not let him give up. He tried again; and this time, as he said himself, he "met with no remarkable failure." [13] Little by little, his confidence grew, and he no longer considered abandoning his chosen profession.

From the beginning Hosea preached extempore. On one occasion, however, he decided to prepare a manuscript; his father and two of his preacher brothers were to be present, and he wanted to impress them. But rather than helping, the manuscript hindered him. He was not used to reading from the page, but preferred to look at the congregation as he talked. As he proceeded, he kept lifting his eyes from the manuscript so as to look into the faces of his audience; when he looked back to the page, he invariably lost his place. Finally, not able to stand it any longer, he took the manuscript, rolled it up and slipped it into his coat, saying as he did, "I shall weary your patience with these notes." Freed of this hindrance, he went on to preach his sermon with great fluency. Sebastian Streeter, who was present, noticed large tears in old Maturin Ballou's eyes.[14]

In September 1791, Hosea went with David down to Oxford, Massachusetts, to attend for the first time the General Convention of Universalists.[15] The convention, despite its name, was made up of a few small, scattered churches in New England. The movement was still new, with only sixteen or eighteen Universalist preachers in the entire United States.[16]

It was at this convention that Hosea met John Murray for the first time. Murray, the most influential of the early Universalist preachers, was ministering in Gloucester on Cape Ann, where a group of staunch supporters had gathered around him and, in 1779, had founded a Universalist church. Using Gloucester, and later Boston, as his headquarters, he continued an active itinerant career, carrying the message of universal salvation into almost every part of the land.

Murray had brought from England the peculiar Universalist doctrine of his master, James Relly of London. Relly's refinement of Calvinism was built around his interpretation of the relationship

of Christ to the human race. He rejected the Calvinist doctrine of
the imputation of Christ's righteousness to the elect. Relly was convinced that Christ was intimately related to man, so much so that
he was actually guilty with man in Adam's rebellion and sin against
God. Thus, when Christ died on the cross, he was justly punished
for sin which was equally his. This formulation relieved the Deity
of the onus of allowing an innocent person to die for the sins of
others; it also gave support to the Universalist contention that all
men benefited from the sacrifice of Christ, rather than just the elect
of the traditional Calvinist system.[17]

John Murray was thoroughly imbued with Relly's thought. A
man of great fervor and emotion, he preached universal salvation
on a Rellyan basis in language which appealed to the heart rather
than the head. He created a stir wherever he went and was roundly
condemned by the clergy of the established order as a rabble-rouser,
whose doctrine lent itself to libertinism. This was the standard
charge made against the Universalist preachers of the day.

Although Hosea had heard of John Murray before they met at
Oxford, he was not familiar with Murray's theological position.[18]
By the time he learned of the Rellyan system, he had become settled in his distinctly different theological position.[19] At their first
meeting, however, Murray could not have realized that this young
man was to lead the denomination from its Calvinistic, trinitarian
foundation to a radically different unitarian base. Hosea was then
preaching a modified Calvinism: he accepted the Calvinistic version
of Christ's atonement for man's sin,[20] but he declared that Christ's
righteousness was imputed not to an elect few but to all mankind.

For the next few years, Hosea taught school and served as an
itinerant preacher. His certificate from the Chesterfield Academy
helped him land his first teaching post—at Bellingham, Massachusetts. He later taught in Rhode Island, at Foster and Scituate,[21] and
spent the summer months making extended preaching trips.[22]

He made a rustic appearance, dressed as he was in homespun.
But he had developed into a handsome young man, with a tall,
athletic frame. He was already gaining the poise and air of authority which were to be so evident in later years. Preaching in many
different surroundings and situations, he developed an argumentative ability which delighted his hearers. They had no trouble understanding him, for he spoke their language and illustrated his

points with stories of the land and its people. His opponents thought him bitter and sarcastic in his approach, but his friends appreciated his wit. To the earthy challenger of his gospel of universal salvation, he always had a ready answer.

"What would you do with a man who died reeking in sin and crime?"

"I think it would be a good plan to bury him." [23]

Wherever he traveled, people liked him and looked forward to his return.

These years on the road were good for Hosea—and so good for the young Universalist movement that when he rode over to Oxford in September 1794 to attend the General Convention, he was energetically received. He had gained a good reputation, and his colleagues were eager to exchange stories and experiences with him.

Hosea received ordination at this convention in a most unusual —indeed, impromptu—manner. He had not asked for it, since he had not been settled in a church. On the last day of the convention, however, he was in the pulpit with the noted preacher Elhanan Winchester, who had come to Universalism from a Baptist background and was noted for his fiery preaching. As Winchester reached the climax of his sermon, his message took on the flavor of an ordination service. He referred to the Scriptures and how they were entrusted to the ordinand. Before Hosea knew what was happening, Winchester, with a flurry of emotion which instantaneously swept the congregation, took up the Bible and pressed it against Hosea's breast, crying out, "Brother Ballou, I press to your heart the written Jehovah!" After holding the Bible for a moment against the startled young man, Winchester ordered Elder Joab Young: "Brother Young, charge him." This, Young proceeded to do. [24]

No one could claim a more memorable ordination ceremony. Hosea was taken completely by surprise. [25] Yet Winchester's impulsive action reveals clearly the respect for Ballou which was prevalent among his colleagues and friends.

The Reverend Hosea Ballou, because he was in such demand as a preacher, decided to give up "keeping school" and devote himself entirely to the ministry. He preached nearly every evening to groups eager to hear the new doctrine of Universalism; [26] now and then he even received money for his efforts. His circuit riding took him from Cape Ann to the Connecticut River, as far north as his native Richmond and as far south as New London and Hartford.[27] (Among his stops was the town of Hardwick in Worcester County, Massachusetts; the contacts he made here were to prove very important a little later.) "I preached in meeting-houses when they could be obtained, sometimes in school-houses, sometimes in barns, and not very seldom in groves and orchards, and often in private houses." [28]

It was a strenuous life. Travel was difficult over the poor back-country roads, and the strain began to show on his health. But preaching was now in his blood, and he could not give it up. To ease the physical strain a bit, he stopped riding horseback and began using a carriage.[29] But he was going through a period of mental strain which could not be eased so simply. He was being shaken at the very foundation of his Christian faith.

CHAPTER V

ORACLES OF REASON

On July 2, 1782, the leader of the Green Mountain Boys, Ethan Allen, put the finishing touches on his *Reason the Only Oracle of Man.*[1] After it was printed two years later, a bolt of lightning struck the print shop; most of the fifteen hundred copies ready were consumed in the resulting fire.[2] Legend has it that many of the remaining copies were burned by the printer because of the book's "atheistical" content.

The pious Christians of the day probably considered the bolt of lightning an act of God, for "Ethan Allen's Bible," as it was called, is a rambling, rollicking, irreverent attack on "priestcraft." Allen minced no words in dissecting and exposing what he considered the many superstitions in Christian belief and practice. Yet his "compenduous system," which is neither compendious nor a system, is genuinely religious. He did not know what his belief could be called, he said, though his friends had labelled him a Deist. He was, he was sure, "no Christian, except mere infant baptism makes me one." [3]

Allen's book is the product of Deism, the Enlightenment religion which was seriously challenging the Christianity of his day. Under the impact of the Copernican-Newtonian revolution in science, the Deists rejected the Christian conception of the universe whose God interfered with the workings of nature and generally was unpredictable in His actions. They substituted a Deity of law and order Who had started the universe on its course and expected man to live in accord with its rules.

As his title indicates, Allen substitutes for the authority of the Scriptures man's reasoning power, which he considers wholly sufficient for man's needs. Man's reason cannot plumb the very depths of being; if it could, he would be God. But with the power of reason, man must see and worship the Deity in the beauty and wonder of His creation:

The evidence of the being and providence of a God, is so full and compleat, that we cannot miss of discerning it, if we but open our eyes and reflect on the visible creation. The display of God's providence is that by which the evidence of his being is evinced to us.[4]

Despite his attacks on traditional religion—which, to say the least, border on the scurrilous[5]—Allen presents a powerful case for a religion of reason.

It is not known where or when Ballou got hold of a copy of Allen's book. It may have been passed hand-to-hand among Universalists because of Allen's universalistic outlook. At any rate, from internal evidence in Ballou's *A Treatise on Atonement*, there can be no doubt that he read it and was heavily influenced by it.[6] Years later, in attempting to trace briefly his change of theological position, he wrote:

I had preached but a short time before my mind was entirely freed from all the perplexities of the doctrine of the trinity, and the common notion of atonement. But in making these advances, as I am disposed to call them, I had the assistance of no author, or writer. As fast as those old doctrines were, by any means, rendered the subjects of inquiry, in my mind, they became exploded. But it would be difficult for me now to recall the particular incidents which suggested queries in my mind respecting them. It may be proper for me here to state one circumstance, which, no doubt, had no small tendency to bring me on to the ground where I have, for many years, felt established. It was my reading some deistical writings. By this means I was led to see that it was utterly impossible to maintain Christianity as it has been generally believed in the church.[7]

Allen taught Ballou to examine everything by the light of reason. Ballou was eminently reasonable; but his heritage of reverence for the Bible, and the piety which was a strong element in his nature, had kept him from questioning the Scriptures too closely. Ballou did not follow Allen in his rejection of the Bible; to the day he died, he made exalted claims for its authority. But he did learn from Allen that reason, too, is a gift from God. As such, it cannot be incompatible with the Scriptures. Reason must be used by man in order to see what the Scriptures really say.

Approaching the Bible in this manner, Ballou saw the truth of many of Allen's criticisms of Christian doctrine. Where, for instance, is to be found justification for the dogma of the trinity? Not in the Bible; and not in reason. Allen observes:

> We will premise, that the three persons in the supposed Trinity are either finite or infinite; for there cannot in the scale of being be a third sort of beings between these two; for ever so many and exalted degrees in finiteness is still finite, and that being who is infinite admits of no degrees or enlargement; and as all beings whatever must be limitted [sic] or unlimited, perfect or imperfect, they must therefore be denominated to be finite or infinite: we will therefore premise the three persons in the Trinity to be merely finite, considered personally and individually from each other, and the question would arise, whether the supposed trinity of finites though united in one essence, could be more than finite still. Inasmuch as three imperfect and circumscribed beings united together, could not constitute a being perfect or infinite, any more than absolute perfection could consist of three imperfections; which would be the same as to suppose that infinity could be made up or compounded of finiteness; or that absolute, uncreated and infinite perfection, could consist of three personal and imperfect natures. But on the other hand, to consider every of the three persons in the supposed Trinity, as being absolutely infinite, it would be a downright contradiction to one infinite and all comprehending essence. Admitting that God the father is infinite, it would necessarily preclude the supposed God the Son, and God the Holy Ghost from the god-head, or essence of God; one infinite essence comprehending every power, excellency and perfection, which can possibly exist in the divine nature. Was it possible that three absolute infinites, which is the same as three Gods, could be contained in one and the self-same essence, why not as well any other number of infinites? But as certain as infinity cannot admit of addition, so certain a plurality of infinites cannot exist in the same essence; for real infinity is strict and absolute infinity, and only that, and cannot be compounded of infinites or of parts, but forecloses all addition. A personal or circumscribed God, implies as great and manifest a contradiction as the mind of man can conceive of; it is the same as a limited omnipresence, a weak Almighty, or a finite God.[8]

Such a common sense approach probably had the force of demonstration in Ballou's mind. This exploding of the doctrine of the trinity naturally raised the problem of the position of Jesus Christ in the scheme of things. Allen amasses biblical texts to show that Jesus was a finite human who did not claim divinity and who attributed to God knowledge that he did not himself possess.[9] This was probably Ballou's first introduction to unitarian thought. It is easy to imagine the eagerness with which he checked Allen's references against his own Bible.

The elimination of the trinity and the reducing of Christ to human status had serious implications. What happens in such a scheme to the orthodox theory of Christ's atonement and the imputation of his righteousness to sinful man? In Allen's view, there was no necessity for atonement. In quaint terms, he examines the biblical story of the sin of Adam and Eve eating the forbidden fruit and dismisses it as ridiculous.

> . . . It is observable, that there are no travellers or historians, who have given any accounts of such a tree, or of the Cherubims or flaming sword, which renders its existence disputable, and the reality of it doubtful and improbable; the more so, as that part of the country, in which it is said to have been planted, has for a long succession of ages been populously inhabited.[10]

Having shown that there was no such fruit and therefore no such thing as original sin, Allen proceeds to the conclusion that there was no necessity for atonement. But he bases this more on the nature of God than on the falseness of the story of the Garden. God is unchangeable, and eternal justice and reason can never be altered. Therefore, God does not need the satisfaction of a sacrifice of an infinite Mediator.[11] Indeed, it was not possible for man to commit a sin of such magnitude as to require such services on the part of Christ, for sin is not infinite but finite. No amount of sin by finite man can possibly equal infinite sin.[12] Furthermore, if sin were infinite, all degrees of it would be so, and it would be no more sinful to kill a man than to kill his horse.[13]

Allen did not mean to minimize the seriousness of sin in human life. He recognized the blight it casts on human affairs. Sin exists because man deviates from the "unerring order and reason, which is moral rectitude in the abstract."[14] This rectitude is not to be had by man overnight, for man gains his knowledge through his senses.[15] Just as with the sciences, so with morality: it is acquired progressively through reason and experience. This might be called the revelation of God, "which he has revealed to us in the constitution of our rational natures."[16] It follows, then, that sin is a misunderstanding of what is right for man. Sin or virtue is found in the intention or motive of an individual, rather than in the end result of his action.[17]

But God overcomes the sins of men, using suffering as a tool. He convinces them in this way that "sin and vanity are their greatest enemies." He shows them that true happiness is to be found in God and *"moral rectitude."* By reclaiming men in this manner, He gives them occasion "to *glorify* GOD *for the wisdom and goodness of his government,* and to be ultimately happy under it." [18] For this reason, eternal punishment is not only unnecessary but impossible; it would defeat the very purpose of punishment, which is to reclaim the wrongdoer.[19] Allen reviles those Calvinists who claim that the eternal condemnation of some of mankind is necessary for the happiness of the elect. Such reasoning is "horrible" and places God in the same class with "the detestable despots of this world." [20] This universalist note was bound to please Ballou.

Allen's *Oracles of Reason* (as he himself referred to the book) forced Ballou thoroughly to re-examine his theological position. The effect of this book on his thought was much greater than these major arguments would indicate. Only a detailed comparison of Allen's book with Ballou's *Treatise on Atonement,* which appeared in 1805, can reveal the extent of his indebtedness in both style and content.

Ballou was not converted to Deism by "Ethan Allen's Bible"; he was capable of standing his ground on point of doctrine. He learned from Allen but was not conquered. All his life he retained his reverence for the Scriptures, but now it was the Scriptures interpreted by reason. Persistently he drove back through the accretions of centuries of interpretation to find the religion of Jesus as it appears in the Bible itself.

Yet the experience was trying to his soul: he was shaken seriously and found it necessary to call for divine guidance. This is made clear by his correspondence on the subject of revelation with Abner Kneeland in 1816.[21] Kneeland was plagued by doubts concerning the authenticity of the Scriptures, doubts brought on by his reading of the works of Deists such as Tom Paine. For such doubts, Ballou proposed the cure that he himself had used:

If you are troubled with unbelief, if this plague have entered your heart, permit me to suggest a remedy. Humility is the first step, sincere piety towards God the second, let these be followed by that for which the Bereans [Acts 17:11] were commended and the deadly virus of unbelief will soon be purged. Will you say; "physician heal thyself?" I reply, I think I have found relief by the use of the prescription, and am so much in favour of it, that I am determined to continue its application myself as well as recommend it to others.[22]

Ballou was able to maintain the piety of his earlier religious outlook against the skepticism of much Deist thought. Yet he always spoke highly of the Deists, believing that they posed a healthy challenge to the religion of his day. Their doubts forced the thoughtful person to examine his own beliefs. In his correspondence with Kneeland he was to say that anathematizing Christians have done more harm to the religion of Jesus "than his open enemies from Celsus down to T. Paine." [23]

Ballou now began the job of theological reconstruction, and Allen was not the only influence on him in this endeavor.[24] In 1784 the minister of the historic First Church in Boston had come out for universal salvation. Fearing an outcry by his more conservative colleagues in the Boston churches—and wanting to avoid association in people's minds with the lower-class John Murray, who was active in the area—the discreet Charles Chauncy had published his book *The Salvation of All Men* anonymously.[25] Ballou was familiar with the book as early as 1797; he refers to it in his correspondence with Joel Foster.[26] Since a forthright statement of universalism by one of the leading figures in the New England church would certainly have been widely circulated among Universalists, Ballou doubtless knew the book several years before his correspondence with Foster.

Chauncy's book supplied Ballou with many new arguments in favor of universalism. With great exegetical skill, Chauncy attempted to demonstrate that the Greek terms for "eternity" and for "eternal" or "everlasting" (αἰών, αἰώνιος) may signify in the New Testament an "age" or "dispensation"—that is, a *limited* period of time. This interpretation would cut the ground out from under the orthodox argument that Jesus and the early Christians believed in eternal misery in another life.[27] Such arguments were very popular with the Universalists and widely used by them. But where Chauncy expressed them as a cautious hope, the Universalists proclaimed them as a certainty.

Ballou was confirmed by Chauncy in his opinion that the texts of the Scriptures must be interpreted in the light of their context. For this technique Chauncy was, in turn, indebted to the English liberal scholar, John Taylor of Norwich.[28]

Like Ethan Allen, Chauncy stressed that sin is not an infinite evil but "the fault of a *finite creature,* and the effect of *finite* principles, passions, and appetites." [29] He also stressed the idea that God, as a loving Father, uses punishment for correction. It is not reasonable to believe that God will torment men eternally "without any *intention* to do them the least *imaginable good,* as must be the case, if the doctrine of *never-ending misery* is true." [30] In a future state of punishment none could be saved; but in a future state of discipline, salvation is possible. [31]

Chauncy sets forth a proposition that was forever after a part of Ballou's thought: sin equals misery. An intelligent and moral agent cannot be happy in sin. Only in the exercise of intellectual and moral powers can man be happy. It is in the very nature of things that this be true. [32] This idea was responsible for Ballou's eventual position that if there is to be misery in a future state of existence, sin must exist in that state.

If Ethan Allen tended to weaken Ballou's faith in Christ as Mediator, Chauncy tended to strengthen it. Allen's position was an out-and-out belief in the strict humanity of Jesus, whereas Chauncy's position was a high Arianism—a belief that the Son was an exalted being created by God before all other things. (Of course, he did not use the term "Arian," and he did not attack the trinity.) Chauncy held that Christ would win all men to himself in this state or in a series of future states and would then deliver up his kingdom to the Father, so that God would be all in all. [33]

In discussing atonement, Chauncy is as interesting for what he passes by as for what he says. He nowhere asserts that God had to be reconciled to men. On the contrary, he stresses that God reconciled man to Himself through the agency of Christ. [34] When Ballou finally hammered out his position on atonement, this concept was to be at its core.

One of the most interesting elements in Ballou's theological thought is his rigid determinism. Never in his life, he claimed time and again, was he tempted to take an Arminian position: he could not believe that man is free either to accept or reject God's proffered grace.

About 1770, Ferdinand Olivier Petitpierre was expelled as minister of the church at Chaux-de-Fonds in the Canton of Neufchatel, Switzerland, for forthrightly preaching the doctrine of universal salvation. In 1786 he published his views in *Thoughts on the Divine Goodness*[35] in Amsterdam. An English translation first appeared in 1788,[36] and various American editions appeared not many years later. Ballou could have had access to the edition brought out at Hartford in 1794 or the one published at Walpole, New Hampshire, in 1801.[37] That he was familiar with the book is certain. Nathaniel Stacy, who pursued his theological studies under Ballou's guidance in 1802,[38] listed the few universalist books in his teacher's library at the time, and Petitpierre was among them.

Even stronger than this external evidence is the internal evidence of *A Treatise on Atonement*. By the time he published this book in 1805, Ballou was thoroughly imbued with Petitpierre's thought. There are reminiscences of Petitpierre, for example, in his treatment of the benevolence of God and His unbounded love for His creatures. Ballou may have been optimistic by nature, but the terms in which he expressed this optimism were very similar to those used by the Swiss.

Petitpierre appears to have been heavily influenced by Leibnitzian optimism regarding this best of all possible worlds. He declared that the Deity is responsible for every happening in the universe, that nothing escapes His direction in space and time and eternity. Everything that happens to man is the work of God, "nor can any event that may concern me hereafter, in time or in eternity, ever take place, without the concurrence of the first cause." [39]

It was Petitpierre who convinced Ballou that "second causes" (that is, men) are instruments in the hands of God. The Father works through men. And because "every thing ultimately proceeds from the first cause," [40] God is responsible even for sin. He uses evil—and Petitpierre did not minimize the fact that evil is real to man—to prepare man for immortality. Thus, what seems evil is ultimately good: ". . . Whatever the sinner intends as evil, the Divine Ruler of events *means unto good*." [41] So the trial and death of Christ, the malignity of the brothers towards Joseph and the folly of the prodigal son were all designed for good.[42]

Ballou was extremely fond of all these examples and used them, especially the Joseph story, throughout life to justify his determinism. But his was a happy determinism. He had supreme confidence that God was in complete control of things and had the good of His children always in view. This was at the heart of his universalism: if all men are to be saved, there can be no free will. He would not admit of any possibility in which the divine will could be thwarted.

Common to Allen, Chauncy and Petitpierre is the insistence that God is supremely interested in the lives of men. It is His intention to "happify" His children whenever possible. This attitude made for a man-centered religion. Far from being willing to be damned for the "glory of God," these children of the Enlightenment insisted that God glorifies Himself by making His children happy.[43]

These were the major strands of Ballou's reconstructed theology. The reconstruction began in the early 1790s and, except for some minor changes during his later life, was complete by 1805, when he published the *Treatise on Atonement*. The steps of this process cannot be traced exactly, but it is known that Ballou was proclaiming his unitarian views by 1795.[44] Edward Turner, soon to be a close friend, heard him at Sturbridge argue against the doctrine of vicarious atonement on unitarian grounds.[45]

But this change of theology did not go unchallenged. There was bound to be opposition on the part of his colleagues in the ministry. Such opposition appears to have manifested itself at the General Convention of 1796 at Winchester, New Hampshire. The venerable Zebulon Streeter, as moderator, had the task of writing the report circulated after the convention closed. His words reflect contention in the ranks:

It is true that different professors of the Abrahamic faith have dissimilar views concerning the modes in which so great a salvation will be individually made known to the purchased possession; but we collectively and separately, seriously, affectionately, meekly, entreat our brethren that they would not give themselves over to vain disputations on the manner in which Jehovah worketh the counsel of his will; rather rest ye contented that God, who hath promised, is faithful to perform; and cheerfully receive all those who are blessed with gifts of edification, however diverse their gifts may be, preferring no one man above his fellow-man, and rendering honor to none, save unto Jesus Christ, the only Holy and the only Reverend.[46]

Ballou said later that he had as much trouble persuading his Universalist elders of "the errors of Calvinistic tenets" as he had persuading the orthodox of the truth of universal salvation.[47] But he was a powerful and persuasive arguer. He preached his liberal views vigorously and was able to win over his colleagues, especially the younger men. Within ten years, the "reform" was complete. There were a few exceptions: the patriarch John Murray, and Edward Mitchell in New York, remained "strenuous" trinitarians and Calvinists all their lives. But, except for rare cases, Universalist preachers have ever since been unitarians, following the lead of their own greatest prophet, Hosea Ballou.[48]

CHAPTER VI

RUTH

One of Ballou's stops on his circuit after he began preaching in 1791 was a section of the town of Hardwick, Massachusetts, that was soon to become the independent town of Dana.[1] By 1794 there were enough Universalists to begin holding regular services. The Baptist church granted them the use of its meetinghouse,[2] and Ballou was invited to "settle" as minister of the group. Since they could not afford to pay him for full time, it was agreed that he could be free to assist other societies.[3] One Sabbath a month he preached in Dana, for which he received five dollars.[4]

His circuit riding in this period took him north into Vermont and east as far as Cape Ann—to the church at Gloucester, left vacant by John Murray, who had moved to Boston.[5] In addition, he found it necessary to till a plot of ground and to keep school in order to eke out a living.[6] Despite this varied activity, he devoted much time to study and to the job of systematizing his theological thought. Like Emerson and Thoreau later, he found much intellectual stimulation in walking in the woods.[7]

Ballou was now twenty-four, and his friends began to think it was time for him to settle down with a wife. He made a fine appearance with his straight, firm build (he was six feet tall and weighed two hundred pounds),[8] and those who got to know him found an "urbanity and pleasantness" about his manner.[9] Caleb Rich was obviously thinking about Ballou's future, for in the late summer or fall of 1795, he invited him to ride out to Williamsburg to meet a young lady named Ruth Washburn, the daughter of Stephen and Sarah Washburn, who were among the first in Williamsburg to have the courage to declare their acceptance of the doctrine of universal salvation.[10]

Ruth, who no doubt had been led to expect the visit, was looking from the window as Caleb Rich approached the house with the tall young man at his side. As she saw the stranger for the first time, her heart told her, "There comes my future companion." [11] Ballou, in turn, was impressed with this tall, graceful young lady of seventeen.[12] Her complexion was clear, her eyes blue; and she had flowing light brown hair.[13] And they were temperamentally suited to each other. Ruth had a sweet disposition and tended to look on the brighter side of things.[14] Who could be a better match for the young preacher who optimistically told of the bountiful love of God? So he came a-courting during the following year and then asked her to be his wife.

Hosea and Ruth were married September 15, 1795.[15] They lived with her family for a few months; then, on a cold winter's day, they climbed into a sleigh and rode off to their new home in Dana.[16] Their happy companionship was to last for almost fifty-five years. Those who knew the couple bore witness that Ruth was a devoted wife, always concerned with her husband's comfort, always interested in his work. She was ever sure that he knew what was best and put complete faith in his judgment.[17]

Life was quite difficult in their early years together, for the combined income from Ballou's various activities was small. Fortunately, Ruth Ballou had been well trained in thrift;[18] her training was immediately put to the test. The newlyweds adopted a plan for very strict management of their limited means. They lived simply, unable to afford even a modicum of luxury in their household furnishings or in their personal attire. They cultivated habits of frugality which were to remain with them even in later years, when their living standards were raised appreciably.

Shortly after their marriage, news arrived from Guilford, Vermont, that a son had been born to Asahel Ballou.[19] Asahel was Hosea's nephew—the son of his oldest brother, Benjamin—yet they were the same age and as close as brothers. Asahel named his son Hosea, 2d, and the boy was always to be equally close to his granduncle.

Early in 1797, Ballou made a journey which lingered long in his memory. He traveled to Hartford to visit his friend Elhanan Winchester, who had ordained him impulsively less than three years before. Winchester, at the age of forty-six, was slowly dying from a disease which baffled his doctors.[20] Ballou spent a week with him, mostly exchanging views on doctrine. The two men discovered that they were far apart on many matters, especially in view of Ballou's new-found unitarianism. But, in the spirit of true friendship, they agreed to disagree and were certain of each other's affection. Ballou was forever after happy that he had made this last visit, for on April 18, Elhanan Winchester died.[21]

When October rolled around, Ballou thought it best to stay as close to home as possible, for Ruth was expecting their first child. This allowed him an excellent opportunity to begin correspondence with a scholar whom he had heard widely praised. Joel Foster was a minister of the Congregational church at New Salem and was well established in the area, having been there for eighteen years.[22] Ballou first addressed Foster on October 4, stating that, being young, he was in need of assistance.[23] But it is fairly obvious that he was seeking to engage Foster in controversy, for among the questions he asked in his letter was this: ". . . Do the scriptures teach us that God intended the eternal misery of any of the human kind, or to glorify himself in their endless wretchedness?"[24] It is difficult to believe that Ballou, for many years a convinced Universalist, could ask this question expecting to be enlightened by the answer.

Foster returned a courteous letter on October 9, accepting the invitation to discuss the proposed questions. He was clearly a liberal, for he replied that it is possible that somewhere in the "divine economy" there is a provision for the restoration of all creatures and that he would not be averse to that belief if it could be shown to be scriptural. He had his doubts, however, about the effect of such a belief on the average individual. To tell people in this life that they eventually will be saved can "only abate their awe and dread of divine punishment, which in all probability would be no great service to them."[25]

Ballou did not have the leisure to reply to Foster until early in November, for family matters had kept him occupied. On October 13, their first child was born. It was a girl, and the happy parents named her Fanny.[26]

The correspondence with Foster is interesting at this date primarily for the light it sheds on the evolution of Ballou's thought. Here is the first glimpse of the biblical interpretation which is to play so prominent a part in *Notes on the Parables* and *A Treatise on Atonement*. Under the influence of Chauncy,[27] Ballou distinguishes between "the law dispensation"[28] of the Old Testament and the "gospel dispensation" of the New.[29] Such passages as II Thessalonians 1:3-10, which pictures Christ as coming from heaven with fire, should not be interpreted to refer to future punishment; they mean, rather, the coming of Jesus in the spirit of the gospel, "for this flaming fire must be of an heavenly nature, or Christ and his angels would not be found in it." [30] Again: "The presence of the Lord destroys all sin and false conceptions. . . ." [31] Not hell-fire but Christ's gospel itself purifies human nature of its sins and corruptions, and man's heavenly nature stands revealed.

Among the other subjects discussed by Ballou and Foster was the problem of free will. Ballou, on grounds of reason, held to a system of "strict fatality," although he was not yet sure that it could be reconciled with all parts of the Bible.[32] (This may indicate that he was already familiar with Petitpierre.)

The correspondence is also enlightening in respect to Ballou's position on the question of punishment in a future life. He appears to have been wavering on this point. To Foster's question, "Do you believe in any punishment at all after this life?" [33] Ballou answers a blunt "No." [34] But he then changes his position. He explains that he answered in the negative because his mind was not made up on the point, but "I am now satisfied in the idea of a future state of discipline, in which the impenitent will be miserable." [35] Here again he appears to follow Chauncy: it is a state of future *discipline*, from which a soul can be saved, not an endless state of *penalty*.

The correspondence between Ballou and Joel Foster, begun in October 1797, was continued through November 1798, and Foster published it in 1799. He presented it as a warning to Christians of the importance of "keeping upon the plain ground of scripture" and the danger of "indulging an unbounded liberty in qualifying the sense of scripture by their own prejudices, contrary to the common use of language, and in support of doctrines which are not according to godliness." [36] Ballou had apparently indicated a willingness to publish when he met Foster for the first time in July 1798.[37] He later reconsidered and wrote Foster that, for the sake of argument, he had expressed some ideas to which he would not want to be held.[38] But Foster had already corrected Ballou's spelling and punctuation (as he had earlier requested) and turned most of the correspondence over to the printer, who had already begun setting the type.[39] Thus Ballou's reluctance seemed "both unexpected and out of season." [40] From Ballou's point of view, however, this first appearance in print was not altogether auspicious.

Barely had Hosea finished his year-long controversy with Foster than he began a preaching engagement in Boston. In October 1798 he had received a letter from John Murray which gives us a revealing picture of the relationship between the two men:

MY DEAR BROTHER,—You are sensible, I presume, that some time past you delivered in this town some matters not *quite* pleasing to me. I cannot act a hypocritical part, and appear what I am not; I have since, however, not only heard you deliver the truth, but have been much delighted by the account I have heard from Gloucester of your labors there. You will see by what follows I am sincere in my *commendations* as in my *censures;* and as I expressed my dislike when I felt it, I am now going to give you full evidence of my *hearty* approbation and my readiness to promote your *interest.* I am going for a few weeks to the southward. I have recommended *you* to my friends to supply my place. I have spoken of you in such a manner as is pleasing to them. I wish *sincerely* you may come unto them directly, and I wait only your answer to set out. I cannot say how long I shall be absent; I contemplate five or six weeks. Were I a *single* man I would leave my *whole* support with you as a compensation for your time; but as I leave two-thirds of me behind, I shall give about half of my promised support. I am willing to allow you ten dollars a Sunday while I am absent. Your *living will cost you nothing;* you may visit the adjacent parts of the country in the vicinity of Boston all the week if you choose it, or visit the friends in this town, where you will be *sure of a welcome.* You will preach to many *strangers here,* and be by this means more abundantly known; and, I presume, if you fare no better than I do when I journey, you will gain *more* towards the support of your family here for the time you continue here, than you would for the same time anywhere else; so that in every point of view it will be your interest to come here. Should you have made other engagements you can plead the necessity of attending on the present occasion as a mere temporary matter, which may not occur again, and that some time back you encouraged your friends in this town to believe you would supply them should they stand in need of you. You will have the goodness to write directly to let us know what we have to depend upon, and if you cannot come send Mr. Coffin or Mr. Lathe. I should hope, however, that you will be able and willing to come yourself; and should you come, Mrs. Murray, who had the pleasure of hearing you sundry times in Gloucester much to her satisfaction, will be glad to see you at her habitation as often as possible. I hope the presence of the Saviour will be with

you, warming your heart and the hearts of your hearers; and should I
ever return I trust we shall rejoice together in this hope. I remain,
Your affectionate friend and devoted servant,

JOHN MURRAY[41]

Ballou accepted, and preached at Murray's First Universalist
Society on Hanover Street for ten weeks. All appears to have gone
very well until an unfortunate incident marred the engagement.
On the afternoon of the last Sunday, he chose for a text I Corinthians 15:26-28:

The last enemy that shall be destroyed is death. For he hath put
all things under his feet. But when he saith, all things are put under
him, it is manifest that he is excepted, which did put all things under
him. And when all things shall be subdued unto him, then shall the
Son also himself be subject unto him that put all things under him, that
God may be all in all.

The "Son" in this passage he interpreted as Christ. Christ, he explained, is subject and subordinate to the Father and one day shall
relinquish all power to the Father "that God may be all in all."

John Murray's wife, Judith, "a most uneasy spirit," was present at the service. She interpreted the "Son" as the "Son of perdi-
tion"—that is, the devil—and believed the text declared that God
would finally subdue him and take control of the kingdom. The
trinitarian and unitarian positions had locked horns. As Ballou
concluded his sermon and was giving the final prayer, Mrs. Murray
sent a message to Jonathan Balch in the choir. Just as Ballou ended
his prayer and was about to announce the hymn, Balch arose in
the choir loft and announced to the congregation: "I wish to give
notice that the doctrine which has been preached here this afternoon is not the doctrine which is usually preached in this house."
Ballou listened attentively to the announcement and then said
simply, "The audience will please to take notice of what our brother
has said." He then proceeded to read the hymn.[42]

The congregation, as may well be imagined, was extremely
upset by this act of rudeness to the preacher. A parish committee
meeting was held immediately after the service to discuss the incident. That evening the committee, along with some of the leading
members of the congregation, formally apologized for the insult.[43]

This effort of Mrs. Murray to save the reputation of the First
Universalist Society probably did not help relations between John

Murray and Ballou. A man of great emotion, Murray tended to be somewhat intolerant of any views not his own. He was not at all happy with Ballou's unitarianism; but, as is obvious from the invitation, he was not unalterably opposed to him. He probably thought that Ballou was capable of learning.

On a visit to Murray's home in Boston, Ballou and the patriarch fell into conversation about the parable of the sheep and the goats (Matthew 25:31-46). It was Ballou's belief that the sheep represented believers in Christ, while the goats stood for unbelievers. Murray attempted to convince him that the sheep were the human race and that the goats represented the devils, who would go into everlasting punishment. Hosea listened patiently as Murray set forth his exegesis of the passage. Then he said quietly, "Father Murray, those who were on the left hand of the throne were accused of not having visited the sick. Do you think that it is so desirable a thing to have *the devils* visit the sick, that they will be condemned to everlasting punishment for having neglected that duty?" [44]

Ballou's ten-week engagement in Boston made for him many friends. A great number had heard him for the first time and were very much impressed. Several of them conceived the idea of starting a new society and inviting him to take the pulpit. When he was approached, however, he kindly but firmly refused. "I cannot," he answered, "do anything to injure Brother Murray, nor the beloved society to which he ministers." And he requested that no more be said on the subject. [45]

On April 4, 1799, the Ballous' second child was born. [46] This time it was a boy. They named him after his father, adding the middle name Faxon.

The General Convention was held at Woodstock, Vermont, that September, and Ballou was honored by being elected to the moderator's chair. [47] But the convention did not proceed without incident. The Universalists had applied for and been granted the use of the courthouse for their gathering, but the sheriff of the county was not happy with the arrangement. He felt disinclined to allow heresy to be preached in the bounds of his jurisdiction. No Universalists were to be allowed to congregate in Woodstock. He planted himself, sword drawn, in front of the courthouse door, determined to keep out any so depraved as to believe in universal salvation.

When it came time for the session of the convention to begin, the Universalists, with moderator Ballou at their head, gathered down the road and proceeded deliberately to the courthouse. As they arrived at the front door, Ballou, with his customary self-possession, looked the sheriff in the eye and said, "Peter, put up thy sword into his place." The sheriff, stunned to hear the words of Jesus addressed to him, lowered the sword and allowed the Universalists to enter.[48]

The Universalists of the Woodstock area were obviously impressed with Ballou's aggressive leadership. Not long after the General Convention, Woodstock and Barnard were added to his circuit,[49] and he was soon invited to make that area his home.

Present at this Woodstock conference was the young man who was to become Ballou's first theological student and who provides the earliest information available regarding his attitude toward theological education. When Ballou, whose circuit now stretched from Barnard, Vermont, to Gloucester, filled the pulpit in Dana once a month, Nathaniel Stacy listened eagerly. He had firsthand experience with the preacher while serving as the assistant in the general store in Dana.

Ballou was observant and well-liked by those who knew him; his "social, affable habits made him an agreeable companion for all with whom he associated, both young and old." [50] He kept an eye on Stacy and obviously thought he had the makings of a preacher. Stacy, who was self-effacing and doubtful of his own ability, was very surprised when, some while later, Ballou walked into the shop of the clockmaker (where he was now an apprentice) and encouraged him to study for the ministry.[51] He was persuaded, and began his study in October 1802.[52]

The resources of Ballou's library were meager. He had very few books; the only Universalist works were Elhanan Winchester's *Dialogues*[53] and *Lectures*,[54] Petitpierre's *On Divine Goodness* and Relly's *Union*. Stacy's main text was the Bible, with Ballou as his commentator.[55]

Soon after Stacy began his study, Ballou was riding a circuit of towns near his home. This made it possible for the young man

to accompany his master—conversing, asking questions and listening
to him preach at various stops.[56]

Ballou obviously believed that one learns by doing; or so it
would appear from the experience of the young men who studied
theology with him over the years. Long before they thought they
were ready, they found themselves in the pulpit. One Sunday
morning in November 1802, when Ballou was to preach in Dana,
he came to Stacy with his hand on his head, complaining of a violent
headache and saying that he could not possibly preach. Would
Nathaniel fill in for him? Stacy protested that the sermons he had
been writing were all at home. After much protest, he agreed to
preach his first sermon, but he was not at all confident of success:
". . . Belshazzar's knees could never smite together more violently,
when he saw the hand-writing upon the wall, than did mine when
I arose to address the congregation!" Yet he preached a fairly acceptable sermon—and thereafter heard no more about a headache.
As a matter of fact, Ballou "preached like an Apostle" at the afternoon service. Stacy never could get him to admit or deny that he
had feigned his headache.[57]

Two more children, a boy and a girl, were born to the Ballous
during their stay in Dana. Massena Berthier Ballou was born on
November 28, 1800.[58] His name was inspired partly by Hosea's
admiration for two of Napoleon's marshals,[59] but also in great
measure by a poetic foible in Hosea's nature. The girl, born in
Dana on January 9, 1803,[60] was christened Cassandana!

The Ballou children had little more than their interesting
names in these years. Like their father when he was a child, they
went without many of the graces of a comfortable existence so that
the work of the Lord could be accomplished. Five dollars a Sunday
—at least when he preached in Dana—and whatever could be
earned by farming and teaching school was the little they had to
live on.

It may have been the financial burden of a growing family
which persuaded Ballou to accept a call from the north. A month
after Cassandana was born, he moved his family to Vermont.

CHAPTER VII

THE SISTER SOCIETIES

Four groups of Universalists united in the Woodstock area to call Hosea Ballou as their minister early in 1803. These "Sister Societies" were made up of the towns of Barnard, Woodstock, Hartland and Bethel; a fifth, Bridgewater, was added to the group a little later. The earliest of these groups was probably at Woodstock, which showed definite traces of Universalism as early as the 1780s and an attempt at organization in about 1786.[1]

At Barnard, Universalist dissenters were given "certificates of dissent" as early as 1792; this freed them from supporting the established Congregational Church. At first they united with the Universalist society at Woodstock,[2] but in 1802 they formed their own church—with thirty-eight members.[3] The local historian of Barnard has called the formation of this church "a militant protest against the established order." [4]

That some of the leading citizens in these towns were involved in the new societies is plain from the fact that at Hartland one of the first settlers of the town, Timothy Lull, cast in his lot with the Universalists[5] when they formed in May 1802.[6] The same was true at Bethel, where Colonel Joel Marsh of the founding family joined the new group.[7]

These "Sister Societies" took such interesting names as The Independent Catholic Society of Woodstock, The Liberal Catholic Society of Woodstock[8] and The Catholic Benevolent Society in Hartland,[9] as well as the usual name, The Universalist Society of——. At first, only the Barnard group was able to build its own meetinghouse.[10] Elsewhere, the meetings were held in private homes or in the courthouse, when it was available, at Woodstock;[11] in the "Square room in Colonel Marsh's house" at Bethel;[12] and in the schoolhouse or at the home of Barnabas Thompson at Bridgewater.[13]

At Hartland the Universalists used the so-called Union meetinghouse, but not without a tussle. "I cannot allow heresy preached in this sacred place!" cried Elder Cheever when the Universalists first proposed using the hall.

"But Hosea Ballou preaches the truth, and no heresy. I have heard him. He is a great man," answered "Old Captain" Williams.

Despite loud opposition from some of the townspeople, Ballou preached his first "formal" sermon at the Union meetinghouse in March 1803. There was no disturbance that morning, possibly due to the fact that "Old Captain" Williams was present—and armed with a club! [14]

As he rode his circuit, Ballou would stay overnight at his parishioners' homes. He journeyed from Barnard to Hartland via Woodstock and would often stay at Seth Darling's place on the outskirts of Hartland. One night he found himself in the company of a Methodist preacher who also was taking advantage of the Darling hospitality. During the course of the evening, the Methodist "discoursed earnestly" with him in an attempt to demonstrate the errors of his theology. Ballou, of course, drew heavily on the letters of Paul for scriptural citations. Finally, the Methodist exclaimed rather heatedly, "I suppose you think St. Paul was the greatest Universalist!" "By no means," he replied, "Jesus Christ was the greatest Universalist." [15]

Ballou undoubtedly had much contact with the Methodists during his stay in Vermont. Like the Universalists, they dissented from the established order in Barnard,[16] and he is said to have attended their meetings at Woodstock. Yet not all of their beliefs were palatable to him. That he could barely restrain himself from challenging the Methodists in their own meetings may be inferred from the fact that it was stipulated that he could speak "if he would wait till his turn came." [17]

The contract of settlement between Ballou and the Hartland society has fortunately survived in the records of that church:

This Indenture between Hosea Ballou on the one part and the Catholic Benevolent Society of Hartland on the other Witnesseth that the sd Hosea shall settle in the town of Barnard and preach to the Universal Societies in Barnard Woodstock and Hartland one fourth of the time in each place and to attend to all the duties of a minister of the Gospel in sd Societies while in Health and in the good Fellowship of the Convention of the Universal Churches and Societies as established in the four New England States and the sd Society promise and engage on their part to pay to the sd Hosea the Sum of Seventy five Dollars in good Salable Neat Stock at cash price on the first day of

Oct. next to be delivered at the Dwelling House of Alexander Campbell in Hartland to be considered as a settlement.

Signed sealed and delivered on the 27 day of January 1803. . . .[18]

The same provisions were almost certainly made in the contracts between Ballou and the other "Sister Societies."

Ballou's finances must have been in a precarious condition. He had chosen to live at Barnard because many of those who had settled there had come from Hardwick; thus he was among friends.[19] But he was not welcomed with open arms by all of the citizens. Because of his bad financial condition, and possibly because he espoused an unpopular religious sentiment, he was treated by the officials of Barnard as a vagrant and served with a notice which was reserved for prospective paupers:

State of Vermont
Windsor County, ss.
     To the constable in the town of Barnard in the county of Windsor, Greeting.
     You are hereby required to summon Hosea Ballou and wife and children and A. Moses now residing in Barnard to depart said town. Hereof fail not but of this precept and your doings herein due return make according to law
     Given under our hands at Barnard this 28th day of July, A.D. 1803

THOMAS FREEMAN
ALEXANDER BOWMAN
Selectmen[20]

He ignored the notice—and heard no more about it.

The latter part of September 1803 was a busy time for Ballou and an important time for the Universalist denomination. At the General Convention of 1802, the Reverend Walter Ferris of the Charlotte and Monkton, Vermont, churches had proposed that the Convention adopt a statement of faith.[21] Up to this point Universalists had been opposed to "human creeds," [22] although "Articles of Faith" had been adopted by a Universalist convention at Philadelphia in May 1790.[23] A committee was appointed to draw up a plan of faith and fellowship and to report the following year.[24] Although he was on the committee, there is no evidence that Ballou was interested in formulating such a statement. With one exception, he seems never to have referred to what became known as the

Winchester Profession. That one exception was many years later—
in 1847.

When the 1803 convention met at Winchester, New Hampshire, not far from Hosea's boyhood home at Richmond, feelings on
the subject of a "creed" were running high. Since John Murray
was not present, one problem—a clear statement on the trinity—did
not present itself.[25] Walter Ferris, who had originally proposed
that a statement of faith be adopted, was (in good parliamentary
style) given the job of drawing up one which would be acceptable
to all.[26]

When the Profession was brought to the convention floor, a
prolonged and heated debate began. Ballou and the rest of the
committee naturally called for its adoption. Among those who
fought against adoption were persons who feared creeds and all the
bigotry that goes with them. The most notable opposition came
from Noah Murray, who rose to say: "It is harmless now—it is a
calf, and its horns have not yet made their appearance; but it will
soon grow older—its horns will grow, and then it will begin to
hook." To this picturesque complaint Zephaniah Laithe, one of the
committee, replied: "All that Br. Murray has said would be correct, had he not made a mistake in the animal. It is not a calf; it is
a dove; and who ever heard of a dove having horns, at any age?"
The opposition finally yielded when a resolution was appended to
the Profession, stipulating that it was never to be altered in the
future.[27] This allayed the fears that it would someday become an
instrument of oppression or exclusion. So the Profession was adopted
on September 22, 1803.

Just five days later, Ballou was reordained and installed as
pastor of the "Sister Societies." It was expedient to reordain him
in accordance with Vermont law, since the ministers of the established Congregational order often disputed the legality of marriages
performed by Universalists.[28] He was presented with his ordination
certificate, signed by those who took part in his ordaining council
and in the service:

In the name of the General Convention of the Universalist
Churches of the New England States:
To all to whom these presents shall come, Christian Salutation
and Benediction:
Now know ye, that Brother Hosea Ballou, of Barnard, Vt., was

regularly ordained, as a preacher of the gospel, according to the Abrahamic faith,—which is that in thy seed, and that seed Christ, shall all the nations, all the families, and all the kindreds of the earth be blessed,—at Barnard, Vt., on Tuesday, the 27th of September, 1803; and he is hereby commended to the whole family of Adam, who are enabled to receive him in the fulness of the blessing of the gospel of Christ.

Given under our hands, at Barnard, Vt., September 27th, 1803.

JOAB YOUNG, *Presiding Elder*
GEORGE RICHARDS
SAMUEL HILLIARD
JAMES BABBITT
WALTER FERRIS[29]

It is significant that the early Universalists thought it necessary to define and propagandize their faith even in an ordination certificate!

Ballou was now supposedly "settled" over these Vermont churches, yet he still spent much of his time traveling.[30] While itinerating, he became involved in a dispute whose effects were to be felt for years after. In June 1805 he was in West Rutland at the invitation of several persons interested in hearing the Universalist gospel preached. Present in the meetinghouse that day was the Reverend Lemuel Haynes, a mulatto, the minister of the local Congregational church. Haynes had been asked repeatedly to come and dispute with Ballou; when he refused, he was charged with "dishonesty and cowardice." [31] Finally he relented and came to the meetinghouse. Ballou invited him to take part in the service, but Haynes declined, saying he had just come to listen. After a bit of urging, however, he agreed to share the pulpit with the guest preacher.[32]

Ballou delivered his sermon on the text I John 4:10, 11:

Herein is love, not that we loved God, but that he loved us, and sent his Son to be the propitiation for our sins.
Beloved, if God so loved us, we ought also to love one another.

The sermon was mostly an elaboration of the text, with (at least, so Universalists claimed) no sectarian overtones.[33] When he had concluded, he invited Haynes to make any remarks he might wish.

Haynes entered the desk and, making no reference to Ballou's sermon, preached on the text Genesis 3:4: "And the serpent said unto the woman, Ye shall not surely die." He cleverly pictured the devil, in the form of the serpent in Eden, as the first Universalist itinerant preacher.

Happy were the human pair amidst this delightful Paradise, until a certain preacher, in his journey, came that way, and disturbed their peace and tranquility, by endeavouring to reverse the prohibition of the Almighty, as in our text, *ye* SHALL *not* SURELY *die*.[34]

Haynes traced the itineracy of "the first Universalist preacher" in his various guises through the centuries, always preaching his "ancient devilish doctrine."[35] The image is witty and lends itself perfectly to satire and sarcasm.

As the author of the foregoing discourse has confined himself wholly to the character of Satan, he trusts no one will feel himself personally injured by this short sermon; but should any imbibe a degree of friendship for this aged divine, and think that I have not treated this Universal Preacher with that respect and veneration which he justly deserves, let them be so kind as to point it out, and I will most cheerfully retract; for it has ever been a maxim with me—RENDER UNTO ALL THEIR DUES.[36]

When Haynes had finished, Ballou thought it best not to answer him, expecting that he would feel sorry for his intemperance after sober reflection.[37] But, far from feeling sorry, Haynes immortalized his words in print the following year.[38] In an "epistle" to Haynes dated April 22, 1806, Ballou reprimanded him for the sermon, which was "fraught with *low cunning* and *spirited satire,* and delivered with an *aspect* perfectly suited to the subject."[39] His reprimand was, as he admitted, in language "full severe";[40] and Haynes replied in a "letter" not designed to smooth ruffled feelings.[41]

The sting of Haynes' sermon was felt for years by Ballou and his fellow Universalists. The sermon went through many editions,[42] and Ballou was still refuting its implications as late as 1834 in a sermon in Philadelphia.[43]

Ballou took part in varied activities in his years as a pastor in Vermont. He was active in the Masonic order, having been attracted when younger by its profession of brotherly love.[44] In June 1806 he preached to the brethren at a Masonic festival at Chester, Vermont, choosing as his text Hebrews 13:1: "Let brotherly love continue."[45] He appears to have been prominent in the lodge, for in 1811 he was elected Junior Grand Warden of the Grand Lodge of New Hampshire, one of the highest offices in the state.[46]

He also made several trips in behalf of the General Convention, visiting various associations of Universalists. This activity made him many friends and helped to spread his influence. His visit to the Western Association meeting, held in June 1806 at Columbus, New York, was particularly stimulating. The crowds attending were so large that the meetings had to be held in a forest! [47] On his way home, he preached to large gatherings at such places as Brookfield (where his friend and former theological student Nathaniel Stacy was propounding the gospel), New Hartford and Utica.[48]

Yet sadness was mixed with the joy of these years. Sometime during 1804,[49] Ballou's brother Nathan sent word from Richmond that their father had passed away. His body was placed next to that of his beloved Lydia, and a matching stone with the letters *M. B.* was placed next to hers. These stones can be seen today in "Benson's Cemetery" on the hillside near the Ballou farm in Ballou's Dell. Universalists have erected also a large, solid, marble stone as a monument to the parents of Hosea Ballou. The inscription reads:

Rev. MATURIN BALLOU
1722   1804

LYDIA HARRIS BALLOU
1728   1773

That same year, a fifth child was born into the Ballou household. Hosea's poetic foible was again to the fore as he named this new daughter Mandana.[50]

A sixth child was also born to them in Vermont. A daughter, Elmina, came into the world in December 1807.[51] Their joy was short-lived, however, for she died within a month.[52] With a heavy heart, Hosea penned the lines for the gravestone:

The graceful flower was lent,
    not given.
Faded on earth, yet blooms in
    heaven.[53]

CHAPTER VIII

"OF MAKING MANY BOOKS . . ."

Opposition to the doctrine of universal salvation was most often based on the parables of Jesus in the gospels. Parables such as that of the sheep and the goats were thought to be certain evidence that Christ believed in and predicted a future judgment, to be followed by eternal damnation for a large part of mankind. After a long day's journey during which he preached several sermons, Ballou more often than not would be approached by someone who wanted to argue with him the question of endless punishment on the basis of the New Testament parables. It was this circumstance which led him to put down on paper his explanations of such passages. By having his views in pamphlet form, he could hand a copy to anyone anxious for the truth.[1]

He began writing his *Notes on the Parables of the New Testament* about January 1804.[2] The necessary leisure came when he was stricken with an illness which was serious enough to keep him indoors but not serious enough to keep him from his desk.[3] The result was an eighty-page pamphlet; he had one thousand copies of it printed.[4]

The parables, says Ballou, are interpreted very differently in various pulpits. Since laymen mostly depend on the preachers for interpretation, this clash of views embitters Christians against one another and causes difficulties among them. He could not clear up all the difficulties, but he would make a start and hoped that a "more able writer" would carry on from there.[5]

The pamphlet is an earnest attempt to elucidate the parables. There is an almost complete lack of the polemics which characterize later editions of the *Notes* and Ballou's other writings. Also lacking is the humor, the witty thrusts at opponents, the parodies and the bits of sarcasm which spice his later works.

From the modern critical point of view, Ballou's explanation of the parables is outmoded. His is an allegorical, mystical interpretation, which seems to have been influenced by the writings of the English Universalist James Relly.[6] It is difficult, therefore, to understand how he expected Christians to agree on their meaning. Yet this allegorical approach allows him to explain in his own manner the texts which were cited against universalism by its opponents. For instance, the unquenchable fire (Matthew 3:12) which consumes the chaff separated from the wheat is God:

We cannot conceive of more than one *unquenchable* fire, and that one is GOD, as it is written, our GOD is a consuming fire; it cannot be supposed that this fire is *quenchable,* neither can we with propriety suppose another *unquenchable* fire, as that would be supposing another nature equal to GOD *himself.*[7]

This divine fire consumes the chaff of human nature—or, as Ballou called it, "the Adamic" nature. With the chaff consumed, what is left is the wheat or heavenly nature of man.[8]

This interpretation cut the ground from under the then prevalent idea that the chaff represented men destined for hell. It also enabled Ballou to express his conviction that human nature, when freed from its corruptions, is akin to the nature of Christ and God. Or, to change the figure:

We are taught that all momentous truth and sublime doctrinal idea of the real nature of man, which absolutely stands in relation to Christ, or his gospel, as meal does to leaven; for, it may be observed, that leaven could have no possible operation in meal, did not the meal, in its own nature, possess a quality that naturally adhered to the leaven.
The final effects of divine grace in the ministry of reconciliation, in which we look for universal submission to Christ in his glorious and ever blessed kingdom, is communicated in that it is said, "until the whole was leavened."[9]

Despite the basic weakness of his allegorical method of interpretation, Ballou recognized an important truth concerning the gospel records. He insisted that in those passages which represent Jesus as predicting the coming of the Son of man on the clouds of heaven, Jesus meant that this would occur within the earthly life of the disciples[10] and not in afterlife; for Jesus had said (Matthew 16:28): "There be some standing here, which shall not taste of death, till they see the Son of man coming in his kingdom." Ballou thus came close to the present day recognition of the eschatological element in Jesus' message. But he understood the Second Coming to apply not to a physical appearance but to a spiritual experience; indeed, he believed it had occurred at Pentecost.[11] (Since the Bible is the word of God, Jesus' prediction could not have been wrong.) These ideas were to be expressed more fully in his *Treatise on Atonement* the following year.

The *Notes* were to prove very popular in Universalist circles. They appeared in an enlarged edition in 1812 and many times thereafter. From this first intentional appearance in print, Ballou learned the power of the press. He was to put it to use many times in the cause of Universalism.

Among his other writings of this period are many hymns. He had a weakness for verse (it cannot be called poetry), yet he never had any training in the art and never really considered himself a poet.[12] It is difficult to understand why he should have offered his "poetic" effusions to the public.

His first indiscretion occurred as the result of action taken by the General Convention. In the meetings of 1805, 1806 and 1807, the Convention appointed him to a committee to issue a hymnbook for use in the Universalist churches.[13] There was a pressing need for such a book. The most popular hymnbook of the day was, of course, that of Isaac Watts; but that great English divine stressed the theme of eternal punishment and "thereby sorely wounded the divine theme of devotional Psalmody." [14] The hymnals compiled by Universalists of the day were little better; their theory of atonement was unsatisfactory[15] in view of the changes taking place in Universalist thinking. "It was a thing much desired by the Convention that the rising generation might learn to sing the praises of the Captain of our salvation, without mixing the alloy of dishonor in the sacred song." [16]

Ballou, Abner Kneeland and Edward Turner were given the task of furnishing a proper hymnbook.[17] They were commissioned to *compile* a book, not to write one. On "mature consideration," however, they decided not to put the societies to the expense of reprinting hymns which were already available. They decided, instead, to write their own! [18] Such a step would have been wise if, on "mature consideration," they had decided that they had the necessary talent; but the talent was lacking.

Of the more than four hundred hymns in the collection, Ballou wrote 193! Kneeland followed close behind with 138. The remainder were supplied by Turner, Sebastian Streeter and the "rustic poet" of Richmond, Silas Ballou.

Since "time makes ancient good uncouth," it is best to turn to Ballou's contemporaries for an evaluation of the Convention Hymn Book. When it appeared in 1808, Universalists found that some of the hymns showed poetic talent but that others were much too argumentative for public worship.[19] The hymnbook was put to the test; it was found lacking. Within five years or so, most of the Universalist societies had discarded it and turned back to Watts or to the book of Murray's First Universalist Society in Boston, despite their objectionable references to the trinity and vicarious atonement.[20]

Ballou continued to write hymns, however, and several of his were popular with Universalists during and immediately after his lifetime. They have not, however, stood the test of time. By 1900 only five of his hymns were included in the Universalist collection;[21] by 1917 only two were included.[22] In the current Universalist-Unitarian collection[23] there is nothing to indicate that Ballou ever indulged in hymnody.[24]

In 1808, Ebenezer Paine of Washington, New Hampshire, suggested to Ballou that they arrange for a debate with several Congregationalist ministers of New Hampshire and Vermont on the points which divided the standing order and the Universalists. The debate never was arranged; but as a result of the effort, a pamphlet controversy began between Ballou and Paine on one side and the Reverends Reed Page of Hancock and Isaac Robinson of Stoddard, New Hampshire, on the other.[25] Paine proved unequal to the task,[26] and the burden of the debate soon fell to Ballou. His was the job of answering Robinson,[27] who managed the debate from the Hopkinsian point of view. Robinson wrote a *Candid Reply*; Ballou countered with *A Candid Review*.[28]

The main question involved in the controversy was whether God is equally good to all. Ballou, naturally, took the positive; Robinson, the negative. Much of the controversy was concerned with procedure in debate; this was especially true of *A Candid Review*.

Such controversies were welcomed by Ballou, who was a born debater. Whereas the modern reader is impressed mainly by the superfluity of words in the controversies of that day, he and many of his colleagues were convinced of their efficacy:

The minds of men in general are much influenced by the prejudices of education; it therefore requires argument to be brought in as plain and direct a manner as possible, in order to get the mind awake so as to think.[29]

This faith in the power of argument was responsible for the style of Ballou's best work of this period, A Treatise on Atonement. Published in 1805, it was the result of almost fifteen years of theological rethinking. His radical changes of thought regarding the nature of sin, the trinity and atonement were now fairly systematized, and he felt justified in presenting his religious philosophy to the world. This he did in a book filled with apt, homely illustrations, which no doubt reflect the sermons he was preaching at this period. Conversational, argumentative, peppered with sudden thrusts of pungent wit, the Treatise appealed to the down-to-earth persons who made up most Universalist congregations. It is not difficult to imagine the ripples of laughter which must have swept his country audiences as he demolished the dogma of the trinity by characterizing it as the "amazing sum of infinity, multiplied by three!"[30]

The Treatise was eagerly awaited by the Universalists;[31] and when it appeared, it had a tremendous effect on them. Ballou's arguments were repeated with the complete confidence that they were "unanswerable."[32] It was especially popular among the young Universalist preachers such as Abner Kneeland, Ballou's good friend, who swallowed it "in total."[33] This book, more than any other effort, established Ballou's reputation as a Universalist leader. From the time of its publication, Universalists increasingly looked to him as their prime spokesman.

The impact of the Treatise was not only swift but powerful. Some years later, when a pirated edition was brought out at Bennington, Vermont,[34] the pirate announced in his own defense: "Such a book is unlike other books,—it belongs to all the world,—no restriction ought to be put upon its publication or its sale."[35] The many legitimate editions brought out during and after Ballou's lifetime also attest to its popularity. Its reception is perhaps best summed up in the words inscribed by an anonymous pen on the inside cover of a first edition now in the possession of the Universalist Historical Society:

> This precious Book
> cannot be read too often,
> nor studied too much.

CHAPTER IX

THE GREAT TREATISE

Ballou's great object in writing *A Treatise on Atonement* was to free the Bible from the encumbrances which have made it "a subject of discredit to thousands." [1] He attempted to clear away conceptions which have "served to darken the human understanding and obscure the gospel of eternal life." [2] In this category he placed the idea that sin is infinite and needs an infinite punishment because the law transgressed is infinite; the idea that "the great Jehovah took on himself a natural body of flesh and blood, and actually suffered death on a cross, to satisfy his infinite justice, and thereby save his creatures from endless misery." [3]

These ideas are not only unscriptural but also—and this is equally important—unreasonable. God created men as reasonable beings; therefore "we ought . . . to believe, that all the truth which is necessary for our belief, is not only reasonable, but reducible to our understandings." [4] Ballou placed himself firmly on the side of the eighteenth-century cult of reason.

The 216-page treatise is divided into three general areas, which pivot on sin, atonement for sin, and the consequences of atonement for mankind. Ballou likens this division to a physical disorder, its remedy and the health which results. [5]

The influence of Ethan Allen's thought is immediately observable as Ballou begins his consideration of the nature of sin. He argues against the prevalent notion that sin is infinite. Since man's capacity to understand is definitely limited, he asserts, it is not possible for man to have a perfect understanding of the law of God. "Sin is the violation of a law which exists in the mind, which law is the imperfect knowledge men have of moral good." Man's sin, therefore, is not infinite—but finite. [6]

Ballou carefully examines the idea that sin is infinite. If the usual theory is true, the interesting situation occurs of finite man thwarting the law of an infinite legislator, God. "With eyes open, the reader cannot but see, that if sin is infinite because it is committed against an infinite law, whose author is God, the design of

Deity must be *abortive*. . . ."[7] Since God is a Being of infinite wisdom, it is unthinkable that the end result of any of His actions could frustrate His will.

Now to reason justly, we must conclude, that if God possesses *infinite* wisdom, he could never intend any thing to take place, or be, that will not take place, or be; nor that which is or will be, not to be, at the time when it is.[8]

Despite the strained grammatical construction, Ballou makes an able case for the all-powerfulness of an infinite God. It is impossible, he says, to conceive of God suffering disappointment in the smallest matter, or it would be impossible for man to have any "satisfactory evidence whereby to prove that any thing, at present, in the whole universe, is as the Supreme intended."[9] This stress on the omnipotence of God is an essential part of his thought; without it, he could not be sure that *all* men would be saved.

He continues to hammer at the theme that infinite sin would frustrate God's plan in creation. If sin is infinite, goodness cannot be greater. If sin is infinite, God Himself cannot be greater. God "cannot be *superior* to that which is *equal to himself!*"[10] If sin is infinite, it cannot be limited in its consequences; and God Himself, as well as all created beings, would be unable to avoid its consequences. If there is such a thing as divine justice, sin must be bounded by it; and if sin is bounded, it obviously cannot be infinite.[11]

Having stated these arguments from reason, Ballou takes note of those who would prove the infinity of sin from the Scriptures. A favorite passage for this purpose is Job 22:5: "Is not thy wickedness great? and thine iniquities infinite?" Ballou turns the exegetical tables on his opponents by putting this text into context. He points out that these are the words of the Temanite whom God specifically refutes in chapter 42:7—

. . . After the Lord had spoken these words unto Job, the Lord said to Eliphaz the Temanite, My wrath is kindled against thee, and against thy two friends: for ye have not spoken of me the thing that is right, as my servant Job hath.[12]

Still on scriptural grounds, he points out that if sin is infinite, no one sin is greater than another. The most trivial offense against society is "equal to *blasphemy* against the *Holy Ghost*." Did not

Christ himself (in Matthew 12:31) speak of a variation in the intensity of sin? [13]

Sin, then, is a violation of a law which exists in the mind; and since man's knowledge is definitely circumscribed, this law of the mind is definitely finite. Man cannot be held subject to a law which is above his capacity to understand.[14]

The influence of Petitpierre's *On Divine Goodness* is very evident as Ballou turns to a consideration of the good use to which God puts sin. Man can never foresee all the consequences of his actions. This is illustrated perfectly by the brothers who sold Joseph into captivity: if their sin had been infinite, nothing good could have come from it, but such was not the case. God was superintending the affair. That which was evil in the sight of men was used by God for a good end.[15]

> . . . What, in a *limited sense*, we may justly call *sin*, or *evil*, in an *unlimited sense* is justly called *good*. We say, of the top of yonder mountain, it is exceedingly high; and of yonder valley, it is low; and this we justly say, by comparing one with the other, in respect to the centre of our earth. But the moment we extend our thoughts to contemplate the millions of worlds in unbounded space, and take the whole in one grand system, the idea of high and low is lost. So is sin finished, when, by divine grace, our understandings are enlightened, and we hear our spiritual Joseph say, "Grieve not yourselves, ye *meant* it unto *evil*, but *God meant* it unto *good*." [16]

Ballou does not deny the seriousness of sin in man's life. Sin is very real, for it is in a man's intention. A man with an evil intention may accidentally do good to a neighbor, but his sin is none the less real. On the other hand, the individual who intends good and sees evil result from his action is not guilty of sin. ". . . It is then an evil *intention* that constitutes an evil *action*." [17] Often he had been challenged by people who said that, if this view were right, it would make sense for men "to do evil, that good may come." But such an objection is self-contradictory, for if a person intends an action for good, it cannot be called sin. "Then it is plain, that to do evil, that good may come, is impossible." [18]

In his examination of the origin of sin, Ballou retells the story of the fallen angels and dismisses it as a "chimerical story from the bard, Milton." [19] This fanciful myth does not provide a satisfactory explanation of the origin of sin. Rather, one must determine the origin of sin on the basis of the Scriptures, using the assistance of reason, "without which, the scriptures would be of no more service to us than they are to the brute creation." [20]

Having rejected the Miltonian interpretation of the origin of sin, he presents a fanciful theory of his own,[21] based on a figurative interpretation of the Adam and Eve story in Genesis. In this he distinguishes between the *creation* of man in Christ and the *formation* of man in Adam. Christ, says Ballou, was the first of God's creations, made in His image and pre-existent to the rest of the created universe. Man was thus *created* in an ideal shape in Christ, though only later was his actual body *formed* of the dust of the ground. In this way, as the Scriptures say, man was created in God's image. Only when he was formed as Adam, did he become subject to all the vanities of human nature.

> He has now, not an immortal, but a mortal constitution; is possessed of natural appetites and passions; and being unacquainted with the ways of his own imperfect self, knew neither the good or evil of a mortal state. If it be said, that man was not mortal, before he sinned, and that he became mortal by sin, it is a saying as distant from good reason as imagination can go. For if man was not *mortal* before transgression, he must have been *immortal*; if he was *immortal*, he was not subject to change, but remains still in the same *immortal* state; and all our notions about the mortality of man is nothing but a groundless chimera. But every day's experience contradicts such absurdities.[22]

Thus Ballou distinguishes between the heavenly essence and the earthly dross in the constitution of mankind. The heavenly part is responsible for man's spiritual yearning; the earthly (Adamic) part, his "carnal mind," is responsible for folly, sin and corruption.[23] By thus interpreting the Garden story figuratively, Ballou rejects a literal belief in the Garden—which, as Ethan Allen observed, cannot be located [24]—and with it original sin.

Ballou does not equivocate. He states flatly that God saw fit to make man "subject to vanity; to give him a mortal constitution; to fix on his nature those faculties which would, in their operation, oppose the spirit of the heavenly nature." But, a critic would protest, this system denies the liberty of the will and, more serious, makes "God the *author* of sin." To this, Ballou readily agrees. He hastily reminds his readers, however, that "God may be the innocent and

holy cause" of that which is in a limited sense sin but which in
God's greater knowledge is good:

> It is not casting any disagreeable reflections on the Almighty, to
> say he determined all things for good; and to believe he supersedes all
> the affairs of the universe, not excepting sin, is a million times more to
> the honor of God. than to believe he *cannot,* or that he does not when
> he can.[25]

Ballou presents a series of homely arguments to refute those
who claim man has freedom of will.[26] Some may argue that sin is
the result of man's freedom, but who gave man this freedom? The
answer is: God, thus demonstrating that God is the original cause
of sin.[27] If it be argued that God gives man freedom of will but
foresees all that he is to choose, the argument destroys itself. For
if the consequences of man's freedom are known, they are certain
"and none of them avoidable." [28] An infinite God must—and does
—control all things.

The spring of man's motivations is his search for happiness. In
all man does, happiness is his main object. He would not form
groups, support government, seek education, study science or even
till the soil if he did not believe he would gain happiness by doing
so.[29] This view is in direct contradiction to the "disinterested benevolence" preached by Samuel Hopkins and his followers. (Ballou
never names these opponents; he concentrates on their ideas.[30])
Disinterested benevolence, says Ballou, is an illusion. The person
who gives of himself or his substance without expecting a reward
is actually rewarded by the happiness that he sees result from his
"benevolent" actions. This is precisely what "Sacred truth" means
by the words: "It is more blessed to give than to receive" (Acts
20:35). Men are motivated by what they expect will result in happiness. The honest and industrious, the indolent and knavish—all
expect happiness from their actions.[31]

Here, then, is the key to sin: man seeks happiness but is often
misguided as to what makes for happiness.

> The objector will say, to admit that our happiness is the grand
> object of all we do, destroys the purity of religion, and reduces the
> whole to nothing but selfishness. To which, I reply, a man acting for
> his own happiness, if he seeks it in the heavenly system of *universal
> benevolence,* knowing that his own happiness is connected with the

happiness of his fellow men, which induces him to do justly, and to deal mercifully with all men, he is no more *selfish* than he ought to be. But a man acting for his own happiness, if he seeks it in the *narrow circle* of *partiality* and *covetousness*, his *selfishness* is *irreligious* and *wicked*.[32]

There is no reason why men should love holiness for holiness' sake, or God for God's sake. Just as in life we can only like what is beneficial to us, so with God. Did not the psalmist write, "O taste and see that the Lord is good" (Psalms 34:8a)? And the apostle, "We love him, because he first loved us" (1 John 4:19)? Man loves God for His attributes of justice, power, wisdom and love. These cause man to love God, for he knows the benefit he derives from these qualities as contrasted with their opposites.[33]

Sin, therefore, is a misapprehension on the part of man as to what makes for happiness. If sin is pictured as pleasure, it will be sought after. Preachers too often err by giving the impression that sin is pleasant and that it is less pleasant to live a virtuous life. They warn their hearers not to risk salvation in a future state by indulging in the pleasures of sin here. But the threat of punishment in an afterlife is no cure for sin in this. The heart will still crave evil, even if the hands do not commit it for fear of punishment.[34]

Ballou denies the existence of a devil. True, the devil has been universally recognized by Christians and "has been of as much advantage to some, as the *Goddess Diana* was to the *craftsmen* of *Ephesus*." But such a being as Christians describe, with such multifarious duties, would have to be omnipresent like the Father; and this Ballou refuses to concede. As for the Old Serpent who beguiled the first woman, this is but a figurative way of describing "the carnal mind, which is enmity against God." Men need no being to tempt them; their passions are sufficient for the task.[35] In the famous temptation, Jesus dealt not with the devil but with his own fleshly appetites. He was tempted in all things, as the Scriptures say, yet he was without sin. "If, therefore, we know how we are tempted, we know, also, how he was tempted."[36] Sin, in short, is the work of the flesh, of the carnal mind.

As a being dependent on his Maker, man tends naturally to worship. But his carnal mind, subject to all manner of fleshly temptation, distorts the true worship of the heavenly nature of man and blurs the true image of God. The false god created by man's

carnal mind will possess all the failings and shortcomings of man
in his earthly state:

[He] will surely possess all the vile passions of the old man, Adam, and
those religious duties must consist in certain rites, which bear no relation to *heaven-born charity,* or *deeds of kindness.* An Almighty, omnipresent, infinitely wise and good, may be talked of; but his wisdom,
power and goodness, must be denied; and he must be a great many
millions of miles off, fixed to a certain place, yet every where present;
infinitely wise and powerful, yet suffers an everlasting violation of his
will; possessed of infinite wisdom, yet, is disappointed in his plans; loves
some of his creatures, and hates others; is pleased and displeased with
the conduct of his creatures; is perfectly unchangeable, yet loves, at
one time, and, at another, hates the same object. Such an idol will
answer for thousands. Now what are the consequences? Answer, one
nation supposes itself the only favorite of God; other people are haters
of him, and hated by him. If my God hates those who hate him, I
ought to do as my God does, and I will hate them too. One denomination of christians has different ideas of the attributes of their God
from another; they are violently opposed to each other; they are at
sword's points, they call each other heretics, and doom each other to the
endless wrath of their *God!* All such religion is of the flesh; the wisdom
of it is not from above, but is earthly, sensual and devilish, and those
who possess it are *tormented day* and *night* with it. Reader, turn over
the pages of history, calculate the rivers of blood which have been shed
on account of religious disputes, and ask yourself the question, is this
religion worthy of a Supreme Being? The devil will have religion, and
will have it maintained as long as he can; but then, he must tell the
people, that it is none of his, but that it came from the true and living
God, or they will not believe it. It is an object with the Old Serpent,
to have a great many denominations, and to persuade them that they
are *individually right,* and *individually wrong,* and to stir up their
minds to maintain their respective tenets, and to wage war with each
other, which he calls *contending correctly for the faith.* Many who
profess to be called by Him who loved sinners, to preach his gospel,
and who pretend to follow the Savior, in the path of meekness, if they
happen to think a little different, in matters of faith, they are filled
with the greatest vehemency towards each other, which they call holy
wrath, or indignation; and you might as well reason with hungry lions,
or tigers, as with them, for they worship the *beast* and they partake
largely of his nature. Did they worship the true God, in the spirit of
the heavenly man, difference, in particular sentiments, would not hinder
their fellowship, and love one to another. All the religion in our world,
founded on the *partial principles of man's inventions,* pointing out particular modes of faith, and forms of worship, is from the carnal man.[37]

The ills of this world, then, are due to the carnal in man over-coming the heavenly portion of his nature. It is the carnal mind which pictures a partial, fickle God. Even the Scriptures are not free from this reflection on the nature of God: some passages show Him as a changeable deity Who is filled with wrath toward sinners and is capable of jealousy, while others reveal a deity Who sends His rain and His sun to the just and unjust alike.[38] In an attempt to reconcile these different pictures of God in the Bible, Ballou asserts that the idea of the changeable God is the conception of the fleshly mind of the old covenant, while the unchangeable God is the conception of the mind "enlightened by the spirit of the new man, and while walking in the spirit of life in Christ Jesus." [39]

Christ is the key. Man is unable to fulfill the requirements of the heavenly law while he is carnal-minded. But in Christ he gains the perfect wisdom and knowledge. It is possible for man "to keep the law of God perfectly" if he is free of "the earthly Adam" and imbued with the spirit of Christ,[40] for the Savior has made possible an atonement.

In his treatment of the subject of atonement, Ballou begins, as he was wont to do, by demolishing those theories with which he does not agree. These erroneous theories, he declares, "besmirch" the character of the Creator.

The usual theories agree in certain fundamentals: Sin is considered an infinite evil, since it violates infinite law. Atonement, therefore, must also be infinite. The transgression of Adam, since he broke an infinite law, requires an infinite penalty. And Adam's sin is counted against the whole human race "before they individually existed." [41]

After this initial agreement, however, the prevalent theories of atonement diverge.

. . . Divines of the greatest abilities, and of the first rank among the literati, have drained the last faculty of invention, in plodding through the dark regions of metaphysics, to bring up a *Samuel* to explain, the *solicism* of *satisfying* an *infinite dissatisfaction!* [42]

Ballou had little patience with the subtle metaphysical arguments of the orthodox divines.[43]

He first considers the Anselmic theory of atonement, which was held by the traditional Calvinists of New England. God, foreseeing through all eternity that men would transgress His infinite statutes, provided a Mediator to suffer the penalty of these transgressions for certain men whom He favored. Since an infinite law has been violated, only an infinite being is capable of making satisfaction. God Himself, therefore, took on the form of man to perform the task.

It is true, they are a little cautious about saying that *God himself absolutely died!* But they say, that Christ, who was crucified, was *really God himself,* which must, in effect, amount to the same thing. And in fact, if the Infinite did not suffer death, the whole plan falls, for it is by an *infinite sacrifice* that they pretend to *satisfy* an *infinite dissatisfaction.*[44]

It is difficult to see how an infinite dissatisfaction—if the word infinite is to hold its meaning—can be satisfied. But this impossibility, according to orthodox theory, did occur. Yet not all men are to benefit by it—just the elect. The non-elect are "left, to suffer *endlessly* for what Adam did, before they were born."[45] Ballou has already shown, of course, that sin is not infinite and that an infinite satisfaction is not called for. But he is ever ready to argue anew on the premises of his "opponent":

I will state it, as it is often stated by those who believe it, which is by the likeness of debt and credit. The sinner owed a debt to Divine Justice, which he was unable to discharge; the Divine Being cannot, consistently with his honor, dispense with the pay, but says, I must have what is my due; but as the debtor has not ability to pay the smallest fraction, Divine Wisdom lays a deep concerted mysterious plan for the debt to be discharged. And how was it? Why, for God to pay it himself![46]

If such a method is used by God, however, it certainly is worthy of the imitation of men.

My neighbor owes me an hundred pounds; time of payment comes, and I make a demand for my dues. Says my neighbor, my misfortunes have been such, that I am not the possessor of the smallest fraction of property in the world; and as much as I owe you, I am worse than nothing. I declare to him, positively, that I will not lose so much as a fraction of the interest, and leave him. A friend calls, and asks me how I succeeded in obtaining my dues of my neighbor; I reply, my neighbor is not, nor will he ever be able to pay me any part of my demand. My friend says, he is sorry that I should lose the debt. I answer, I shall not lose it. I have very fortunately, in my meditations on the subject, thought of a method, by which I can avail myself of the whole, to my full satisfaction; and I think it is a method which no person in the world, but myself, could ever have discovered. My friend is curious, and impatient to know the mighty secret, never before found out. The reader may guess his confusion, on my telling him, that, as I have that sum already by me, I am now going to pay up the obligation, before the interest is any larger! This has been called the gospel plan, which contains the depths of infinite wisdom.[47]

To the objector who says a distinction must be made among the persons of the Godhead, Ballou replies that they are so essentially one that it is futile to pretend that the second person could pay the debt to the first.[48]

Again, for the sake of argument, Ballou grants that this system of atonement is true. On this basis, he examines the morality of the transaction. (The question of morality had played an important part in his own rejection of the traditional idea of atonement.) He questions "the propriety" of allowing an innocent man to suffer in place of the guilty: "It is scripture, reason, and good law, never to condemn the innocent, in order to exculpate the delinquent." In a picturesque illustration, he asks how the American people would respond if the President of the United States were executed in place of a would-be assassin, even at the President's own request.[49]

The Creator's partiality in this plan of atonement is also shocking. There is no justification for the idea of election, either in the Scriptures or in reason. Ballou expresses indignation at the idea that God could be less ethical than His creature, man.

Have we not reason to believe our Creator possessed of as much goodness as he has communicated to us? Can we rationally believe, that he is wanting, in those principles of goodness which he has placed in our understandings? [50]

Why should God show partiality to a small fraction of Adam's progeny, when they are all in the same situation? "The sacred oracle declares God to be no respecter of persons; if this is true, he is not a partial being." [51] He piles up scriptural texts to back up his claim of God's impartiality[52] and points out that, if there were such a being as the devil, he would be less wicked than an Anselmic God. For the devil can only *strive* to make man miserable, but the God of the orthodox—an omnipotent God—deliberately destined millions for an eternity of torment.[53]

Again, Ballou compares the ways of such a God to the ways of
man. Some argue that God has the right to treat His creatures as
He pleases, simply because He has such power. God cannot be
.constrained by a moral code; on the contrary, His every action is
right because He does it. But this same principle, applied to men's
affairs, becomes "tyrannic majesty": "Every thing that can be done,
is moral holiness; and every thing that cannot be done, is sin, or
moral evil." [54] In effect, might makes right.

Ballou next turns to the Grotian theory of atonement as held
by the Hopkinsians and some of the Arminians (though he does not
mention either group by name). This theory holds that Christ died
not for the salvation of men but for the sole object of glorifying the
Father. God's supreme object in everything He does is to glorify
Himself. Christ died "for the honor of divine justice, and the glory
of his Father." Yet his death also satisfied the penalty of endless
punishment incurred by mankind, which had transgressed an infinite law. Since this is true,

it is now just and right for God to acquit as many of the sinful race of
Adam, as is consistent with his grand object, which is himself; yet, by
no means rendering it unjust for God to punish, to all eternity, as many
as is necessary, in order for the satisfying of the same grand object.[55]

Ballou uses a common sense approach in refuting Hopkinsian
claims. If God is infinitely glorious, it is a waste of time for Him
to try to enhance that glory. If he is attempting to secure and
maintain His splendor, His infinite glory is perishable! To those
who say that God's object is to manifest His glory to intelligent
beings without reference to its effects, Ballou answers that this is
absurd, for no rational being could operate without consideration of
the effects of his actions.[56]

Before turning to consider a third theory of atonement, Ballou
digresses on the subject of endless punishment. Here he develops
an idea hinted at in the *Literary Correspondence* published in 1799,
an idea which was to play an increasingly important part in his
later thought. Endless punishment cannot keep a sinner from
sinning, for sin and misery are irrevocably bound together. Endless punishment

would fix the delinquents in a situation, in which they could do nothing
but sin, to an endless eternity. No moral being can be miserable, as

suffering conscious guilt, without sin; therefore, in order for endless misery to be inflicted, *endless transgression* is *necessary.*[57]

The final "erroneous" theory of atonement to be considered is that held by the Arminians. This theory grants that Christ's suffering and death were completely efficacious for all men. Adam's transgression and the resultant original sin were wiped out by Christ. Adam and his progeny are now on probation. Unlike Adam before the Fall, man now knows the difference between good and evil; but he also has strong appetites which lead to sin. A "portion of the divine Spirit" is his, however, and this helps him to oppose those appetites and overcome them. Adam had the power as a moral agent to choose holiness and happiness; man now has that same power. Man is capable of repentance, and the heavenly Father is willing to forgive.[58]

Ballou considers this position completely inadequate. "The sum of this plan of atonement, made salvation *possible* unto *all men,* but *certain* unto *none.*"[59] He insisted on the certainty of salvation for all men. Under the Arminian system, there is no certainty. If man failed on his first try, there is no reason to believe he will succeed now. There can be no certainty that *any* of Adam's posterity will achieve salvation.[60]

Christ suffered to give man another chance. God revealed himself in the prophets, and sent His Holy Spirit into the world to guide men to truth. All this was done—

but *all* upon *uncertainties!* After all, man has it in his *power* to frustrate the whole plan of grace, and render it abortive! O! ye angels of celestial purity, had ye known this, ye would not have sung, on the auspicious birth-day of Emanuel, *"Great joy, which shall be unto all people."*[61]

Having shown why the usual theories of atonement are inadequate, Ballou sets forth a system which is designed to show the loving-kindness of the Father to all His children. First it is necessary to make clear what is meant by atonement. Ballou defines it as reconciliation or satisfaction. The question then arises: "Who is the unreconciled or dissatisfied party?" Is it God, or is it man? "It is a being *unreconciled to truth and justice,* which needs *reconciliation;* and it is a *dissatisfied being* which needs *satisfaction.*"[62]

To demonstrate that it is man, rather than God, who needs

reconciliation, Ballou turns to the story of Adam. Would the first man have hid from God after his transgression if he considered God his friend? Adam's sin produced two misconceptions which have continued in men's minds ever since: first, that God is man's enemy as a result of Adam's sin; and second, that man must reconcile God by his works. The first of these errors is illustrated by Adam's attempt to hide from God; the second, by his attempt to clothe himself by the works of his own hands.[63]

With his carnal mind, man misunderstands God. He looks on Him as a tyrant Who desires vengeance. "A consciousness of sin, without the knowledge of God, represents *Deity* as *angry*, and full of *vengeance*. . . ." This attitude is fully seen in the Scriptures where God is often seen in a fit of jealousy and wrath—and then calming down and changing His mind toward man.[64] Yet, while Adam changed as a result of his experience, there is no evidence that God changed. His fatherly interest and love continued. In the cool of the day, He clothed Adam in skins and promised him that "the seed of the woman should bruise the serpent's head." God cursed not man but the serpent. How, then, could He need reconciliation?[65]

An important argument against the idea that God changed His attitude toward man is His attribute of unchangeability. "To say, that God loved man any less, after transgression, than before, denies his *unchangeability*; but, to say, that man was wanting in love to God, places him in his real character."[66] God foresaw, in His infinite wisdom, that Adam would sin. It was no surprise to Him. But He continued to love Adam, for, as He is infinite in all His attributes, he could not love man at one time and hate him the next.[67]

Because God is unchangeable love, He seeks to win back erring man to Himself; and this is the key to the necessity for an atonement. God sent Christ to renew man's love to Himself. Christ's death is the *result* of God's love to man, not the cause. To this point Ballou cites John 3:16-17:

For God so loved the world, that he gave his only begotten Son, that whosoever believeth in him should not perish, but have everlasting life. For God sent not his Son into the world to condemn the world; but that the world through him might be saved.

This passage demonstrates that "what Christ did for sinners, was a consequence of God's love to them."[68] The belief that Christ was a proxy in whom the world was tried and condemned, and in whom man suffered as a penalty for transgression, is wrong. God's purpose in sending Christ into the world "was the salvation of the sinner, and not for the removing of any dissatisfaction in himself" towards mankind.[69] Ballou piles up his texts in order to prove his point[70] and sings a paean of praise to the Father for His love.

What an infinite difference there is between the All-gracious and Merciful, and his lost and bewildered creatures? He, all glorious, without a spot in the whole infinitude of his nature; all lovely, without exception, and loving, without partiality. Who can tell the thousandth part of his love to his offspring?[71]

As for man, Ballou asserts that the theory of atonement held by the individual has practical consequences in life. The most abominable actions of men have stemmed from a mistaken notion of the Deity. Persecution, among other crimes, has resulted from the belief that God is an enemy of wicked men. If Christians believed that God loved and had compassion for the ignorant and for those who have strayed, how different would be their actions toward their fellows![72]

What is the nature of the Mediator who performs atonement? Here Ballou's unitarian ideas come to the fore.[73] In his introduction, Ballou noted that he would not attempt a full refutation of the doctrine of the trinity "as I think that has frequently been done, and well done."[74] He probably had in mind Ethan Allen's *Reason the Only Oracle of Man* and Thomas Paine's *Age of Reason*. He would touch on the trinity only where the problem bears on his theory of the Mediator.[75]

His approach to the dogma of the trinity is direct and unsubtle. The trinity does not make sense; it is not reasonable. But, for the sake of argument, he will admit that Jesus is a member of the trinity. It follows that Christ, as the son of God,

is the *son* of *himself,* and is his own father; that he is no more the *Son* of *God,* than *God* is his *son!* To say, of two persons, exactly of the same age, that one of them is a real son of the other, is to confound good sense. If Jesus Christ was really *God,* it must be argued, that *God*

really died! Again, if the Godhead consists of *three distinct* persons,
and each of those *persons* is *infinite,* the *whole Godhead* amounts to the
amazing sum of infinity, multiplied by three! If it is said, that neither
of these three persons alone is infinite, I say, the *three together,* with
the addition of a *million* more *such,* would not make an *infinite being.*[76]

Having thus dismissed the trinitarian dogma, Ballou presents
a unitarian—or rather an Arian—view of Christ. He bases his arguments squarely on the Scriptures in order to prove that "the Mediator
is a *created dependent* being." [77] The dependence of the Mediator
on God is shown by his frequent prayers to God. Jesus recognized
the Father as a superior: "The Son can do nothing of himself, but
what he seeth the Father do" (John 5:19). He acknowledged his
Father as superior in wisdom: "But of that day and hour knoweth
no man, no, not the angels of heaven, but my Father only" (Matthew 24:36).[78] Ballou bolsters his belief that the Mediator is in-
ferior to the Father with a whole series of texts from the Old and
New Testaments.[79]

Christ, as the Mediator, is the representative of God. Just as
a minister of the President of the United States at a foreign court is,
in effect, "the *power* that sent him," so Christ is, in effect, God
on earth in the task assigned him.[80] When his mission is accomplished, he will deliver up his kingdom to the Father, "that
God may be all in all" (I Cor. 15:28).[81]

Ballou tries to be honest with the Scriptures. He does not deny
that, in places, Christ is referred to as *"God, Lord,* and *ever-lasting
Father,"* nor does he deny the propriety of such appellations. But
he does deny that they equate Christ with the self-existent Jehovah.[82] St. Paul could not have known Christ as *"essentially* God,"
for he specifically calls Christ a man (I Tim. 2:5). This would have
been improper, to say the least, if Paul had known him to be otherwise.[83]

Is Christ, then, just a man? Yes—but. Ballou would consider
Jesus "no more than equal with men," were it not that God "anointed
him above his fellows." [84] But Christ was dependent on God for
this exaltation.[85] Again:

It will be said, Christ taught the people, that *he* and his *Father*
were *one.* I grant he did, and if that proves him to be essentially God,
the argument must run farther than the objector would wish to have it.
See St. John xvii. ii, Christ prays that his disciples may be *one,* even as
he and the *Father* are *one.*[86]

It is obvious that the oneness of the Father and the Son is not a metaphysical oneness but a "union and agreement in the great work which he has undertaken." [87]

Christ's anointment "above his fellows" truly exalts him in Ballou's eyes. Christ is, as the Scriptures say, the "image of the invisible God, and the first born of every creature" (Colossians 1:15). He is pre-existent:

> . . . The Mediator is the first human soul which was *created,* as Adam was the first man that was formed; and . . . he is, *in Spirit,* the Father of every human creature, as much as Adam is *in* the *flesh.* Therefore, Christ saith, as it is written, "Behold I and the children that thou hast given me." [88]

Christ is not of the trinity, yet this does not lessen his power to save mankind. There is no doubt that the Mediator has the power and ability to perform the task of atonement.[89] And man needs the saving work of Christ, for he himself is not capable of performing the task of reconciliation with God. If the job of reconciling *"all things"* to God was given to Christ, "it is not reasonable to believe we have power to perform it ourselves." [90]

What is the nature of this atonement performed by Christ? Ballou first tells what it is not. Christians in general are, like the Pharisees, so bound to the letter of the law that there is a veil before their minds. They believe that the temporal death of Christ was the atoning act which freed them from sin. It is the literal blood which, they believe, has efficacy to cleanse from guilt. This is sheer carnal-mindedness.[91] When Christ said—and here Ballou paraphrases John 6:53—"except ye *eat my flesh,* and *drink my blood,* ye have no *life* in you," did he mean this to be taken literally? If so, what would the orthodox Christian make of these words (paraphrased from John 6:63): "The *flesh* profiteth nothing; the words which I speak, they are *spirit* and they are life."

The apostles were devoted to the spirit, not to the letter. The church has been led into its "wilderness of the letter" by "an *hireling priesthood.*" [92] Ballou here reveals a prejudice against the "priests" of orthodoxy which plays a part in his preaching throughout his life. The clergy have misguided the people.

To escape this carnal-mindedness, the Christian must take Christ's death figuratively to represent the death of the letter of the law. The death of Christ's body allows for the destruction of the letter and the releasing of the spirit.[93] The shedding of the blood of Christ has no other meaning.

What, then, is atonement? It is reconciliation, a renewal of love. When the soul is freed from the law of sin, it embraces the law of the spirit of life in Christ, which is love.

. . . It is by the force and power of the law of love, in Christ, that the soul is delivered from the government of the law of sin; the process of this deliverance is the work of atonement, or reconciliation.[94]

This spirit of love is the *logos,* which was made flesh and dwelt among men. The *logos* was hidden behind the letter of the law and the "cabalistical" allegories of the prophets, but it broke forth in Christ.[95]

Only love can overcome sin:

There is nothing in heaven above, nor in the earth beneath, that can do away sin, but love; and we have reason to be eternally thankful, that love is stronger than death, that many waters cannot quench it, nor the floods drown it; that it hath power to remove the moral maladies of mankind, and to make us free from the law of sin and death, to reconcile us to God, and to wash us pure, in the blood, or life, of the everlasting covenant. O love, thou great Physician of souls, what a work hast thou undertaken! All souls are thy patients; prosperous be thy labors, thou bruiser of the head of carnal mind.[96]

Through his conception of the power of love, Ballou was able to break away from the exclusive Christian outlook. In his awareness that the power of love is not exclusively Christian lay the seeds of modern Universalism.

The power of atonement, "the divine grace of reconciliation," can be communicated to those who have never heard the name of Jesus. This love is no doubt abundant even among those who have been taught that Christianity is an imposture. It cannot be restricted to "names, sects, denominations, people or kingdoms."[97] Such a conception was absolutely necessary if Ballou was to believe in the salvation of all mankind, but he was by no means giving up Christ. Only through this "second Adam" can the rejuvenating love be felt.[98] Christ as love is at work in the hearts of those who have never heard his name, even in the hearts of those who have heard it and reject it!

Ballou was a practical man. He had only to look about him

to realize that the atonement of Christ did not perform miracles. But it was never intended to "perform impossibilities" in men's lives. One cannot expect it to make men agree and live in peace with each other if they are destitute of the love which is an essential part of it.

. . . It is calculated and designed to inspire the mind with that true love which will produce peace in Jesus. As atonement is a complete fulfilment of the law of the heavenly man, it causes its recipient to love God and his fellow creatures, in as great a degree as he partakes of its nature.[99]

He compares the soul when atoning grace is absent to the land that is suffering drought. Streams and springs are dried up; the green fields have lost their allure. The soul without "the rain of righteousness" is barren. But atoning grace makes all the difference: "The soul is like the earth that drinketh in the rain that cometh oft upon it. . . ." All is revived; and like a garden "well watered and cultivated," the soul produces precious fruit.[100]

The presence of atoning grace in an individual can be determined by a simple test. Ask him if he loves God, and why? If he answers that he loves God because it is his duty and he fears God's rod, he does not possess atoning grace. He does not, cannot really love God. His profession of Christianity and his performance of the endless round of church duties amounts to nothing. He lacks the one important element: love.[101]

But if he answers that he loves God because of His "divine beauties and excellencies," that he delights in obedience to God's commands because they are "joyous and not grievous," then he is filled with atoning grace. Regardless of his denomination, if he regards the Deity in this manner, he is fulfilled.[102]

Atoning grace produces all which the bible means by conviction, or being born of the Spirit; it brings the mind from under the power and constitution of the earthly Adam, to live by faith on the Son of God, and to be ruled and governed, even in this life, in a great measure, by the law of the spirit of life in Christ Jesus. It opens eternal things to our view and contemplation; it brings heaven into the soul, and clothes the man in his right mind; it inspires the soul with divine meekness and boldness, at the same time. It was this that enabled the apostles of our Lord to preach the gospel, in defiance of the rage of their enemies, and gave them immortal consolations in their sufferings for the cause of truth. It causes the christian to love all God's rational

creatures, and to wish their saving knowledge of the truth; it produces
good works in their purity, and all the morality worth the name is
founded on it. Its divine power is stronger than any possible opposition,
and the gates of hell cannot prevail against it; it opens a door of everlasting hope, and conducts the soul, by way of the cross, to immortality
and eternal life. This dispensation of atonement is manifested through
Christ, for the reconciliation of all things to God, in his glorious kingdom of holiness and happiness.[103]

The question arises as to God's partiality in His dispensation
of grace to mankind. Ballou's argument is weak at this point:

The divine efficacy of this atoning grace may be communicated to
the most vile and profligate person in the world, and stop him in his
full career of wickedness; it can show the sinner, in a moment, the
deformity of sin, and the beauty of holiness. In other instances, the
morally virtuous are led a long time in concern and great trouble, about
themselves, before they find him of whom Moses and the prophets did
write.[104]

His only recourse is to fall back on the usual answer of Christian
piety—that God "does all things well, and in the best time and
way." [105]

Having discussed the nature of atonement, Ballou turns to the
consequences: holiness and happiness for all mankind. He sum-
marizes in three points the basis for his belief in the doctrine of
universal salvation: (1) Man was created by God in Christ. In
other words, man was originally possessed of a heavenly nature. (2)
God later reduced man to a state of flesh and blood, in which state
he became subject to the *"law of sin"*—that is, the governing principles of the fleshly man.[106] (3) God has revealed His intention
of returning man to his heavenly status "forever to be under the
governing power of the law of the heavenly constitution." [107]

Before proceeding, Ballou feels compelled to take note of the
theory that a portion of mankind must suffer in order to make the
saints in heaven more happy. He is revolted by such an argument.

. . . What reason can be given, for such an idea? How do we look
on a person, in this world, who manifests joy and happiness in the
misery of one of his fellow creatures? Do we say, he manifests a godlike
disposition? Surely no. From whence came charity; from heaven, or
hell? [108]

If any portion of the human race were to be endlessly miserable,
the rest of men would be so too, tormented by their knowledge of

their brothers' torment. A "well disposed" man cannot bear the suffering of others without suffering himself. No one in the world has exhibited more of this compassion than Jesus.[109]

A similar theory—that an all-merciful God cannot be at the same time a God of justice—Ballou also scorns as invalid. There is no scriptural proof of this proposition, and there is nothing self-evident about the maxim usually quoted in its support: "A God *all* *mercy* is a God *unjust*." [110]

At this point, Ballou develops an idea that, a few years hence, was to become known as the death-and-glory theory and was to play an important part in disrupting the peace of the Universalist denomination. Some persons declare that many men die not in a state of grace and that there is no alteration for better after death. Ballou admits that this would be a powerful argument against universal salvation, *if* it could be proved. ". . . All our christian people must [then] remain eternally as unsanctified, as they are in this world of infirmities." [111] But no Scripture can be cited in proof. Ballou himself believed strongly that there was an alteration of the person immediately after death. The soul will be instantly enlightened and converted from sin to holiness. God will purify the soul at its entrance to eternal life. [112]

Ballou is aware that there is a huge stumbling block between the Christians of his day and the doctrine of universal salvation. To surmount it, he enters on a long discussion of the meaning of biblical words usually translated in such terms as "everlasting" and "forever." [113] He cites case after case from the Bible to show that these words were used in reference to many things which have not proved to be everlasting. Used in connection with suffering and misery, therefore, they do not mean what divines have interpreted them to mean.

He then considers the use of the word "fire," asserting that in the New Testament it is used metaphorically.[114] While his arguments are not always convincing to the modern mind, he at least recognizes the important truth that many of the passages used by his opponents as references to an afterlife really refer to this earthly state. The "consuming fire" of which Jesus spoke purges man of his carnality and reveals the basic heavenly strain in his nature. The "power of gospel grace to remove all *excrescenses* from our *hearts* and *consciences"* is demonstrated by the figure of the wheat and the chaff.[115]

Wheat, though concealed from vulgar eyes, by chaff, yet, by the experienced, in the raising of grain, is perfectly well known; and we do not condemn wheat and throw it away, because nature has so ordered, that it is encompassed with chaff while growing in the field. So man is not to be valued the less by the wisdom of God, on account of the imperfections of his earthly nature. And we may, with great propriety, argue, that, as chaff is necessary for the growth of wheat, until it comes to maturity; so are all the imperfections of man, viewed by divine wisdom, until the creature comes to that experience, which was intended in a state of imperfection.[116]

Ballou never overlooked the sins of men and the corruption to which they are vulnerable. But the darker side of man's life did not blind him to man's heavenly, divine potentialities. He believed that men come to the knowledge of moral principles by degrees and that it is man's nature to seek happiness on these principles.[117]

Ballou reiterates his belief that man turns to sin because he thinks it will make him happy. Happiness is his main goal, and he will seek it by the most direct means.[118] So long as he is under the mistaken notion that sin will produce happiness, he will sin. But once he realizes that the path of virtue will "happify" him, he will be virtuous. "I wish the reader to keep in mind, that I hold sin and misery inseparably connected, and holiness and happiness so, likewise." [119]

In this last section of his *Treatise,* Ballou alternates between the scriptural argument for universalism and an assertion of the benevolent nature of God. But when all is said and done, he cannot condemn the reader who feels that, despite all Ballou has written, the doctrine of universal holiness and happiness cannot be true. "The time has been, when I believed as little of the doctrine as you now do; I never adopted the belief of universal holiness and happiness out of *choice,* but from the *force* of *real* or *supposed* evidence."[120] He realizes the opposition that those who profess the new belief will face. Some will be excommunicated; others will be avoided by their neighbors; still others will be violently opposed. There will be division even within households.[121] But what are these travails compared with the blessedness which comes from the belief in the goodness of God and the Savior?

The fulness of times will come, and the times of the restitution of all things will be accomplished. Then shall truth be victorious, and all error flee to eternal night. Then shall universal songs of honor be sung to the praise of him who liveth forever and ever. All death, sorrow and crying, shall be done away; pains and disorders shall be no more felt, temptations no more trouble the lovers of God, nor sin poison the human heart. The blessed hand of the once crucified shall wipe tears from off all faces. O, transporting thought! Then shall the blessed Savior see of the travail of his soul, and be satisfied, when, through his mediation, universal nature shall be brought in perfect union with truth and holiness, and the spirit of God fills all rational beings. Then shall the law of the spirit of life in Christ Jesus, which maketh free from the law of sin, become the governing principle of the whole man once made subject to vanity, once inthraled in darkness, sin and misery; but then, delivered from the bondage of corruption, and restored to perfect reconciliation to God, in the heavenly Adam. Then shall the great object of the Savior's mission be accomplished. Then shall the question be asked, O death, where is thy sting? But death shall not be, to give the answer. And, O grave, where is thy victory? But the boaster shall be silent. The Son shall deliver up the kingdom to God the Father; the eternal radiance shall *smile,* and GOD *shall be* ALL *in* ALL.[122]

CHAPTER X

PORTSMOUTH

In the early years of the nineteenth century, Portsmouth was the largest town in New Hampshire. Universalism had first been brought there by John Murray, and one of his disciples, Noah Parker, was the first resident preacher. After Parker's death in 1787, the Universalists were without a preacher until 1793, when they succeeded in calling George Richards, a teacher who had substituted for Murray in the Boston pulpit when the latter was off preaching in Gloucester. On Murray's permanent removal to Boston, Richards was free to accept a call to Portsmouth.[1]

With a permanent minister among them, the Universalists organized and were officially incorporated in June 1793 by act of the General Court of New Hampshire.[2] When the society began its corporate life, it had only eighteen members,[3] but by 1807 it was in a position to build a meetinghouse on newly purchased land.[4] This move proved to be unwise, however, for it left the society unable to meet Richards' full salary of $500 a year for the next few years.[5] He finally resigned [6] and moved to Philadelphia.

With this financial cloud over its head, the Portsmouth society elected a committee "to go or send to Salem to confer with the ministers which may be assembled there at the Instalation [sic] of Mr Turner in June next, on the subject." [7] Ballou was in Salem on the appointed day, having come from Vermont to deliver the sermon at his friend's installation.[8] The sermon, as printed, is not very impressive; but the committee was much taken with the tall, imposing, thirty-eight-year-old preacher. It invited him to fill the pulpit at Portsmouth for several Sundays. The Portsmouth people heard Ballou, agreed with the opinion of their committee and voted to

offer him the sum of Eight hundred dollars pr. year together with the contribution money, as an inducement for him to settle with us as our Minister, the expenses of removing his family &c from Barnard to this place to be paid by the Society.[9]

It is interesting that the society offered a salary of $800, after having failed to meet Richards' salary of $500. Ballou may have known of this trouble, for he insisted that one quarter of his salary be paid in advance and that he be given the rest punctually in quarterly payments. This the society voted to do.[10] He then wrote the society a letter:

DEAR BRETHREN IN CHRIST,
    With deep concern I have taken into consideration your friendly call bearing date August 21st, 1809 for my settlement with you in the ministry. Many and important have been the objections to my removal from those United Societies, with whom I have been happily connected almost seven years, without experiencing the smallest disaffection either with the body at large, or even an Individual. But such are the ways of *divine Providence* and *Grace,* that human Wisdom seems to have nothing to do, but submit to the economy and wisdom of God. In having pleased the great head of the Church to put it into the hearts of my friends in Vermont to grant their consent to your request, as you have seen by their answer; it devolves on me to decide the main question, whither [sic] I consent to your invitation or not. From the first of my having this subject under consideration I have invariably considered it of that importance, which rendered it necessary to watch with profound attention whatever might transpire in divine Providence to assist in a correct decision. In this way I have come to the conclusion that the *Call* from the Society is a *Call* from my divine *Master,* and in obedience to him, I joyfully accept it; Altho. I am sensible that my cares are enlarged by it; yet, I pray God that his Grace may be sufficient for me.
                                        Yours in Christian love
                                        HOSEA BALLOU[11]

That fall Ballou moved his wife and five children to Portsmouth[12] to begin his first real settlement over a church. He was installed on November 8, 1809, with Edward Turner preaching the sermon on the text II Tim. 1:8a: "Be not thou therefore ashamed of the testimony of our Lord." [13] The first few years of this ministry were to be very successful. Ballou preached twice, sometimes three times, every Sunday[14] to large congregations.[15]

Shortly after he arrived in town, Ballou visited Dr. Joseph Buckminster,[16] minister of one of the Congregational churches. He expressed the wish that he might have friendly relations with his fellow ministers in Portsmouth.[17] The older man appears to have taken a liking to the newcomer, for on December 28 he sent him a note expressing his concern. Ballou, he fears, is incurring danger to his soul by preaching the heresy of Universalism. No matter with what "human ingenuity or plausible and sophistic reasoning" such ideas are preached, they have not divine authority.[18] He does not want to dispute with Ballou, for he believes that no good can come from controversy. When people have made up their minds and party passions are involved, it is not likely that opinions can be changed. Opinions can only be changed by *"that still small voice"* speaking to one in "retired reflections." [19] But he entreats Ballou "in friendship and affection" to reconsider his Universalist preaching and its dangerous consequences to himself and others. He asks him to "anticipate the day of judgment, and realize yourself called upon to give an account of your stewardship." [20]

Ballou appears to have been impressed by Buckminster's concern for him. He answers the letter in terms of warm appreciation,[21] but expresses his belief that universal salvation can be proved, as well as any doctrine can, from the Bible.[22] Furthermore, he takes issue with Buckminster's statement that party passions will prevent a fruitful discussion.[23] He believes that "candid and temperate" men can receive "light and edification" by such a process.[24] Let Buckminster write down his reasons from the Scriptures for rejecting the idea of universal salvation. He promises to give them prayerful consideration and acknowledge whatever light he gains—and, by the same token, to state wherein he disagrees.[25]

If Ballou, who relished controversy, thought he could pull Buckminster into a dispute, he was mistaken. The old man courteously declined to debate with him. He is concerned to appear before his Judge with "unstained garments"; for this reason and no other, he had felt it his duty to warn Ballou against heresy. He had hoped his expressions of concern would lead Ballou to reconsider his positions. Although he must admit that he was tempted to break his resolution and debate with Ballou, he has decided that, if the arguments of such giants as Edwards have not prevailed, nothing he can say will have any effect.[26]

Ballou was not one to give the opponent the last word. He answered Buckminster, expressing his joy and supreme confidence in Universalism as the truth.[27] And with an exchange of very formal notes,[28] the correspondence came to a close.

Ballou also impressed one of the other Congregational ministers in town. Old Joseph Walton was pastor of the Independent Congregational Church. He thought highly of Ballou's natural abilities and gifts, and was particularly taken with his deferential attitude toward himself.[29] Unlike his Congregational colleague, Buckminster, Walton was perfectly willing to enter into a disputation and to trade text for text. His disagreement with Ballou resulted from his attendance at two funeral services conducted by the young man.[30] He was disturbed by Ballou's message on these occasions and wished to admonish him in a friendly manner concerning his errors of omission and commission.[31]

In a letter dated November 19, 1810, Walton objected to Ballou's contention that death was designed by God for the good of man. How can such a view be reconciled with such biblical passages as Romans 6:23, which states that "the wages of sin is death"? He points to the Genesis story of the forbidden fruit to prove that sin is responsible for death and that "sin is the work of the devil." [32] He accuses Ballou of perverting the Scriptures[33] and charges him with not having preached in either service the need for repentance[34] or belief in the resurrection of the dead.[35]

In his reply, Ballou takes up Walton's charges one by one. As to death, he believes it was designed for the good of mankind. It was designed by God, so it must be good, or God must be considered man's enemy.[36]

I view *death*, sir, as an appointment of God, a friendly messenger, sent to dissolve a tabernacle of corruption and vanity, at the dissolution of which, "the dust returns to the earth as it was, and the spirit unto God who gave it." [37]

He bases this belief on such passages as the words of Paul to the Philippians (1:21): "For me to live is Christ, and to die is gain."

As to the lack of a call for repentance in his sermons, he believes in the passages which call for repentance as much as he believes in the rest of the Scriptures. But he does not subscribe to the idea that repentance must be taught by threats of eternal damnation.

Preaching repentance, I conceive is *teaching* men and giving them such divine instruction as bring their minds to discover more glorious things than the sins and carnal vanities of this world; which *teaching* produces a returning of the mind to the things of God and his ever blessed kingdom.[38]

It is not even necessary to use the word *repent* in order to preach repentance. A preacher "warmed with the spirit of eternal love" may successfully preach repentance without ever mentioning the word.[39] For repentance is the gift of God and does not depend on "creature agency"—that is, on man's actions.[40] Ballou thus squarely places himself against revivalism.

Concerning the resurrection he has little to say. He affirms his belief in it as it is taught in the Scriptures.[41]

The correspondence continued, taking on a sharpness of tone in places, but the expressions of friendliness and goodwill on the part of both men are strikingly genuine. Their friendship clearly surmounted their clash of opinions.

The correspondence between Ballou and the two stalwarts of orthodoxy was published in 1811 by Abner Kneeland. Why he put it into his friend's hands is not known. Perhaps he had his hands full preparing new editions of his *Notes on the Parables* and *A Treatise on Atonement* for the press.

Near the close of 1809, John Murray was stricken with paralysis. Since it was apparent that he would never be active again, it was necessary to obtain a colleague for him. Edward Mitchell, like Murray a conservative trinitarian, was persuaded to leave his pastorate in New York to come to Boston. He was settled as Murray's associate in September 1810;[42] but Ballou, next to Murray the most prominent preacher in the denomination, did not take part in the installation. An idea of the relationship between Murray and Ballou at this period may be gleaned from a letter from George Richards to Edward Turner:

I do not find that Ballou was called to the ordination of Mitchell and as a late letter from Brother John [Murray] expresses his joy at having got rid of "a *Socinian, Deistical, Sadducean Universalist,*" I have thought whether he did not thus point to a certain neglected individual.[43]

In January 1811, Ballou joined with Edward Turner of Salem, Thomas Jones of Gloucester and Abner Kneeland, now of Charlestown, to form a new association of Universalist ministers in towns along the coast. Jones was elected the first moderator, and the group named itself the Gloucester Conference, though it met in various places. Questions for discussion were submitted by the members

and assigned as the topics of papers to be read at succeeding meetings.[44] These papers, along with sermons, excerpts from books and
similar materials, were printed in a quarterly published by the
group under the title *The Gospel Visitant*. It lapsed after the first
volume was issued.

Among the papers read by Ballou was one on I Peter 3:18-20:

> For Christ also hath once suffered for sins, the just for the un-
> just, that he might bring us to God, being put to death in the flesh, but
> quickened by the Spirit: by which also he went and preached unto the
> spirits in prison; which sometime were disobedient, when once the
> longsuffering of God waited in the days of Noah, while the ark was a
> preparing, wherein few, that is, eight souls were saved by water.

From his presentation, it is apparent that he then believed in
some form of punishment in a future life.[45] But he insists that the
text cannot possibly be used to support the theory of eternal punishment. The plain meaning of the text can be seen if it is read in the
light of I Peter 4:6: "For this cause was the gospel preached also to
them that are dead, that they might be judged according to men in
the flesh, but live according to God in the spirit." It is clear that the
gospel is brought by Christ even to those spirits who died unreconciled to Him.[46] This very passage, which Ballou himself rein-
terpreted a few years later, was to provoke a great dispute in the
denomination.

Ballou found a settled ministry quite different from circuit
riding; there were many parish responsibilities he had not en-
countered before. Among these was the religious education of the
children. In those days, Sunday schools had not yet been established,
and instruction was carried on at home by means of catechisms.
In 1810, Ballou issued one for the use of the children of his
church.[47] Being opposed to creeds, he decided that the passages for
the children to memorize should be entirely in the language of the
Scriptures.[48] In selecting these, he took the opportunity to instill
into their minds, among other things, the distinction between the
creation of man and his formation in the dust.[49] And the entire
book has, of course, a decided Universalist flavor.[50] Unfortunately,
since the answers were all in scriptural language, it was not always
easy for a child to understand them without the help of a good
teacher.[51]

In 1812, Ballou published an enlarged edition of the *Notes on the Parables.*[52] From a pamphlet of eighty pages, it grew to a book of 278 pages. His interpretation of the parables has not changed, and the text of the first edition remains untouched; but added after the exposition of each parable is a section labelled "Illustration." Here the polemics missing in the first edition appear almost immediately. With all the skill at his command, Ballou attempts to show that the parables do not support the orthodox doctrine of eternal punishment.

There are occasional flashes of brilliance in this edition. A good example is a parody of the parable of the Good Samaritan, in which Ballou substitutes for the Samaritan "a certain learned divine." The Samaritan of Jesus' parable helps save the man accosted by thieves without asking any questions, but the "learned divine" questions him on his creed, whether he is willing to perish for the glory of God. Obviously the "certain learned divine" is a Hopkinsian!

Yet this edition of the *Notes,* on the whole, lacks the witty, pungent, homely illustrations of the *Treatise on Atonement.* Ballou confines himself primarily to marshaling a legion of texts from both the Old and the New Testaments to support his allegorical interpretation of the parables. Written before the birth of historical and textual criticism of the Bible, these *Notes* were far in advance of their times. But they have nothing to offer the modern reader.

In this same year, 1812, Ballou published a second edition of *A Treatise on Atonement.* It is simply a reprint of the 1805 edition, without even a new preface.

These publications were the occasion of an attack on Ballou by George Forrester,[53] a Calvinistic Baptist preacher who was a teacher in Portsmouth. Forrester did not carry on a serious discussion but resorted to ridicule. Ballou answered his "uncouth invective" [54] with considerable restraint in a series of letters published under the title *An Attempt with a Soft Answer to Turn Away Wrath.* The controversy ended with a brief reply by Forrester.[55]

The same year found Ballou engaged in a much more important controversy with members of his own church. The contention arose due to the War of 1812. Portsmouth was badly affected by the war, and the Federalist shipowners were strongly opposed to it. The majority of Ballou's church were Democrats (then called Republicans), but there was a sizable group of wealthier and more influential members who were Federalists.[56] Trouble began when

Ballou responded to a call by President Madison for a day of national humiliation and prayer. Although Ballou was a Republican[57] and had decided political opinions, for ministerial reasons he never expressed his views outside the family circle.[58] He believed that politics should definitely be kept out of the pulpit.[59] But on the day of humiliation and prayer, his patriotic feeling got the better of him. He preached a forthright, emotional sermon in favor of the President and the war.[60]

He took as his text John 18:36: "If my kingdom were of this world, then would my servants fight." Carefully he drew a distinction between the kingdom of Christ, which is not of this world and so does not use force to gain its ends, and the kingdom of this world, where force is sometimes a necessary expedient. Despite persecution the early Christians had propagated the gospel; but the church fell when Christianity was recognized by Constantine. From that

fatal moment . . . though an overflowing flood of Christian profession succeeded to cover the Roman provinces, an undulating tide of pagan superstitions found its way into the vitals of the church; and, laying hold of the civil sword, has set up and maintained, for ages, the kingdom of antichrist.[61]

The church may not use force, but it is permissible for the civil government to do so, not in an unjust war but "in the necessary defence of any of its rights which might possibly be infringed." [62] He justifies the lately declared war against England with several examples from the Old Testament. Force may be used to defend the rights of the individual, national rights and independence—and to defend property "against the depredations of wanton, unprincipled plunderers." [63]

Ballou's labeling of the mother country as "unprincipled plunderers" did not sit well with the monied Federalists in the congregation, nor did his emotional defense of the President against the "abundance of contumely, which has appeared in the public prints, designed to destroy public confidence, in our chief magistrate." [64] He fumes against the "outrage" the British have perpetrated on American citizens and quotes at length inflammatory passages from the President's message on the subject of British impressment of American seamen.[65] He urges full support of the war, for justice is on the side of America, and God will not fail to support the side of justice.[66]

Despite the unrest in the church caused by this sermon, it was published "by Request of the Wardens." [67] (It is safe to assume that at least the majority of the wardens were Republicans!) The newspapers of the town also spread word of the sermon. Depending on their party affiliation, they praised or denounced it, but no attempt was made to refute its arguments. ". . . The opponents of the war described it as an illiterate performance, and found fault with the metaphors and phraseology." [68]

During the next winter, the anti-administration party in Portsmouth formed the "Washington Benevolent Society," using the name of the beloved father of the country as a rallying point against Madison. Ballou, who did not approve of this tactic, was on the sidewalk one day when the society staged a parade. Asked what he thought of it, he replied that it reminded him of a passage of Scripture. Asked which passage he meant, he quoted Isaiah 4:1: "And in that day seven women shall take hold of one man, saying, We will eat our own bread, and wear our own apparel: only let us be called by thy name, to take away our reproach." [69] The report of this incident did not help to endear him to the disaffected members of his church.

The opposition to Ballou among the antiwar party came to a head at the annual meeting of the church the following June. The embargo imposed in the war had severely damaged the economy of Portsmouth and other seacoast towns, and the society was having trouble paying the debt incurred by the building of the new meetinghouse. Despite this trouble, it voted to set Ballou's salary at the usual $800 for the ensuing year. [70] But the monied Federalists did not let this opportunity pass without attempting to make trouble for their minister:

> Mr Isaac Waldron Jr, Capt Lewis Barnes Mr Mark Simes & others presented to the meeting their protest against their contributing in any way to the support of Mr Ballou &c, which protest was read, & by them requested to be recorded on the records of the society. [71]

But they were not successful. Ballou had the backing he needed to defeat the opposition:

> Voted, That the protest offered by Isaac Waldron Jr, Lewis Barnes, Mark Simes & others shall not be entered on the records. [72]

Waldron and Barnes then attempted to block the assessment on the pews, not wanting their tax money to go to Ballou's salary. Their move, however, "was negatived" by the moderator.[73]

The state of the Portsmouth society was bad, emotionally and financially. Animosity to the minister was so intense that several persons declined to serve as officers of the society.[74] The financial plight was severe; a special committee was formed to receive all money held in trust by the wardens, to collect all accounts receivable and to pay all debts, even if it were necessary to borrow money.[75] It is interesting to note that the society then owed almost $1,000 to Mark Simes in debt and interest on the new meetinghouse.[76] Simes was one of those who had attempted to cut off Ballou's salary.

As a result of all these troubles, several of the disaffected members withdrew from the society.[77] The greater part of the congregation remained loyal to Ballou, but his ministry was under a cloud. He would not leave town under this pressure, however, even when the society had trouble paying his salary. To supplement his income, he turned again to his avocation of teaching. He had a large family to support: two more daughters had been born, and another child was on its way. Elmina Ruth was born on April 3, 1810, shortly after the Ballous came to Portsmouth. In her name they sought to preserve the memory of the baby who had been lost to them two and a half years before. Clementina was born on July 10, 1812, shortly before the trouble began over the "war" sermon. Fiducia came into the world on May 1, 1814.

With a wife and seven children (soon eight) it is no wonder that Ballou was hard pressed for money. From the fall of 1813 to the spring of 1815, he conducted a private school. Quarters were readily available; the other half of the double house in which they lived was inhabited by a sea captain, who was often at sea.[78] Ballou called to Portsmouth to assist him his bright, seventeen-year-old grandnephew and namesake,[79] Hosea Ballou, 2d, who not only taught school for him but also began the study of divinity under his tutorship.[80] This was the beginning of a long and deep association between the two men.

CHAPTER XI

SALEM

At the end of April 1815, Ballou received a letter from a committee of the new Universalist Society in Salem. Edward Turner had gone to Charlestown in June of the previous year, and the Salem church had been without a minister ever since. At a special meeting of the society,

it having been intimated that your ingagements where [sic] not so in Portsmouth but that you might receive an invitation from any other Society, under that impression it was Voted unanimously to give you a Call to be our pastor and that a Sallerey of Eight hundred Dollars was Voted for one year.[1]

Ballou's reply encouraged the Salem society to hope that he might be available, but he pointed out that, with his large family, $800 was scarcely enough to support him in Portsmouth, and living costs were higher in more fashionable Salem. Furthermore

Should the Society in Salem think proper to find me a comfortable house to live in, and as much firewood as a prudent family would consume, in addition to what has been already generously offered, the *conditions* would be acceptable. There would be some expence in moving which the Society would undoubtedly assist in at least.[2]

Salem replied that the best it could offer was $800 a year, to be paid in quarterly installments as requested, and his moving expenses.[3]

Portsmouth obviously knew nothing of this correspondence, for on May 22 the society held its annual meeting and voted to offer him the usual $800 for the year.[4] When it heard that Salem was attempting to woo its pastor away, it voted to match the Salem offer up to $900.[5] This was a sizable increase; but Ballou knew from experience that, no matter how much was promised he would probably never collect it. He therefore requested a dismissal from the church.

The Portsmouth society, meanwhile, was corresponding with Salem in an attempt to persuade them to withdraw their invitation.[6] This the Salem church refused to do. It felt it had acted properly in its negotiations with Ballou; and his services were badly needed in Salem, which had been without regular preaching for a long time. "Since Brother Ballou gave his answer and it was made known here a number of applications have been made for pews in the meeting and the spirits of our friends seem to be revived. . . ." [7]

Salem was, of course, a seacoast town and had suffered as much as Portsmouth as a result of the late war. Edward Turner had had a very difficult time collecting his salary; he had often complained that he was destitute and that his family was in need.[8] This bad financial situation was probably responsible for his resignation and removal to Charlestown. Ballou could not have been ignorant of the problem, for he was a very close friend of Turner, and his position must have been exceedingly unpleasant at Portsmouth if he was willing to move on with so little security. But he felt a warm spot in his heart for the Salem society. When it began building its new meetinghouse on Rust Street in 1808, he had been chosen to place the cornerstone.[9] When Edward Turner had been installed there in June 1809, he had served on the examining council and had preached the installation sermon.[10]

Beyond this, the Salem situation offered a challenge. The society was discouraged, having been without a preacher for an entire year. And there was work to be done at nearby Danvers, where a newly organized group of Universalists was meeting in a schoolhouse. Ballou was to preach to this new group every fourth Sunday.[11]

At last all negotiations were completed; and with great expectation, the Salem society installed its new minister on June 21, 1815.[12] It was immensely proud of him, but it was less impressed with the appearance of his family. Hosea and Ruth, frugal by taste and necessity, found it difficult to clothe themselves and their eight children in a manner acceptable to aristocratic Salem. Some of the more interested church members decided to take action. The result was recorded in a personal notebook by one of the leading members of the church:

When Mr Ballou first came here he and his family were destitute of many articles of wearing apparil . . . or Such articles as to make them appear decent in the Street, and in order to have our minister appear as respectable as to dress as others the Society took up a Subscription, and collected Money Enough to furnish Mr Ballou with many very useful articles for his family, among which Mr and Mrs Ballou were both furnished with Superfine Black Broad cloth Cloaks & Hat & Bonnet to correspond, which when worne, they made a much more respectable appearance than when they came, and they also were much improved in their manners before they left us.[13]

But this commiseration was short-lived. When the time came for the quarterly salary installment, Ballou had to ask for it:

To the Committee of the universalist Society,
Brethren, as the means for the support of my family, which were on hand at the time I came to this town, have hetherto [sic] met my expences [sic], I have not called on the Society for any part of my Salary; but those means having now failed, it will be necessary to call for a quarter's Salary next week, when my first quarter will have terminated.
Yours with due respect,
HOSEA BALLOU[14]

His financial situation was not much, if at all, improved by his move to Salem. The balance of what was owed him by the Portsmouth church was not paid until May 1816.[15] Since Ballou never liked to borrow money, he found it necessary to request a raise in salary when, in April 1816, the Salem church voted to request him to serve another year.[16]

As to the Salary, I am *confirmed* in the opinion which I formed before I came to this Town, that the sum agreed on for the first year is too small to meet the expenses of my family, in that way of living which convenience and the respectability of the Society require.[17]

Salem voted to offer him $900 for the coming year.[18] He accepted this figure,[19] but the society fell further and further behind in its payments to him.

Ballou's years in Salem were filled with controversy. The orthodox groups in the area were quite hostile to the Universalist faith. Samuel Worcester had attacked Universalism from his pulpit at the Tabernacle Church as early as 1811. Ballou, then in Portsmouth, had written an extended review of this sermon,[20] but there is nothing to indicate that the two ever met when Ballou moved to Salem.

Ballou did, however, come into conflict with one of the other Congregational ministers in town. He seems to have attended a meeting at the church of the Reverend Brown Emerson[21] and heard him preach on Romans 5:18, one of Ballou's favorite universalist

texts. Emerson labored to prove that this text could be applied only
to the elect. Ballou was so incensed at this misuse of the Word of
God that he published an open letter to Emerson,[22] with an introduction addressed, by way of explanation, to his own church and congregation. He is writing, he says, because he is

> fully convinced that our blessed Redeemer has placed me among you,
> for the purpose of watching the motions of "spiritual wickedness in
> high places," and of opposing thereto the spiritual "weapons of our
> warfare."
> . . . .
> I can give no good account of my divine master, if I shun to meet the
> enemy in the most direct and open manner.[23]

The *Letter* is primarily concerned with a defense of the
scriptural validity of the doctrine of universal salvation and a refutation of the idea that such passages as Romans 5:18 refer only to an
elect. He also rebuffs the calumny that Universalists claim there is
no distinction between the righteous and the wicked set forth in
"all the scriptures." [24]

Emerson did not condescend to answer Ballou; but one Benjamin Dole, no doubt of his congregation, published an open letter
in reply. Styling himself "an illiterate mechanic," [25] he explains
that he is writing because Ballou's "pamphlet has fallen below the
attention of men of talents and science." [26] Dole's tone is that
which one might expect from "an illiterate mechanic":

> I shall not attempt to follow you through all your windings, nor
> drive you from your false refuges; neither will I endeavour to uncover
> all your hiding places. When the overflowing flood shall come, it will
> sweep away your refuge of lies.[27]

Dole writes in defense of election and the other standard doctrines
of Calvinism.

Ballou's most extended controversy of this period was with the
Reverend John Kelly of Hampstead, New Hampshire, who was
alarmed at the rapid spread of Universalism[28] and what he believed to be its deleterious effect on the morals of the people. So
alarmed did he become that he found it necessary to publish to the
world his *Solemn and Important Reasons Against becoming a Universalist*. Ballou, ever ready to take up the cudgels for the faith,
replied to Kelly's charges.[29] He demonstrates his mastery of the

polemical style in his refutation of the "opinion" that God's anger
was pacified by the blood of Christ.

> *Atonement* signifies *reconciliation.* The opinion that God received
> atonement, or was reconciled to man by Jesus Christ, is nothing but
> the old doctrine of the mother of harlots, which enabled her clergy to
> sell indulgences.[30]

Kelly responded with more of his reasons against becoming a
Universalist,[31] and Ballou offered more vindications of divine benevolence.[32] Kelly had hoped to stem the tide of Universalism; but,
as is usually the case in such matters, the publicity given it by his
attack only helped to inspire further interest in the "heresy." [33]

Not all of Ballou's time was spent in battle against the enemy.
These years in Salem saw two important rounds of correspondence
with friends.

Ballou's old friend Abner Kneeland had become disenchanted
with the church and Christianity, and was being lured into skepticism by the writings of the Deists. He asked Ballou to help him
in his unbelief, to show him cogent reasons why the Deists were
wrong in their disparagement of the Bible and the revelation usually
associated with it. Their correspondence[34] makes tedious reading,
for Ballou had great trouble keeping Kneeland on the subject.
It is quite revealing, however, with regard to Ballou's attitude
toward Deism. He believed it had a good catalytic effect on
Christians, forcing them to examine their traditional beliefs.[35]

Ballou takes his stand squarely on the authority of the Scriptures, expressing complete confidence that the testimony of the
apostles is true,[36] that the prophecies of the Old Testament were
fulfilled in the coming of Christ[37] and that the miracles of Christ
are proof of the truth of Christianity.[38] It is obvious from his repeated references to Paley[39] that he depends heavily on that Angli-
can divine for his major arguments in countering Kneeland's
doubts.[40]

Near the close of their cycle of letters, Kneeland professed to
have been convinced by Ballou's arguments.[41]

> The question may be still asked, why do you now believe? To
> which I give this plain and simple answer. It is because, notwithstand-
> ing the *incredibility* of the miracles of Christ, and of the apostles, and
> the resurrection, the truth of which, these miracles go to confirm and
> substantiate; yet, the idea that this story should ever have been told in

the manner it is, without having truth for its foundation, in spite of all my *incredibility*, is still more *incredible!* [42]

This is a shaky foundation for faith, and it was to prove so a few years later, when Kneeland was engulfed completely by the tide of infidelity. During the interim, however, he once again became a servant of the church and accepted a pastorate in New York.[43]

Of much more significance and lasting consequence was the correspondence between Ballou and his friend Edward Turner, of the church at Charlestown, on the subject of future punishment. Their letters appeared intermittently for a year—April 1817 to April 1818—in *The Gospel Visitant*, which they had revived.[44] The debate seems to have been instigated by the contentious Jacob Wood,[45] who had recently been accepted in the ranks of Universalist preachers. Wood carried to Edward Turner a proposal from Ballou that the two men conduct a "friendly investigation" [46] of the subject of future punishment, with the aim of determining whether it is taught in the Scriptures.[47] The fact that Ballou and Turner were friends and shared the same opinions would insure a cool, dispassionate debate.[48] Ballou extended to Turner the privilege of choosing the side he would like to defend.[49]

Turner, a mild, gentle person, agreed to the debate and chose the affirmative side of the question. Having always been inclined to believe in a future punishment, he felt that—with his limited ability at argumentation—he could best defend the side in which he believed.[50] But this choice may also have been deferential; he may have felt that Ballou tended to favor the other side of the question: that there is no future punishment and that chastisement for sin is limited to this life. The two men had been close friends for twenty-two years, ever since Turner first heard Ballou preach a unitarian sermon at Sturbridge in 1795. Turner would certainly know in what direction Ballou's thoughts were running. From Jacob Wood's later actions, it is safe to assume that he also sensed Ballou's inclination to reject the idea of punishment in a future state.

Such a rejection was the logical outcome of Ballou's theory of man. If, as he had set forth at length in the *Treatise*, man's carnal mind is responsible for sin, it is logical to assume that when man's carnality is dissolved at death, he will enter the eternal state bearing only the marks of his heavenly nature. Would this heavenly nature then be subjected to punishment for the sins of the earthly life?

But Ballou also held that sin equals misery and that misery cannot exist where there is no sin. If there is no sin in an afterlife, there can be no punishment!

That Ballou had tussled with this problem before is obvious from his correspondence with Joel Foster, which was published in 1799. At that time, Ballou was wavering on the question of punishment in the future life. When Foster forced him to take a stand, he declared that he believed in a limited, disciplinary future punishment, as opposed to an endless penal suffering.

In the *Treatise on Atonement*, six years later, Ballou was purposely vague on the subject of future punishment. This was possible in a work which, after all, was designed mainly to refute the idea of endless punishment and other favorite tenets of orthodoxy.

In the years following the *Treatise*, Ballou apparently accepted some form of punishment in the afterlife. His exposition of I Peter 3:18-20 before the Gloucester conference of ministers suggests this, and in his review of Samuel Worcester's sermon *God a Rewarder*[51] he wrote:

> As believers in God who will have all men to be saved, and to come to the knowledge of the truth, and as deniers of ENDLESS UNMERCIFUL PUNISHMENT, we do by no means assume the place of judgment, or pretend to say how long God may, for gracious purposes, chasten or punish the rebellious. We believe that chastisement will be exercised by the faithfulness of our merciful father in heaven, as long as sin in us renders it necessary, and no longer.[52]

If Ballou had any doubts on this point at the beginning of his correspondence with Turner, by its close he had made up his mind once and for all, and he vigorously defended this position for the rest of his long life.

The debate started with a broadside of challenges; but as it proceeded, Turner declared the whole question could be resolved into one point:

> If it can be proved from reason and scripture, that "death NECESSARILY produces such a moral change in the mind of the sinner, as to make him at once a willing, obedient and happy subject of the moral kingdom;" then it will follow that the doctrine of future punishment is proved false.[53]

In short, if Ballou's theory of the heavenly and carnal natures of man could be proved true, Turner would concede that there is no future retribution.

Ballou did not take up this challenge directly. Throughout the course of the debate, however, he insisted that belief in a future punishment is not an essential feature of the gospel faith.[54] If the Deity had considered it so, He would have put it beyond dispute by proclaiming it from the time of Adam to the present. But no such proclamation can be found in the Scriptures.[55]

The climax of the debate was reached when Turner asked Ballou how I Peter 3:18-20, with its reference to "spirits in prison," could be reconciled with his new position.[56] Turner undoubtedly remembered his earlier interpretation of this obscure passage as favoring the doctrine of future retribution.

Ballou's exegetical skill was sorely tested by Turner's question, but he proved equal to the occasion. As he pondered the problem, reading the passage over and over in context, suddenly "the light broke in" on his mind.[57] The interpretation he came to was quite different from that of "the Papists" and the Winchester Universalists (for whom the "spirits in prison" were souls in a kind of purgatory) and of Protestants in general (for whom the "spirits" were the souls of the people of Noah's day, who were in hell in the lifetime of Peter).[58] As Ballou now read the passage, the "spirits in prison" were simply the Gentiles. Peter was reporting that, after Christ's death, his spirit was made manifest to the Gentiles. The reference to "spirits in prison," then, did not justify the theory of a future state of punishment.[59]

The hurdle had been removed from his path. Forced to study the question of future punishment in order to score as a debater, he had convinced himself on the truth of the position he had arbitrarily taken. At last he could see the logical outcome of the premises he had started with so many years before. This correspondence with Turner was another of the turning points of his life. As he later wrote to a friend:

While attending to this correspondence, I became entirely satisfied, that the scriptures begin and end the history of sin in flesh and blood; and that beyond this mortal existence the Bible teaches no other sentient state but that which is called by the blessed name of life and immortality.[60]

CHAPTER XII

THE CALL TO BOSTON

John Murray was dead. He had passed away in September 1815,[1] leaving a vacuum in Boston. The First Universalist Society was not without a minister, but Paul Dean was exceedingly ineffective. Many of his congregation wanted to hear an aggressive Universalism preached, but Dean preferred to keep his Universalism to himself and avoid the censure of his orthodox brethren. Furthermore, he was out of step theologically with almost the entire body of the Universalist ministry: he was a trinitarian, rather than a unitarian.[2]

Apart from Murray, Ballou had long been the most prominent Universalist leader in the nation. It was inevitable that an attempt would be made to draw him to Boston. The city was growing rapidly and could easily support more than one Universalist church. A group of his admirers therefore joined together and, on December 13, 1816, were incorporated as the Second Society of Universalists in the Town of Boston.[3] This group had the express hope and intention of attracting Ballou to its pulpit.[4]

The Second Society erected a spacious brick building on School Street, diagonally across from the present City Hall.[5] Though an exceedingly plain building—it might almost be called barnlike—it was excellent for its purpose: to bring the message of universal salvation to many people. With a spacious main floor and with galleries on three sides, it could seat almost a thousand persons.[6] It cost $22,000 and was dedicated on October 16, 1817,[7] with Thomas Jones of Gloucester preaching the sermon.[8]

The School Street Church—as it soon became known—extended to Ballou a unanimous call to become its minister[9] at a starting salary of $1,300 a year, plus occasional donations of fuel.[10] He accepted and was installed there on Christmas Day, 1817—but not without hard feeling on the part of some members of the Salem society, whom he had served about two years. These critics felt that he had not acted an honorable part in his negotiations with Boston and accused him of not being open on the subject.[11] But he must have felt a move was imperative, not only because of the great advantage of a pulpit in Boston, but because his financial condition was very poor. When he left Salem, the Standing Committee gave him two notes for money owed him, a total of $660.[12]

Although his higher Boston salary allowed his large family—for the first time—to live comfortably, Ballou was anxious to receive the money owed him by Salem. His first son, Hosea Faxon, was now married[13] and striking out on his own in the then wilderness of western Massachusetts. Hosea wanted to help the boy and pleaded with Salem for the money:

> Brethren, I am in great want of some assistance. My oldest son is in a new country, has a family and nothing but his hands to depend on for support. I greatly desire to help him. I am persuaded that you will so far enter into my feelings as to assist me to one hundred dollars, at least, by the first of September next. Your affectionate and faithful Servant, *Hosea Ballou.*[14]

This letter to the clerk of the Salem society, written nine months after his departure from Salem, was not given the courtesy of a reply. More than a year later he wrote again.

BROTHER NEWEL [sic],

It is now going on nearly twelve months since I stated in a letter to the Clerk of your Society the necessity that my family was in for want of what is due me from the Society in Salem—to which statement I have never received any reply. In that communication I requested that the Society would be so good as to accommodate me with an hundred dollars by the first of September last, as my necessity for the money was very pressing.

I will not undertake to make you acquainted with the painful feelings of my mind, occasioned by the entire neglect with which that Society has seen fit to treat me. A Society for whose benefit I directed my most zealous and active labours, until stern necessity humbled me before God, to ask of him relief in the way his wisdom should direct. But wish you to communicate to the Society my most fervent request, that measures may be taken, which may issue in my receiving what is my due. This request is made with reference to my first duty, which is to provide for my family; it is made with reference to that brotherly conduct which is indispensible [sic] for the maintenance of christian fellowship, and with that principle of moral rectitude which requires us to do as we would be done by. Some reply from the Society favourable to this request would be received with great satisfaction, by the Society's most humble

SERVANT HOSEA BALLOU.[15]

Although these letters were read to the church and referred to the proper authorities,[16] no action appears to have been taken. By 1821 the money was still owed—with interest.[17] Whether Ballou ever received it is problematical.[18]

The Salem society, meanwhile, had fallen on evil days. It promised Ballou's successor, Joshua Flagg, $700,[19] but Flagg could not collect his money and finally left in desperation. His successor, Barzillai Streeter, was promised only $400 a year.[20]

Despite their financial disagreement, Ballou seems to have remained in friendly relations with Salem, at least for a while. After Joshua Flagg resigned, he helped the society fill its pulpit on a number of occasions and appears to have paved the way for the call of Barzillai Streeter.[21]

The most serious opposition to Ballou's move came from Paul Dean. He "distinctly informed" Ballou that he did not want him to come to Boston.[22] Some claimed that he was afraid that Ballou's outspoken universalism would force him to take a stand on matters concerning which he would prefer to remain silent.[23] There was also the practical consideration that Ballou's presence would have an adverse effect on his church. In any case, the relationship between the two men was always very strained, despite many efforts on Ballou's part to overcome Dean's animosity.[24]

Dean was naturally invited to play a prominent role in Ballou's installation as minister of the new church. If there was resentment in his heart, it was not apparent in the smooth-flowing, well-chosen words of his sermon:[25]

> With peculiar satisfaction do I receive you as one, come to second my feeble efforts to testify the Gospel of God's universal grace in this metropolis. . . . Your lot has cast you in a pleasant place, and I trust God has, and ever will give you here a goodly heritage.[26]

It was an aggressive Universalism that Ballou introduced to Boston. Immediately he took the battle to the enemy's territory, choosing for the text of his evening sermon on the first Sunday of 1818 the words of Paul, II Thessalonians 1:7-9—words usually interpreted as referring to the day of judgment:

> . . . When the Lord Jesus shall be revealed from heaven with his mighty angels, In flaming fire taking vengeance on them that know not God, and that obey not the gospel of our Lord Jesus Christ: Who shall be punished with everlasting destruction from the presence of the Lord, and from the glory of his power.[27]

Ballou attempted to show that this passage refers not to a last judgment but to the judgment of Jesus' own generation. The "flaming
fire" he interpreted as the fire of God's love: the Lord chastises man
because He loves him and wants to correct his ways. This opposition to the traditional doctrine of the last judgment, and this
proclamation that God is a God of love, sounded the keynote for
Ballou's long ministry in Boston.

When the sermon was published,[28] it fell into the hands of a
Methodist preacher, Timothy Merritt, who complained that

at one dash he strikes out the doctrine of a future judgment, the displeasure of God against the sinner, and all future punishments, thus
opening the gates of heaven to the most depraved among mankind, and
showing a broad, instead of a narrow way, to eternal life.[29]

As far as Merritt could see, Ballou's reasoning amounted to this:
"Jerusalem and many of the Jews were destroyed; therefore there is
no future judgment." [30]

This was the beginning of a round of "replies" and "vindications," [31] during which neither man really attempted to understand
the other's position. Merritt's parting words show the tone of the
controversy:

Should his opponent [Ballou] write again, and use sophistry,
declamation and evasion, instead of discussing the merits of the cause,
he [Merritt] will consider his production as already answered, and take
no further notice of it.[32]

With such a controversy on his hands immediately after his arrival
in Boston, Ballou soon felt right at home.

In order to accommodate the crowds who wanted to hear him,
he preached three times every Sunday.[33] Practically all the seats
were taken in the morning; in the afternoon, many persons were
standing in the aisles; in the evening, the aisles were crowded.[34]
Many of these hearers were visitors in Boston who came to hear
Ballou out of curiosity. Those who went away convinced of the
truth of his doctrine took Universalism home with them to their
communities and were responsible, in many cases, for the birth of
new societies.[35] There is no doubt that Universalism was given great
impetus by the presence of its greatest preacher in the metropolis.

From August 1818 to July 1819, Ballou presented on alternate
Sabbath evenings a series of lecture sermons.[36] Many of these

were preached on texts about which people had questioned him.
Others were preached on specific topics by request.[37] His purpose
was to demolish the interpretations of texts used to justify belief
in eternal misery: "We are not only at liberty to reject all ideas
which have been established by tradition without proper evidence,
but it is our religious duty so to do." [38]

Although Ballou's style in the *Lecture Sermons* does not appeal to the modern taste, it was extremely popular in his own day,
when biblical preaching was in fashion. The approach is argumentative, with a heavy accent on scriptural proof; the sermons abound in
citations and quotations. Occasionally, but not often, he waxes
poetic over the love of the Father to His children. On rare occasions,
the sermonizing approaches the aesthetic, though on the whole it is
of pedestrian style. The attendance during this series was uncom-
monly large; every part of the auditorium was crowded.[39] The
sermons were printed by Henry Bowen, a member of the congregation, and had a wide circulation.[40]

The sermons are largely an exposition of the leading ideas
found in the *Treatise on Atonement*. The infinite love of the Father
for His children; atonement as the reconciliation of man to God;
Jesus as a demonstration of God's love for man; the finite nature of
sin—all is here, with but one important exception. Ballou does not
mention the trinity. He attacked that erroneous doctrine on several
occasions, but he obviously felt it was not essential in his pulpit
presentations—or so it would appear from the many sermons which
were put into print over the years. His main concern was to preach
the joyful gospel of God's universal love for His children.

On the evening of July 4, 1819, a young bootmaker's apprentice was walking down School Street on his way home. As he
passed the Second Universalist Society, he noticed the lights and
realized there was a meeting inside. Curiosity lured him in, and
he found it necessary to ease himself into the crowded aisles. Up in
the pulpit he saw a tall, impressive preacher comparing the love of
God to the love of parents for their children.[41] Thomas Whittemore was moved by this message of love to God and man. He did
not know then that the man in the pulpit was to change his life
completely.[42]

CHAPTER XIII

THE UNIVERSALIST MAGAZINE

Ballou had been in Boston for more than a year when Henry Bowen, a member of his church and his publisher, came to him with an idea. Ballou's sermons had been selling well, and Bowen felt that they might have stirred up enough interest in Universalism to justify the publication of a weekly newspaper. Bowen was then publishing an unsuccessful quarto sheet, *The Weekly Magazine and Ladies' Miscellany*. Ballou was doubtful that a Universalist newspaper would be any more of a success, but Bowen figured he had little to lose.[1] And so was born *The Universalist Magazine*, the first Universalist newspaper in America.

The first issue appeared on Saturday, July 3, 1819, with Ballou as editor and Bowen as publisher. Ballou set forth his editorial policy on the first page. The *Magazine* was to deal with the "momentous subjects of DOCTRINE, RELIGION, and MORALITY." [2] He invited readers to submit any of their thoughts which might promote the "growth" of these "essential concerns," whether or not they agreed with his own position on these matters. Members of all denominations were invited to contribute, for the Universalist is no sectarian. "He keeps his eye on the divine Master, who is the same to all nations, to all sects, and to all denominations." [3]

As might be expected, however, the *Magazine* became primarily the organ of the Universalist denomination. The first few issues were written largely—and anonymously—by Ballou, but numerous correspondents soon began contributing material. The paper was largely devoted to selections from sermons, letters and debates on subjects of interest among Universalists, along with notices of births, deaths and marriages, the laying of cornerstones and similar denominational affairs. Of particularly great value was the inclusion of the calls and notices of conventions and association meetings, and the reports and circular letters which came forth from such gatherings.

Many articles were devoted to refuting the charge that Universalism leads to licentiousness. And the Universalists of the day were much incensed over attacks in the orthodox press, such as the report of the "Death-Bed Exercises of a Woman Who had Lived a Universalist" but had renounced the heresy just in time. The woman's daughter described the scene in the Chillicothe, Ohio, *Weekly Recorder:*

> She said she was struck with death's cold chills—the darts of the "king of terrors" were piercing through every nerve. She found her *universal plan* would not answer, and renounced it, observing, "The bridge on which I trusted has fallen under me—I am now dying and have no hopes of myself." O my friend, my pen cannot describe, nor your imagination conceive the horrors of her mind. Her screams of dying anguish, and groans of black despair were too much for poor human nature to endure.

But the dying woman found her peace in the prayers of her family and in her own renunciation of Universalism.[4]

Such dangerous stories had to be refuted. The editor of the *Magazine* found in this story

such marks of erroneous education, such strong indications of superstition, such blind fanaticism, such palpable absurdities, such a preference to vain imaginations in comparison with the word of God and his moral attributes, that to neglect considering the subject in a way to show its total want of propriety seem a neglect of duty.[5]

On the other hand, he reported with great satisfaction the story of a young woman who, just a few hours before death, had written a letter to a Universalist friend "expressing her firm belief in the doctrine which she before disputed, and detailing the treatment she received in consequence of her avowal of her faith." [6]

There were humorous things, too. The pages of the *Magazine* are spiced with an occasional "Original Anecdote" which makes the reader smile—at the expense of the orthodox. There is the story of a little boy who heard his elders complain that Universalist preachers are indulgent toward sin. Finally he gained permission to attend a Universalist meeting. When he returned home, the elders asked how he liked the preacher. Not at all, he confessed, and swore that he would never go again, for "you told me he would let me commit as much sin as I pleased, but he says more against sin than our minister does." [7] Then, too, there were the little children who were taken to hear a Methodist preacher. In his sermon he dealt out to sinners "with a liberal hand . . . the awful denunciations, and unmerciful punishments" of hell. When they returned home, their mother examined them on what they had heard. Her "little son between five and six years old," stepped up to her, "and looking very earnestly in her face said, 'Ma'am, did you ever hear a man swear so in all your life.' " [8]

The *Magazine* attempted to be helpful regarding puzzling texts from the Scriptures. Ballou invited his readers to submit them to the paper, so that he and the paper's many correspondents might try their skill at explanation.

Although many persons contributed to the *Magazine,* it must have been a strain on Ballou's own writing arm to keep its four pages filled every week. His penchant for rhyming was given full latitude; many a "fugitive" verse was penned to fill the "Poets' Corner." And many columns were filled the first year by a "Dialogue between a Universalist and a Limitarian," [9] which ran serially and was doubtless written by Ballou. Time after time the Universalist leads the Limitarian to the discovery of new truth, until finally (in the last issue of Volume One) he is ready to embrace the true way. He gives his friend the right hand of fellowship and offers "up to our heavenly Father my hearty desires that you may still labour with success in the vindication of the truth as it is in Jesus." [10] Universalists followed with bated breath the stilted language of this dialogue, not only to see the outcome, but also to gather ammunition for their own battles with the orthodox.

Articles and clippings from various other religious papers of the country helped to fill the *Magazine.* Excerpts from the "fire and brimstone" sermons of the New England clergy were quoted, only to have their propositions exploded by the penetrating observations of the editor.

The pages of the *Magazine* offer a fairly good check on what Ballou was reading. A full complement of extracts is included in its columns, and he draws on one of his favorite books, Charles Chauncy's *Salvation of All Men,* for "Proofs of Universal Salvation." [11] In view of his own continuing liberalization of thought, it is interesting to find many extracts from the writings of the radical English Unitarian, Joseph Priestley.[12]

Ballou is outspoken in his criticism of the doctrine of the trinity and in his advocacy of unitarian ideas.[13] His own attacks are supplemented by excerpts from various well-known Unitarians, American and English. In the third and fourth issues of the paper, he includes two long excerpts from the famous Baltimore Sermon, *Unitarian Christianity*, which his celebrated fellow-Bostonian William Ellery Channing[14] had delivered in May of that year. Priestley's friend, the prominent English Unitarian Thomas Belsham, is quoted at length,[15] and the story of the martyrdom of Servetus at the hands of Calvin and his Genevan cohorts is excerpted from Robinson's *Ecclesiastical Researches*.[16] This sympathetic treatment of Unitarianism is significant. Unitarian preachers, writers and publications appealed generally to the more wealthy and socially elite in Boston and New England. The promotion of liberal religion among the common people of the area was the accomplishment of the Universalists and such forces as *The Universalist Magazine*.

Editorially, Ballou was conservative in all things except religion. The editorial columns of the *Magazine* shun political and social issues; they are devoted, with rare exceptions, to the religious and moral questions which were of special interest to the Universalists.

The rare exceptions to this rule can be stated very briefly. On one occasion, Ballou spoke out on "A Subject of Regret"—the use of intoxicating liquors:

> Why should the reasonable creature man become his own enemy, disregard his rational being and happiness, and destroy all that is noble in himself by indulging in intemperance? This, though to the reasonable mind, one of the greatest outrages ever committed on propriety and decency, has become one of the most frequent, which are practised in our country. This is certainly a subject of regret. Parents, be cautious that the example you set be not such as may lead your sons into this vice. Young men, you are too noble, too glorious, in your reasonable nature to render it fit that you should be governed by appetite and passion. Be careful that you keep in the path which reason dictates, and you will shun intemperance, and avoid its bane.[17]

With this outburst, his comments on the subject ceased. He carried on no crusade against liquor.

When the question of the continuation of the religious establishment was posed in the Massachusetts Constitutional Convention in late 1820 and early 1821,[18] Ballou, of course, came out against the establishment of Congregationalism.[19] Its proponents said that religion must have the arm of the state to support it, or people will not be religious. Establishment was essential for the salvation of their souls. But this was as ridiculous as to propose that the state must compel young men to marry, or that laws were needed to force men to till the soil and "to compell the merchant by law to see and attend to his business." Man worships from the same motivation as he does these other things: "his hopes of gain are quite sufficient without any such law." [20]

Daniel Webster, said Ballou, had a better argument. He spoke in favor of establishment simply on the basis of state policy. But, Ballou observed, if it is to be a matter of state policy, the state constitution must define the doctrine of Christianity. He suggested sarcastically that this might "be done in thirty-nine articles, or more or less as the constituted authority should see fit to determine." [21]

Aside from these instances, the *Magazine* took no stand on political and social issues. Let us reform *religion*, Ballou implied, and all other reforms will follow. Let us help men to see the true God, the loving Father, and they will love Him and their fellow men.

The Universalist Magazine was not without opposition. Interestingly enough, the first opposition came from a Unitarian! The editor of the *Boston Kaleidoscope* proposed certain questions which, he believed, cast doubt on the truth of Universalism.[22] (He did not limit himself to Universalism, however. He advertised that the front page of his paper would be devoted to explaining and defending "what is now called *rational* and *liberal Christianity*," [23] as distinguished from Roman Catholicism, Calvinism, Hopkinsianism, Universalism, and Deism.) Little did he realize what he was getting into. Before he knew it, he was involved in a dispute with Ballou. A flood of words descended upon him from the columns of *The Universalist Magazine* until he finally—and probably in desperation—called off the controversy.[24]

The editor of the *Christian Advocate* announced in an open letter to Henry Bowen (he meant Hosea Ballou) that he hoped the conspiracy against Christianity in France, which had brought down God's displeasure, would have discouraged anyone from attempting it again. But now, "using all the allurements of *smooth language*," Ballou was making his own damnation sure by deceiving "the simple and unthinking." [25] The editor of the *Ulster Plebeian* of Kingston, New York, announced that he had consigned his two complimentary copies of the *Magazine* to the flames for fear they would fall into the hands of his family and corrupt them.[26]

Reactions to the paper, pro and con, came from all the United States.[27] To promote the *Magazine,* Bowen sent complimentary copies not only to the editors of other newspapers and periodicals but also to the various post offices throughout the country, hoping thereby to drum up interest and increase his subscription lists. The opposition to this procedure, bitter as it was at times, had its humorous aspects:

PROFANITY

"Answer a fool according to his folly."

THE following, which was returned on one of our Subscription Papers, as it appears, from J. SHAW, Post Master, Bradleysville, (S.C.) shows not only the bitter spirit of the opposition, but the profanity in which it is willing to indulge.

Infernal Pit.

My Good Friend,—Continue as you have done widely to disseminate your very princely Magazine, and be assured that you shall shortly have one of the most exalted thrones amongst us.

Yours with all the love of a Fiend,

NICK LUCIFER.

REPLY; We have for a long time been of opinion, that it was not necessary to go into the future world to find the *infernal pit* so much talked of, and we are now furnished with a demonstration of the correctness of this opinion; the above letter came by mail directly from that pit, where it appears there is a Post Office and a Post Master. We have the satisfaction also to be certified that the Universalist Magazine does not please those who are in this *infernal pit,* for the number of the Magazine we sent there, was sent back with the above letter; but it was not scorched, nor was the smell of fire or brimstone on it.[28]

Opposition never fazed Ballou. He imbibed it and loved every moment of it. And *The Universalist Magazine* throve on it also. At $2.50 a year, it managed to pay for itself without advertising; and although it continually carried notices of money owed by subscribers, it appears to have been making a good profit.[29] More important, it was a great stimulus to the Universalist movement.

CHAPTER XIV

THE BOSTON YEARS

Ballou's ministry in Boston covered a span of almost thirty-five years. They were busy years, as can be said of most of his life. Writing, editing, pastoral work, family life and, of course, preaching filled his cup to overflowing.

He had not been at School Street long when he decided to replace the inadequate hymnbook used by his society. The so-called Convention Hymn Book was a grand failure; Universalists had gone back to the standard collections, with all their objectionable references to the trinity and atonement. Ballou suggested to Edward Turner that it was time for a change. Turner agreed, and the two spent much of the winter of 1820-21 collaborating on a new collection.[1]

This time the original offerings were limited to about fifty.[2] Universalist hymns by Abner Kneeland, Sebastian Streeter, Mrs. Murray, Ballou and others were interspersed among hymns from Watts, Doddridge, Tate, Rippon's Collection, Wesley and other standard hymnals. Their aim was to produce a collection which would allow the worshiper to "sing with the spirit and with the understanding also."[3] Yet they were not narrowly sectarian in their approach, as can be seen by their inclusion of such stanzas as this by Abner Kneeland:

> The blessing of the Father, Son,
> And Holy Ghost be giv'n;
> The three who do unite in one,
> And record keep in heav'n.[4]

Early in May 1821, *The Universalist Magazine* carried a notice that the Ballou-Turner hymnbook, titled *The Universalists' Hymn-Book,* was "now in press."[5] The new collection was well received when it appeared, and a new edition was called for in 1824. It remained in general use for the next ten years, until it was replaced by the collection by Sebastian and Russell Streeter.[6]

Even in those days, when ministers were expected to spend a great deal of time in the study, there was much pastoral work to be done. Despite the pressure of writing and preaching, Ballou never neglected this aspect of church life. He was frequently called upon to visit the sick—often persons who had little or no connection with his society. As the faithful pastor, he never hesitated to lend a helping hand, for he sought to practice as well as preach the doctrine of universal love.[7]

But his first love was preaching. At fifty he was at his prime in the pulpit. Only for special occasions did he prepare his sermons in written form before delivery, and even then he never took a manuscript into the pulpit.[8] He delivered his sermons extempore. His old sermon workbook, which is still extant,[9] contains hundreds of sermon sketches in closely scrawled sentences. Each text is stated, and the message derived from it is outlined very briefly. With the exception of two collections which were stenographically recorded as he delivered them,[10] his published sermons were written out after delivery.

As he sat in the pulpit before the sermon, he was buried in thought, no doubt developing his message in his mind. His countenance was anything but bright, and persons seeing him for the first time wondered if this was really the great preacher of the love of God to man. He looked so cross! When Lucius R. Paige, as a young man, arrived in Boston to study divinity with Ballou, he went first to hear him preach. As he sat in the pew looking up at his future teacher, he was amazed: "I thought him the crossest man I had ever seen." [11]

But there was a dramatic change when Ballou stood up to deliver his sermon. His face was suddenly alive with happiness. With his spectacles on, he would read through his text—and then read it a second time for emphasis. Next he would remove his glasses and carefully ease them into their case. He would take out his handkerchief, fold it and lay it across the open Bible in front of him. This ritual held the attention of the congregation, which waited with increasing eagerness for his first words. Then, very slowly and deliberately, in a low voice, he would introduce his subject.

His first sentences were involved, at times confused. As he began to warm to his subject, however, they became more conversational, more direct. His thoughts and words became sharper and hit his hearers with driving force. His voice rose; his right arm extended; his face shone; and as he reached the height of his discourse, "his words came in an impetuous flow." [12] There was no escaping the power of his words: "You felt as if his hand were on your shoulder, and he were speaking directly to you." [13]

The force of Ballou's preaching can be sensed, though imperfectly, in this excerpt from one of his sermons:

Before this discourse is closed, it is necessary to make some remarks on what the opposers are endeavouring to insinuate against these plain and glorious truths of the gospel.

They are not disposed to meet these things in the way of open and candid investigation; but they will go from house to house, and from ear to ear, and whisper about licentious doctrine. They will endeavour to stop the people's ears and blind their eyes, lest they hear with their ears, and see with their eyes and be converted.

What, no future judgment! Is there to be no distinction in the world to come, between the righteous and the wicked? Are saints and sinners all to fare alike? It is then no matter what we do? We may indulge without restraint in all manner of iniquity. We may neglect the duties of religion; lie, steal, defraud; indulge in drunkenness and gluttony, together with base uncleanness, and all is just as well. Nay, better; for who, were it not for the terrors of condemnation in a future state, would be at the expense and trouble of public worship and religious duties, or refrain from the indulgence of sensuality? Such is the dust these enemies of the gospel throw into the air.

"Be not deceived; God is not mocked; for whatsoever a man soweth, that shall he also reap. For he that soweth to his flesh, shall of the flesh reap corruption: but he that soweth to the spirit shall of the spirit reap life everlasting." Notice carefully; "he that soweth to his flesh, shall of the flesh reap corruption." He must receive his wages from the master he serves; he must reap his harvest where he sows his seed.

Go to our prisons and places of correction; you will find hundreds who believe in a day of judgment in the next world, and have no doubts that punishment everlasting will be inflicted on the wicked, accordingly as they have been educated to believe; but they all intend to repent before they die, and that is early enough according to the argument of our opposers. These miserable wretches believe as they have been taught; and they act as if they were fully convinced, that religion, virtue, justice, temperance and godliness were nothing but so many obstructions to their present happiness, and of no use this side the eternal world. O fatal delusion! "Stolen waters are sweet, and bread eaten in secret is pleasant. But he knoweth not that the dead are there; and that her guests are in the depth of hell." These sinful riots are in the darkest regions of hell.

Look round on society. Do misery and wretchedness mark the footsteps of religion, virtue, temperance, prudence, industry, economy, justice, love and mercy? No, my brethren, this is not the case. But it remains true that "the way of the transgressor is hard," and that "there is no peace to the wicked."

The religion of Jesus is represented by many beautiful figures; such as bread for the hungry, water for the thirsty, a feast of fat things for all people.

. . . .

After all, what is this religion which is founded on the fear of future misery? Is there any real sincerity in it? Is there any of the true love of God in this religion? "Perfect love casts out fear; he that feareth is not made perfect in love." You provide for your companions and your dependent offspring because you love them, and your duty is perfect delight. Can you honestly say, that you would not give your children bread when they are hungry, if you were not afraid of everlasting punishment hereafter?

Away with this deception. Let us learn to love God because he has first loved us; let us cautiously obey his commandments, in keeping of which there is great reward.[14]

Ballou was perfectly capable of humor in the pulpit, also; but he usually elicited smiles, not through a well-told joke, but by an ingenious argument[15] or by his good-natured approach to a problem. While he was preaching at Milford, Massachusetts, in December 1821, during the meeting of the Southern [New England] Association, the sun came blazing through the uncurtained windows of the meetinghouse—right into his eyes. He began speaking of God's impartiality, of His goodness to all men, and mentioned as an illustration the glorious sun "which nearly blinds me with its abundant light." Someone took the hint and hung a coat over the window.[16]

His preaching was invariably argumentative. No matter what the subject,[17] he presented it as if someone were disputing him. Even his prayers had an argumentative flavor. One of his feminine hearers once remarked that she did not "usually enjoy Mr. Ballou's prayers so well as those of some others, for the reason that he seemed to be arguing with God."[18] Yet his prayers were fresh, unsullied by cant and stock phrases.[19] If he did argue with God, he at least did so in an original manner.

Ballou's early lack of education and polish was obvious in his writing and preaching. His early writings—even his masterpiece, the *Treatise on Atonement*—are in the language of a country lad. But they had spontaneity, brilliance of argument and wit. As the years passed, he became more practiced in the art of writing and overcame, to a certain extent, his rough-and-ready writing style—but often at the expense of spontaneity.

His elocution and pronunciation in the pulpit were no doubt improved by his experience in the blossoming cultural metropolis of Boston. But during his early years in Boston, his preaching smacked of his country upbringing. A student at the Boston Latin School, who heard Ballou for the first time in 1825, recorded this extraordinary example: "Brethering, I perceed to dev-il-ope and illusterate the follerin p'ints." [20]

Uncultured as his language was, Ballou had a powerful effect on his listeners. His preaching was said to have drawn "thousands on thousands" of converts to Universalism.[21] Many of these were clergymen from other denominations.[22]

Many theological students came to Ballou during his years in Boston. The most notable was Thomas Whittemore, who had first heard him preach at the installation of Abner Kneeland at the church in Charlestown in 1811.[23] Thomas was then a boy of twelve, and the experience meant little to him. But he was a young man of nineteen when he wandered into the crowded School Street Church in 1819, and he was then much impressed with Ballou's message of love to God and man.

Whittemore had no intention of studying for the ministry; it had never entered his mind. When he first met Ballou personally, he was a poorly educated apprentice to a bootmaker named Abel Baker.[24] One day in 1820, Ballou entered Baker's newly purchased shop on Mason Street.[25] Whittemore was impressed with the preacher's friendliness and soon found the courage to ask him for help with his English. Ballou[26] was obviously impressed with the intelligence and humor of this "Boston rough," [27] for he agreed to tutor him. This was in April 1820.[28]

A short time later Whittemore, who was passionately fond of music, was playing the violoncello in the School Street choir,[29] where he was continually impressed by Ballou's preaching. His studies were proceeding satisfactorily, and Ballou even published in the poetry column of *The Universalist Magazine* a little opus by his pupil called "Reflections Over the Grave of an Infant." [30] Soon Ballou was publishing all of his contributions, and the lad was reading proof on the *Magazine* when Ballou was out of town.[31]

One day Ballou asked Whittemore whether he was planning

to enter the ministry. "No," he replied, admitting that his faith had been shaken by what he thought were traces of Calvinism in the Bible. Ballou suggested that he read Paley's *Evidences* to correct his misapprehensions. Between Ballou and Paley, Whittemore soon became convinced that the Scriptures were not Calvinistic. He became eager to preach, and during the summer and fall of 1820 he spent all his spare time reading in divinity.[32]

Ballou realized that his young friend had no money to prepare himself for his new career, but he had an idea for raising some. At the close of the Sunday service at School Street on the last day of the year, he announced that he had a special subject to discuss with those who cared to stay for a few minutes. The result was a collection of $150 to cover Whittemore's room and board for one year.[33] The next day, Whittemore entered Ballou's family as a theological student.[34] He felt very much at home there, for Ruth Ballou treated him like one of her nine children. (There were nine now; the last child, a boy, had been born on April 14, 1820.[35] He was named Maturin Murray Ballou, after Hosea's father and John Murray.)

Whittemore planned at least a year's study in theology before taking to the pulpit, but Ballou had other plans. He believed that the best way to learn the art of preaching is to practice it. For this reason, and because there was a dearth of preachers among the Universalists, Whittemore—unqualified as he felt—accepted a call to the church at Milford after only three months training! [36]

Ballou had a habit which sometimes disconcerted people. When something disturbed him, he would groan. Not long after Whittemore had moved to his pastorate in Milford, the young man was invited to preach at the Third Universalist Society in Boston. He accepted the invitation and, much to his delight, found his old teacher present for the occasion. Ballou sat in the pulpit while Whittemore delivered his sermon.

> I preached what I thought was as good a sermon as I could give, from the text, Matt. 11:28-30, "Come unto me, all ye that labor," etc. Several times during the sermon, I heard father B., who sat behind me, groan quite audibly. I thought perhaps he was sick; but I learned afterward what was the cause of his trouble. I went home with him to spend the night; and all the way to his house he said but little to me, but kept talking to himself, as if "treasuring up" something. When we arrived at his house, he began about the sermon. The substance of his

remarks was, that it was in bad taste, words were mispronounced, new words were coined, bad metaphors occurred, etc., and instances of these things were pointed out. I, of course, was crest-fallen, for up in Milford I was a great man. Finally, said he, there was one good thing in the sermon. "What was that, sir?" said I, glad of a little praise. "The text," said he, "the text; and that was the only good thing in the whole!" [37]

Although Ballou was now settled in one of the most prominent churches of the Universalist movement, he was as active for the greater cause as ever. Throughout his Boston years he traveled widely, preaching evening after evening as he had in his circuit-riding days. "If you want to keep the bell a-ringing, you must keep the tongue a-thumping" was the homely philosophy he preached to the little group of faithful gathered at the schoolhouse in Woburn, Massachusetts.[38] If universal salvation is to be believed, it must be preached vigorously and often, in language that the people understand: "As in Adam all died, even so in Christ shall—half?—a double l spells all; shall all be made alive." [39]

Ballou kept his "tongue a-thumping" in many of the towns around Boston. Through his efforts, a Universalist group was gathered in Roxbury in late 1818. He preached his first sermon there on November 29; and early in the next year Paul Dean joined him, preaching on alternate Sunday evenings at the town hall.[40] By August 1820, the new society was strong enough to lay the cornerstone for a meetinghouse, on which occasion "the Throne of Grace was implored in a fervent and affectionate manner by the Rev. Mr. BALLOU, of Boston." [41] He also found time to nurture a new group at Cambridgeport, which met in a schoolhouse. By the end of 1822 this group had dedicated its new meetinghouse, with Ballou preaching the sermon.[42]

Even the island of Nantucket heard his message of God's universal salvation. He spent ten days on the island in 1820, after which he returned to the mainland and boarded a stagecoach at New Bedford for Boston. There was one other passenger aboard. The stranger struck up a conversation.

"You just from the island, I suppose?"

"Yes."

"Well, they say old Ballou is over there, preaching his heresy. Did you see him?"

"Yes, I saw him," Ballou answered amiably.

"Well, he's a rough old fellow. I don't like him."

"Why not?"

"Because he preaches that all men will be saved and go to heaven in their sins, and no man in his senses can believe that!"

"But, sir, did you ever hear him preach?"

"No; I hope not," said the man determinedly.

"Then you may be misinformed as to what he does preach," Ballou suggested mildly. "Now I think he would say, if he were here, that he did not believe nor preach as you have represented."

"But what does he believe, then?"

"I think he would say that sinners are to be saved *from* their sins, not *in* their sins. Christ came to save the world from sin, not in sin; and furthermore we are told in the Scriptures that 'he that is dead is free from sin,' and he that is freed from sin must surely be holy, and consequently happy."

The stranger was silent for a moment. Then: "Sir, if I may be so bold, where do you live when at home?"

"I live in Boston, sir."

"Whose church do you attend?"

"Mr. Ballou's church, sir."

"What is your name?"

"My name is Ballou." And despite Ballou's friendly manner, the man, at a loss for something to say, left the coach at the next stop.[43]

In late December and early January, Ballou made his first trip as far south as Philadelphia. On the way he filled preaching engagements in New Haven and New York. New Haven, the seat of Yale College, seemed to him "the bitterest place I ever visited, and manifests the most unreasonable opposition to every thing which looks like charity." [44] In New York he preached at the Pearl Street Church,[45] sharing the pulpit with Edward Mitchell, one of the few stalwart trinitarians left in the denomination.

At Philadelphia he was entertained by his old friend Abner Kneeland, who was now ministering to the church on Lombard Street. Ballou's eleven sermons were so well attended that the Grand Saloon of the Washington Benevolent Society was used for his last appearance. This hall, which had a capacity of several thousand, was so crowded that he had trouble walking to the rostrum.[46]

The sermons Ballou preached in Philadelphia were taken down in shorthand and published.[47] He had an opportunity to examine the first three in transcript before he left Philadelphia, and Kneeland "examined and corrected" the rest, yet they were printed substantially as delivered extempore.[48] The reader is struck immediately with the difference between these and most of his other published sermons. Here one can virtually hear him speaking to a crowded auditorium. The repetition, the emphasis and the construction are notably different from those of the sermons which he himself wrote out after delivery. The formal (in places, stilted) style of the *Lecture Sermons,* for instance, is nowhere in evidence.

As a general rule, Ballou avoided bringing the question of the trinity into his sermons; and in his final sermon, in which he offered a long catalogue of the false doctrines fostered by the church, he did not mention the trinity.[49] This is particularly striking, for he preached this same sermon in his own pulpit when he arrived home, and there he included the trinity along with the other corruptions of Christianity.[50] But the omission in Philadelphia may have been a human error, due to the crowd and excitement at his last address.[51]

The Philadelphia sermons are, in essence, one sustained song of God's love for His children. God will never cease to love man; He will continually advance him in knowledge.[52]

. . . Love God constantly, and abundant will be your peace—abundant your joy—abundant your satisfaction and delight. And in the room of tending to what our opposers sometimes assert, to licentiousness, to a corruption of morals, and an indulgence of unbridled passions, it will always tend to lead us to conduct ourselves with the utmost propriety in relation to our heavenly Father—in relation to all mankind as brethren, and in relation to ourselves.[53]

. . . Let each of us say, "If God loves me, I will imitate my Father in heaven, and if the gospel embraces us all, let me do the same and embrace my fellow creatures in the affection of the soul; and let me live in this religion, walk in this perfect law of liberty, and be blessed in my deeds." [54]

Ballou made this journey to Philadelphia when a controversy about the probability of punishment in the afterlife was beginning to wax hot in Universalist circles, but he showed admirable restraint in broaching the subject. He approaches the problem by refuting the argument that sin is not punished in this earthly life.

"God has ordained laws on earth by which vice is punished, and we see the wicked *are* miserable beings, in the present tense." The way of the wicked is hard. Our experience is that only the virtuous man, he who obeys the commandments of God, is happy.

"If you will look . . . and see the dreadful calamities which afflict the wicked, you will see, that God has inseparably connected sin with misery, and righteousness with happiness in the present life." And—thinking perhaps of some of his Universalist opponents as well as the orthodox—he adds:

Hence then, when you are told that sin is not punished in this world, you must know it is false; and when you are told virtue does not make a man happy in this world, you are told what every man knows to be untrue. When this doctrine is preached, the people are not fed with knowledge or understanding.[55]

This appearance was the first in a long series. Ballou traveled to New York and Philadelphia periodically for the rest of his life and was at times tempted to move to that area.

A yearly event in his life, ever since he had joined the movement, was the Universalist General Convention held each September. From 1791 to 1825 he never missed a session,[56] and after that he missed very few. The brethren became so accustomed to his presence that it was established practice to reserve for him the last sermon of the Convention, and he often served as moderator or clerk of the gathering. It was as moderator of the General Convention of 1822 at Warner, New Hampshire, that he had the pleasure of granting his own son Massena Berthier, then twenty-one, a "letter of fellowship." [57] Massena was not to be as distinguished a preacher as his father, but he served the cause long and well.

Now that Ballou was living in the city, his routine was naturally much different from what it had been in his earlier ministries. Physical exertion, which he always valued highly, could too easily be neglected in his new surroundings. Determined that this should not happen, he made it a practice to get as much exercise as possible. Thus the townspeople might observe the celebrated preacher cutting his own firewood into the proper lengths for stove and fireplace and carrying it into his home.

Ballou lived true to his own beliefs. He indulged himself very little; even his favorite snuff was put aside when he became convinced that it was responsible for clogging his nasal passages. Pleasure or not, once he had made up his mind that it was detrimental to his health, away it went. No habit was to be allowed to master the force of his mind.[58]

So, too, with his pipe. Ballou had not developed the smoking habit until, during a siege of indigestion, his family physician suggested that he enjoy a good full pipe after every meal. This would relax him and improve his digestion. He followed the doctor's orders faithfully for several years, three times a day. Then one day the family noticed that the familiar object was not in father's mouth. Had he forgotten it somewhere?

"No. I have been thinking that I am becoming a slave to this habit, inasmuch as I find that I have to do it *regularly* every day at certain periods. It is no longer a medicine, but a pleasant habit, and I shall leave it off until I find that I require it again for my health's sake." [59]

The Ballou household was happy and well disciplined. Hosea ruled with a gentle but firm hand. It was always understood that his word was law; his slightest suggestion was taken as a command. Ruth, as always, was concerned to make him comfortable and content. She pursued her household duties equably, even when Hosea was most demanding.[60]

Ballou was too preoccupied with his thoughts and his many professional activities to indulge often in recreation with the children. Occasionally he would play at their games with them; but soon he would remember a task to be done or an idea which should be jotted down in his sermon workbook, and he would leave them as suddenly as he had come.[61] Nor could he devote much time to the pastimes approved by society. An occasional game of checkers with a close friend was about his only concession, and even then he was not really interested or involved in the game, caring little whether he won or lost.[62] How much better to pass the time in good conversation—which for Ballou meant a meaty theological discussion!

CHAPTER XV

ULTRA-UNIVERSALISM

In his *Treatise on Atonement*, Ballou had written that the atonement of Christ was never intended to "perform impossibilities."[1] It could not be expected to transform men's lives and make them agree and live in peace with each other if they were destitute of love. The truth of this proposition was amply demonstrated in the Universalist denomination itself in what came to be known as the Restorationist Controversy.

In the early years of Universalism, the great task, in which the whole denomination was united, was to overcome the arguments of the partialists—those orthodox believers who claimed that God was partial, that He would save relatively few of His children and would doom the rest to endless punishment in the future life. There was little controversy over a secondary question: whether there was any punishment at all in the afterlife or whether earthly life provided sufficient retribution for men's sins.[2]

During the early 1820s, however, the denomination was split by a controversy over this secondary question. One group of ministers held a so-called restorationist point of view—a conviction that men might die in sin but that all their souls would be restored to goodness after a limited period of suffering in a future life. A second group, led by Ballou, carried the belief in universal salvation (and in the perfect love of God for His creatures) to its logical extreme. According to this ultra-universalist position, the corruptions of the flesh are dissolved along with the body at death, and only the heavenly nature of man returns to the Father.[3] Sin finds its punishment in this life; there is only bliss in the hereafter.

Caleb Rich had set forth the ultra-universalist doctrine as early as 1816. The question did not come into prominence, however, until the correspondence between Ballou and Edward Turner was published in *The Gospel Visitant* in 1817-1818. And even after that, the doctrinal question was not always the central issue. To a great extent, Ballou's personality dominated the controversy as it did the denomination. The two camps, while differing intellectually on the question of future punishment, differed also on their attitudes toward Ballou. The ultra-universalists tended to be his ardent supporters. The Restorationists tended to resent him personally. Throughout the controversy, they were intent on reducing his influence in the denomination.

There is no doubt that much of the agitation which resulted from the Ballou-Turner correspondence was due to the restless Jacob Wood. Indeed, while the debate was in progress, he published *A Brief Essay on the Doctrine of Future Retribution,* in which he challenged both the exponents of eternal punishment and the believers in no future punishment.[4] Quoting the great men of the past, Relly and Chauncy, he attempted to show that the doctrine of no future retribution gave "encouragement to sin":

> I will not call those who believe in this system *"stupid animals,"* and "regret the time spent in writing to them," as a modern Universalian writer has, but I really think the opinion very erroneous. The many gross absurdities to which the doctrine of immediate universal salvation is liable, and the vicious effects which it is calculated to produce, render it a doctrine justly deserving of disapprobation and contempt.[5]

To his essay Wood added "An Appendix, containing extracts of Letters from most of the Principal Universalian Ministers in New-England on the Subject of Future Misery."[6] He claimed to have received answers from practically all the ministers in the denomination and asserted that, with *"very few* exceptions," they took a position similar to his own.[7] Hosea Ballou, 2d—who, unlike his granduncle, always retained a belief in a future state of punishment—later claimed that Wood published nearly all the extracts without the writers' consent.[8]

In September 1817, two weeks or so after the publication of his essay, Wood's church at Charlton, Massachusetts, played host to the General Convention. At that time, he attempted to round up support in order to bring the question before the Convention. If the Convention would not take a stand in favor of restorationism, a secession was to be staged. But he did not introduce the subject, as he had led his colleagues to believe he would.[9]

When Ballou moved to Boston, he brought with him his new opinions regarding punishment. His first published sermon in Boston was a forthright declaration that the sins of men are punished in this life, not in the hereafter; and this was followed by a long line of sermons dealing with the same subject. The problem was discussed vigorously in several of his *Lecture Sermons;* in one of these, he actually refers to his published controversy with Turner.[10]

Ballou believed that the hell mentioned by Jesus was to be found in this world. There is no reason to doubt that Jesus was referring to hell on earth when he taught (in Mark 9:43-44):

> And if thy hand offend thee, cut it off: it is better for thee to enter into life maimed, than having two hands to go into hell, into the fire that never shall be quenched:—Where their worm dieth not, and the fire is not quenched.

It was evident to Ballou from such passages "that a state of extreme trouble and affliction is, in the language of scripture, called hell." [11]

Essentially, Ballou's was the Old Testament belief that the Lord rewards and punishes men during their lifetime for their virtues and sins. He insisted that the lot of the wicked is a hard one; that even with no punishment in the afterlife, man does not escape the consequences of his actions. He often transcended this notion of external punishment and declared that virtue and wickedness hold reward and punishment in themselves:

> . . . As a man loves the truth, and speaks the truth, he enjoys the divine sunshine in his breast; and in addition to this sure and ample reward he generally is believed by others, and confidence is placed in his word. In the same proportion as a man is honest in what he does, he has the enjoyment of his own conscience, which is a treasure that the honest man prizes far above silver or gold.
>
> . . . .
>
> As wickedness is exactly the reverse of righteousness, so the recompense of the former must be the reverse of that of the latter.
>
> If we have no love to God we cannot enjoy him. The thought that he exists and exercises universal dominion, and controls all things by his Almighty power is a source of infelicity. The soul, in room of being refreshed with the sweet waters of life is suffused with anger, wrath, strife, and bitterness. In the room of peace, there is trouble. "The wicked are like the troubled sea, when it cannot rest, whose waters cast up mire and dirt. There is no peace, saith my God, to the wicked." [12]

Although Ballou was outspoken on this matter in his own pulpit, he exercised great restraint in discussing it in *The Universalist Magazine.* He may have realized that a debate on the subject would bring great harm to the denomination. At any rate, during the first two years of his editorship there is barely a mention of the idea of no future retribution.[13] In a dispute with the editor of *Kaleidoscope*, who challenged him on this point, he wrote simply: "We are sensible we cannot prove that sin and misery will exist in a future state of being."[14] He also reprinted from *The Gospel Visitant* his exegetical labor on I Peter 3:18-20,[15] of which he was no doubt quite proud, and printed a compendium of a School Street sermon on Genesis 3:4, in which he referred briefly to his belief that sin is punished in this life rather than in the next.[16] But he never believed that all Universalists must share his view on this matter.[17]

In a reply to a correspondent of the *Magazine* at the beginning of October 1820, Ballou mentioned that the "impaired state" of his health would force him to keep his reply brief.[18] His bad health appears to have continued into the next year. He suffered from indigestion and from pains in his back and near his heart, which led him to believe that he had heart trouble.[19] Soon his mental outlook was affected; when not under tension (as in preparing a sermon) or stimulated by the conversation of friends, he suffered from depression. The doctors decided that he was suffering not from heart trouble but from an overtaxed mind, which in turn affected his digestion. He would have to slow down and reduce the number of his activities.[20]

Under the circumstances, he decided to give up the editorship of the *Magazine*. He announced his decision in June 1821, at the conclusion of Volume Two. But he promised "an undiminished ardour for the promotion of that heavenly doctrine, so honourable to God, so consoling and edifying to every true believer."[21]

The editorship of the *Magazine* was given to a man named Foster, who, it is said, was "improperly recommended to Mr. Bowen." Foster was, in Thomas Whittemore's opinion, "utterly ignorant of Universalism, and every other kind of theology, and unfit, in every respect, for such a post."[22] This estimate is borne out by the changes in the *Magazine* itself during his tenure.

Whereas Ballou had been careful to keep to a minimum any mention of the problem of future retribution, Foster encouraged a great proliferation of letters and pieces on the subject. On the front page of his very first issue, the dogs were let loose;[23] and under various *noms de plume,* Turner, Wood, both Hosea Ballous, Dean, the editor himself, the clever Dr. John Brooks of Bernardston and numerous others carried on a heated debate. Each side called on the other to prove its position from the Bible; each claimed the other had that duty. It is interesting that the *nom de plume* under which Ballou chose to write was "H. B." There was no mistaking those initials!

After the initial explosion, the heat died down; the debate vanished from the newspaper from the middle of August to December 1821, although its columns were filled with other controversial matters. But the controversy was not over. In December, letters appeared advocating a belief in no future punishment. Thereafter, letters and replies sprang up "like weeds" in its columns.

On December 15, there appeared a review by Ballou in which he scored the bad reasoning of a recent restorationist pamphlet.[24] For this he was bitterly attacked by Jacob Wood, writing under the *nom de plume* REASON.[25] Ballou answered the attack, showing REASON to be unreasonable, bad-tempered and a distorter of facts.[26]

Wood then, over the pen name "Restorationist," made certain "proposals" which exacerbated the controversy still further.[27] In March 1822, writing in behalf of himself and several brethren, he said he wished the controversy to avoid the nature of "a desultory, promiscuous news-paper dispute," which he believed it had been up to that point. To this end he proposed:

1. That a brief statement of the evidence that all misery is confined to this life, be written by one who believes in that doctrine, and published in the Magazine, and that we will engage a similar communication in proof that misery will extend beyond death. [Footnote: "It is understood that this evidence will be both positive and negative. That is, each party shall have right to anticipate the contrary arguments, and refute them."]

2. That both these communications shall be lodged in the hands of the Editor of the Magazine before either is published, so that no alterations may be made in them afterwards, by reference one to the other.

3. That both these communications shall be submitted to the public to draw their own conclusions, without any controversial replies on either side.[28]

These proposals, though inadequate to quell the feelings roused by the controversy, might have been accepted as the work of a sincere group of peacemakers if Wood had not observed, in his character-istically insulting manner:

If the advocates of the doctrine of *no* future misery are honourable and conscientious in their cause, they will be willing to meet us on this just and equal ground.

He clearly had Ballou in mind, for he added:

It is wished that the gentleman who shall accept this invitation, will be one who is qualified to do full justice to his side of the question; and we hope that honor will restrain all others from interfering.[29]

Ballou considered Wood's implied questioning of the honor and conscientiousness of the ultra-universalist group a slap at himself. He lost his usual equanimity and was unable to humble himself enough to overlook the brash insult. In a letter to the editor, which appeared in the following issue, he writes that, if the framer of the proposals will reveal his real name and the name of his brethren, he will inform them why he will not accept their proposals and "give them and the public to understand what I think of their suspending my *honor* and *sincerity* on the condition which they suggest." [30]

Wood replies that if Ballou can offer a good reason for wanting to know the names, he will give them; but he believes that anyone "who is *sincere* and *honorable* in his cause, will not hesitate to defend it in opposition to *any* signature." [31] The haggling over names and "honor" continued briskly,[32] while other correspondents fought over such matters as whether the "proposals" would not unfairly choke off debate.

Meanwhile, Bowen was receiving numerous complaints from readers who were tired of seeing the paper filled with unprofitable controversy.[33] He asked Ballou once more to take over the editor's chair. Ballou agreed but insisted on help. At the beginning of May 1822, Bowen announced that Ballou would resume the editor-ship with two associates, Hosea Ballou, 2d (who was a restoration-ist) and Thomas Whittemore (who shared the elder Ballou's ultra-universalism).[34]

The two junior editors—Ballou abstained because of his per-sonal involvement—called off the debate which had been raging over the Wood proposals, but they carefully pointed out to their readers that any and all communications on the more important subject of future punishment would be printed.[35] Wood wrote a severe letter under the name "Restorationist," the "substance" of which was reproduced editorially by Hosea, 2d, and Whittemore. Wood then claimed he had been misunderstood by the editors; further, he asked why his replies to several correspondents had not been printed and threatened to use the columns of another paper if not accommodated by the *Magazine*.

The junior editors explained why they did not insert the letter verbatim: ". . . It is addressed to us in a style which approaches too near that of mockery, to be received from any correspondent who does not give us his real name." [36] They added politely that if anyone cared to accept "Restorationist's" proposals for debate, they would print the notice of such an acceptance.[37]

Despite Wood's threat to go elsewhere with his correspondence, he carried on in the columns of the *Magazine* a lengthy debate with Dr. John Brooks,[38] until finally, in December, a note from the editors announced that "for sundry reasons" they thought it best to end the controversies between Wood and Brooks and others.[39] The editors apparently took this action because they were aware that the Restorationist group—Jacob Wood, Edward Turner, Paul Dean, Barzillai Streeter, Charles Hudson and Levi Briggs—had met and prepared an article attacking the *Magazine's* policy as unfair. The article had been sent for insertion in the *Christian Repository* of Woodstock, Vermont.[40]

Some weeks earlier, the Restorationists had held informal meetings at Wood's parsonage in Shirley, Massachusetts.[41] They had agreed that a statement should be published concerning the editorial policy of *The Universalist Magazine* and that Wood should write it.[42] Wood was then seeking a secession from the denomination, but this "impetuosity" was restrained by Edward Turner, Ballou's old friend, who hoped that a separation could be avoided. Turner was convinced, however, that "the controversy, if it did not soon subside, would end in one." [43] He felt that it was up to the editors of the *Magazine* to refrain from advocating the idea of no future punishment[44] and to "set a conciliatory example by refraining from controversy." [45] Party passions blind: the truth is that the *Magazine* carried correspondence on both sides of the issue.

The article which Wood wrote in behalf of the group was published in the *Christian Repository* of December 1822. It was in two

parts. In the first, an "Appeal" signed "Restorationist," Wood claims
that the believers in no future punishment (he calls them a "party")
are using convention meetings, pulpit exchanges and other occasions to force their opinions on those Universalists who believe in
limited future punishment.[46] He accuses the editors of *The Universalist Magazine* of unfairness in their handling of the dispute and
protests that they had choked off the controversy in such a way that
their own side was given the last word.[47] He speaks of the many
attempts at reconciliation and the Restorationists' desire for peace,
but ends ominously:

   . . . Be it ever remembered, and I appeal to the foregoing facts to
substantiate my assertion, that, if a separation be the final result, *we*
did not seek it, and *they* must be considered as its legitimate authors.[48]

This "Appeal" is followed by a declaration "To the World" over
Wood's signature. He speaks of the *"modern corruption"* that
Universalism has suffered and claims that the belief in "final restoration of all men by Jesus Christ, through faith and repentance"
is quite a distinct doctrine from the belief in universal salvation at
the *beginning* of a future state. These doctrines are "incapable of
being reconciled together." Belief in no future punishment is "sub-
versive of a just sense of our accountability to God, and the proper
distinction between virtue and vice, and, consequently, lessens the
motives to virtue, and gives force to the temptations of sin." [49]

In some "explanatory remarks" added to the "Declaration,"
Wood uses language not designed to conciliate brethren. He links
the believers in no future punishment with "many ancient heathen
philosophers" and warns that their system subverts the doctrine of
salvation by Christ.[50] He attacks as "absurd" the belief that men,
when freed of the body, will "come into the actual possession of
their native glory" without first having exercised repentance and
faith.[51]

After the appearance of the "Appeal and Declaration," as the
article soon came to be known, the editors of the *Magazine* attempted to persuade the Restorationists to withdraw it—but to no
avail.[52] Edward Turner later wrote to his daughter:

   The editors of the Magazine complained bitterly, and charged us
with breaking fellowship with them. This we denied. I offered to submit
the whole affair to Committees chosen from our respective parishes, and

abide their decision. They refused, and immediately published "a Reply" to our "Appeal and Declaration." [53]

The "Appeal and Declaration" was reprinted in the *Magazine* on January 25, 1823, with a brief preface written by Ballou[54] on behalf of all three editors. He listed the names of those associated with it.[55] Despite the rhetoric, his words were sincere.

Christian brethren, it is a most, painful heart-agonizing task to put into your hands, what we know must produce in you surprise and grief of no ordinary character; but you are assured that this *gall and wormwood* has for years been tasted by those who saw the first germ of this *root of bitterness*. Yes, the shade of many a night has witnessed the anguish which preyed on the heart of him, who writes this notice, and his pillow has received the tears of grief occasioned by the increasing symptoms, which portended the unhappy schism, which is now made manifest to the public. We expect the daughters of the uncircumcised will triumph; but what is this in comparison with those inward sighs, which force our tears on the defection of those we love? [56]

In the next issue the editors made their "Reply." Written by Hosea, 2d,[57] it is a stinging indictment, two-and-one-half pages long.[58] Hosea, 2d, reviews the controversy at length, reveals the names of the Restorationist group and condemns their use of the divisive term "party." He shows the utter inconsistency between Wood's claim that the Restorationists had labored long for reconciliation and his statement that there can be no reconciliation. He claims the Restorationists had breached the rules of fellowship by publishing complaints against their brethren without first laboring with them.[59] On several occasions, he reveals, the editors had tried in person to calm the troubled waters, only to be rebuffed.[60]

The most severe part of Hosea, 2d's Reply is his recounting of Wood's devious tactics in his attempts to damage the reputation of Hosea Ballou and the School Street society. Wood boasted that Ballou "had got to come down" and complained that "nine tenths of Br. Ballou's society are infidels." But he then hypocritically shifted the full blame to Turner and Dean. When Benjamin Whittemore, Mandana Ballou's future husband, asked Wood why Turner and Dean opposed Ballou, Wood attributed it to "ENVY." Said Wood, "Br. Whittemore, I know human nature so well as to know that envy is the cause of the impending schism." He also had told one of the editors of the *Magazine* of the envy of Turner

and Dean toward Hosea Ballou. Hosea, 2d, goes on to accuse
Wood of an attempt, with the sanction of Dean and Turner, to
organize a secession from the General Convention in 1817. He
points to the "harshness" of Wood's *Brief Essay* of the same year.
As for Dean, he writes, "Mr. Dean has reported, *secretly*, that Mr.
Ballou retained nothing of Christianity but the *name*. . . ."[61]

After this stinging rebuke, the public part of the controversy
was temporarily stilled. Whittemore later wrote that the effect of
the "Reply" had been "stunning." ". . . It seems to have had the
force of demonstration among the people." At any rate, the Restorationists made no public answer.[62] But behind the scenes there was
much activity. In the middle of February, while the elder Ballou
was out of town, the Restorationists and the junior editors got
together and reached a "settlement" of their differences. In effect,
this was a statement that neither side meant to injure the feelings
or the character of the other. The statement was put in writing and
signed, and the junior editors agreed to publish it in the *Magazine*.[63]
This attempt at harmony failed, however, when Ballou got
back to town. The "settlement" was not printed as scheduled.
When questions were asked, the junior editors announced in the
issue of March 15 that, although they had signed an agreement with
the authors of the "Appeal and Declaration" and had agreed to
publish it on February twenty-second, they later discovered misstate-
ments of facts in the agreement. Furthermore, they realized they
had no right to sign such an agreement without the senior editor,
since they had bound themselves not to print anything regarding
the "Appeal and Declaration" without the consent of all three.[64]
What Ballou said when he discovered that his friends had taken
action without him can only be conjectured. But at this point he
was not in a conciliatory mood. He was still stinging under Wood's
insults and upset by the actions of his old friend Turner.
The Restorationists claimed a breach of faith on the part of the
junior editors and accused Ballou of putting stumbling blocks in
the way of reconciliation. Turner later said that he made several
attempts at reconciliation, but that "Mr. Ballou continued to declare
that nothing short of a total retraction of our writings would satisfy
him."[65] Ballou denied that he had done anything to influence his
colleagues' action. "I told them if they had subscribed to matters of

fact to abide by their agreement; but they both said that what they
had subscribed to was false. I then told them that they must see to
that." [66]

The friendship between Ballou and Edward Turner was shat-
tered. It had been unaffected by the initial correspondence on future punishment; at least, they remained close enough to collaborate
on the hymnbook of 1821. But Wood's machinations seem to have
cast a shadow on that hallowed tie of twenty-five years. When, at
the height of the controversy, Turner was dismissed from his church
in Charlestown, he became convinced that the editors of the *Magazine* had conspired with one of the prominent families of his parish
to overthrow him.[67] On February 4, 1823, he wrote a biting letter
to Ballou:

> That you are a man who preach [*sic*] with great *éclat*, and are
> attended by multitudes, I am sensible; but I have long since discovered
> that these things are not always to be envied, nor always the tests of a
> preacher's usefulness.[68]

Ballou mourned the loss of this friendship. He answered the
letter several days later:

> Had you been a young man, whose friendship I had enjoyed
> but a short time, the case would have been widely different; I could
> have endured it, and could have admonished you; but you were an old,
> tried *friend*, experienced in all matters which related to brotherly walk,
> and when I saw the ground you had taken, I returned home and to my
> pillow, and then gave secret vent to a heart broken with grief for the
> loss of a friend, who for more than twenty years had possessed my
> warmest affections.[69]

Attempt at reconciliation was complicated by the fact that, the
following month, the Standing Committee of the Second Universalist Society of Boston passed an angry resolution. Since Wood,
Turner and Dean had published charges against its pastor and other
Universalists of like thought without first attempting to reach an
understanding, and since they had accused their pastor of unchristian
views "pernicious to the morals of Society," the committee requested
Ballou not to exchange pulpits with these gentlemen until they had
"recalled" their complaint.[70] Turner, on his dismissal from the
Charlestown church, had taken a splinter group with him and was
preaching at the Town Hall. He resented the fact that Ballou

would not exchange with him. Yet Ballou could not reasonably be in the position of encouraging a splinter group, nor could he violate a resolution of his own School Street Church.

As late as 1827, Ballou and Turner were exchanging letters on the subject of Turner's dismissal from Charlestown. Turner persisted in the belief that Ballou had had a hand in his downfall. Ballou appealed to him not to continue to believe and spread the story that he was at fault.

I hope that you are now convinced *that I had nothing to do in that agency which caused your removal from Charlestown.* You know that I never faulted you for your belief. I never complained of the tenets of your faith. I notice this, because several respectable brethren have told me that you and Mrs. Turner contend that I was the cause of your leaving Charlestown. If this information be correct, I hope you will both be generous enough to exonerate me from such a charge.[71]

The Southern Association, meeting at Stafford, Connecticut, took official cognizance of the "Appeal and Declaration" by unanimously voting that the Association express to the authors its disapproval of their action. Of the entire Restorationist group, only Paul Dean had attended the Association meeting, but he had left for home before this action was taken. The Association therefore elected a committee to communicate with the absent brethren and inform them of its action. Six months later—at the next meeting of the Association, at Milford, Massachusetts—the committee reported that it had had no success. Later in the day, however, a feeling of good fellowship was in the air; and a committee of reconciliation, including Ballou, was appointed to draw up terms of settlement.[72] A sweetly worded statement was the result. It was signed by the three Restorationists present—Edward Turner, Barzillai Streeter and Charles Hudson.[73]

A settlement with Paul Dean was a little more difficult to obtain. His animosity to Ballou extended at least as far back as the latter's settlement in Boston. According to Whittemore, Ballou had held out the olive branch until "it had withered in his hand." He then lodged a complaint against Dean at the General Convention of 1823 at Clinton, New York. In a maneuver to offset this, Charles Hudson lodged a complaint against Ballou. The Convention, loath to take action in such delicate matters, exonerated both men. Dean immediately asked permission to withdraw formally from the denomination. His request was granted.[74]

The wound was healed, however, the following June at the meeting of the Southern Association, held at Attleboro, Massachusetts. Dean and Wood were both present. Wood agreed to the terms of reconciliation which had been signed by Turner, Streeter and Hudson at the previous meeting, so the cause of complaint against him was removed.

Dean, who had quit the fellowship the year before, now sought readmission. The majority of those present were in favor of admitting him. Ballou, eager to heal all the wounds caused by the controversy, worked publicly and privately for unanimous consent to his readmission. Among those opposed was Thomas Whittemore, who could only see the seeds of future controversy in such action. Ballou took him aside and attempted to persuade him. "I believe," he said, "Brother Dean is sorry for what has happened; I *cannot* vote not to receive him; if we err at all, let us err on the side of forgiveness. Withdraw your opposition, Brother Whittemore, for my sake; perhaps the joys of former days will return." [75] Whittemore had his doubts, but he gave in.

Dean was again given fellowship. The brethren must have been very happy as Ballou preached, with Paul Dean and Jacob Wood, who were to offer prayers, seated on either side of him.[76]

Ostensibly, peace had been restored. Attention shifted from the conflict of personalities to the realm of ideas. In 1827, Charles Hudson, minister of the church at Westminster, Massachusetts, and one of the more able of the restorationist "party," attacked Ballou's theories in *A Series of Letters*. He criticized Ballou's interpretation of many texts, usually construed to signify a future punishment, as referring to the fall of Jerusalem in 70 A.D. Ballou, showing unusual restraint, did not reply. In fact, he claimed in a letter to Abner Kneeland that he had not even read Hudson:

> As to the license and its latitudes, which the writer, to whom you allude, has taken with my publications, I am unacquainted, having never read his work. Having been informed, by the best of judges, that it contained no new arguments on the merits of the subject to which it professes to be devoted, and having so often answered those which have been in use, I have not been disposed to go over grounds which I was sure would present neither fruits nor flowers, pleasant to the taste or eye.[77]

Walter Balfour, however, did stand up in Ballou's defense. Balfour was a Scotch Presbyterian who had come from Scotland to Charlestown with letters of introduction to the Reverend Jedidiah Morse, the well-known opponent of liberalism in the Congregational order and founder of those twin institutions of reaction, the Park Street Church and Andover Seminary. Balfour preached for a time in the Baptist Church but soon came under the influence of Universalists. In 1823 his conversion was noted in the columns of *The Universalist Magazine.*[78]

Balfour, like Ballou, used his exegetical skill to prove that there was no such place as hell in the thought of the writers of the Scriptures. Like Ballou, he came under the guns of the restorationists. In 1828–1829 he carried on a long debate with Hudson via the press.[79]

Unfortunately, words were soon again replaced by action. On January 1, 1831, Adin Ballou (a younger and very distant relation) began to publish a Restorationist organ, *The Independent Messenger.* Much space was devoted to discussions of the advisability of withdrawing from the Universalist denomination.[80] Adin Ballou was soon involved in a heated controversy with Thomas Whittemore and his powerful *Trumpet,* successor of the *Magazine.* A sharp-tongued controversialist who would give no quarter, he was fully a match for the dynamic but blunt Whittemore.

This agitation, plus what was considered discriminatory action by the General Convention against the Restorationist-dominated Providence Association, led to the secession of the Restorationists in August 1831.[81] Among their number were Jacob Wood and Ballou's old antagonist Paul Dean. Edward Turner was not involved. After a brief pastorate at Portsmouth, he had become a Unitarian and spent his closing years in various small churches.[82]

The secessionists were not a large group; only eight ministers were involved.[83] Many persons of restorationist sympathy, including Hosea Ballou, 2d, remained loyal to the Universalist denomination. These men felt perfectly free to hold their own belief in fellowship with those who disagreed with them. But the great swing in the denomination was to the no future punishment view. Ballou seemed to be riding the wave of the future.

CHAPTER XVI

DEATH AND GLORY

Ballou returned from a preaching visit to New York and Philadelphia in June 1828 to find that his editorial chair had vanished.

Thomas Whittemore had been considering a move to either Philadelphia or Cincinnati. He had finally decided to stay at Cambridgeport, but his pastorate there did not provide sufficient outlet for his boundless energy. Seeking more activity, he had conceived the idea of publishing a bigger and better Universalist newspaper in Boston.[1] That this was unethical, considering his connection as associate editor of *The Universalist Magazine,* appears not to have crossed his mind. In any case, he had teamed up with Russell Streeter of the Watertown church and began mapping plans for a new paper.[2]

When the announcement of their proposed venture was first issued in April, quite a stir was caused in Universalist circles in the Boston area. Many believed that Whittemore and Streeter were encroaching on the territory of Henry Bowen and the *Magazine.*[3] Ballou was very upset by the announcement: he believed that the field should have been left to Bowen, or that Bowen should at least have been informed in advance.[4] Whittemore, in his biography of Ballou, does not tell whether his old teacher and friend was personally affronted by his actions.

While Ballou was away, a compromise was reached between Whittemore and Bowen: the old paper was absorbed by the new,[5] which took the name *Trumpet and Universalist Magazine.* The first copy was issued on July 5, 1828. Unlike the old *Magazine,* the *Trumpet* was full newspaper size, carried advertising and dealt with secular as well as religious concerns. Under Whittemore's vigorous editorship (Streeter withdrew after three months[6]), the paper was truly a "trumpet" in the Universalist Zion for more than thirty years—until Whittemore's death in 1861.

Whittemore writes[7] that Ballou expressed his approval of the new paper, but it is notable that he appears to have made no contribution to its columns for the first few years. It seems likely that he resented Whittemore's actions. He eventually became reconciled, however, and contributed many letters, articles and reviews.

Ballou was not long without an editorial post. Hosea, 2d, because of the success of his *Ancient History of Universalism* (published in 1829), became convinced that the denomination was ready for a heavier and more scholarly fare than was being served by the existing papers and periodicals.[8] He persuaded his publishers, Marsh and Capen, who were members of the School Street Church, to originate a serious bimonthly journal with articles of lasting interest to Universalists. So was born *The Universalist Expositor.*

The magazine began to appear in July 1830, with the two Hosea Ballous as co-editors.[9] Many of the contributions by the elder Hosea seem to have been adapted from sermons; others of a more pretentious style were written expressly for the *Expositor.* The contributions by Hosea, 2d, are of a scholarly nature.[10] In July 1831, L. S. Everett joined the Ballous as a co-editor. This relieved the aging Hosea of the burden of having to write prolifically in order to keep the columns filled. He made comparatively few contributions to the second volume.[11]

Universalists generally did not appreciate the *Expositor,* and lack of patronage forced the suspension of publication at the end of the second volume.[12] But agitation, especially among the ministers, led to the revival of the journal by a different publisher in January 1833. The new version, under the title *Expositor and Universalist Review,* was under the proprietorship of—and edited by—Hosea Ballou, 2d, and Thomas Whittemore.[13]

1833 was a notable year for Ballou. His oldest boy, Hosea Faxon, had decided to become a preacher: he had been farming in the summer and teaching in the winter, but now was anxious to join his father and his brother Massena in proclaiming the gospel of God's love to man. On June 30, Ballou had the pleasure of giving the charge to his son at his ordination.[14] Hosea Faxon at thirty-three was tall, straight and strong. People noted his "marked resemblance" to his father, not only in his face and build, but also in his mental characteristics.[15] He was to gain a distinguished record of public service in Whitingham and Wilmington, Vermont.[16]

The General Convention of Universalists, at a spirited meeting in 1832, had voted to become a nationwide organization. Up to that point, it had been mostly confined to New England; but by 1833 sentiment was in favor of making it a general convention in fact as well as in name, with representatives from the various state conventions. (Ballou's attitude was not registered, since he presided at the meeting as moderator.[17]) At the meetings the following year, the action was made official, and in 1834 the first General Convention of Universalists in the United States was held at Albany, New York. It was a notable meeting, with fifty preachers present—then a very large number indeed.[18] The honor of the moderator's chair was voted to the most distinguished preacher of the order, Hosea Ballou.

In November 1834, Ballou made one of his frequent visits to Philadelphia. As on his first visit to the city, his sermons were taken down in shorthand and published, this time by the disowned Quaker Universalist Abel Thomas.[19] In the preface to the *Nine Sermons*, Thomas explains that he "exercised the privileges of an editor" in cutting out repetitions and expanding wherever necessary in order "fully to express the meaning of the preacher." [20] So it is difficult to determine in these sermons how much is Ballou and how much is Thomas.

Ballou preached at both the Lombard Street and the Callowhill Street Churches, but the most interesting sermon in the group is a lecture that he delivered before the newly formed Young Men's Universalist Institute. Here he is seen in a more formal mood. The burden of the lecture is that one must have sufficient knowledge to combat the three antagonists of Universalism—the Calvinists; the advocates of Free Will, or Arminians; and the skeptics (those who have renounced Christianity and even question the existence of a "First Cause").[21]

As the sixty-three-year-old preacher looked out on the young faces before him, his mind ran back over his many years of preaching the gospel of universal salvation. He could not but compare the past with the present:

> . . . My young friends, be not discouraged at the embarassments which lie around you. There are those who vindicate our doctrine, who have seen it in a very different state from what it is now. When your

humble servant commenced his career in life, he does not know that he could count ten individuals who had opened their lips on this continent, in advocating our doctrines; and there were not more than two or three regular societies formed, professing to believe as we do. What a change has he lived to see! I have been engaged in the conflict for more than forty years, and I now invite you to enter on the prosecution of the work before you. I have not met with any thing, in all the means which have been arrayed in opposition to our faith, nor in all the errors which have existed, both on the right hand and on the left, that has produced one moment's discouragement in my mind. Perfect confidence in the truth of God, and in the fact that truth is great and will prevail, has inspired me with courage to go forward, and prosecute the Christian warfare.[22]

In a sense, the years 1832 and 1834 saw the completion of Ballou's theological system. The latter part of 1832 saw the publication of his "Works," and in 1834 was published his detailed examination of the doctrine of future retribution. The Works included two volumes of sermons—the *Lecture Sermons* of 1818–1819 and a collection of "fugitives" under the title *Select Sermons* —and revised editions of the *Notes on the Parables of the New Testament* and *A Treatise on Atonement.*

The revised *Notes* of 1832 are, in some cases, quite different from the earlier editions in their interpretation of the parables. Ballou at times abandons the allegorical, cabalistical interpretation and follows a more natural approach. But the earlier view still mars much of the book, and Ballou himself admits in the preface that the revision is not as thorough as he had wished. He pleads lack of ability and lack of the good health and leisure necessary to accomplish such a task. He is convinced, however, that those passages which are left untouched will not harm anyone, for they are still the result of honest conviction.[23]

In the case of the *Treatise*, his revisions were more thorough. From 1805, when it was first published, to the edition of 1832, the text was left untouched; but now he attempted to bring it up to date. He did not completely recast it, for he wanted to retain the language common people can understand.[24] Instead, he excised from the old text those elements of which he no longer approved and, in some cases, rewrote paragraphs from his new point of view. This naturally resulted in an unevenness of style; the reader moves from words written with Ballou's 1805 vocabulary to those written in 1832.[25]

A comparison of the editions of 1832 and 1805 reveals that a constant liberalization had taken place in his thought over the years. This modification is seen at work in the preface of the edition of 1828,[26] in which he expresses doubt concerning some of the statements he was to change in the edition of 1832.

Ballou had made a distinction between the creation of man in Christ and his later formation in the dust. He had attributed the cause of sin to the later, carnal part of man's nature rebelling against the earlier, heavenly part. In 1832 he abandons this fanciful dual-conception of creation and formation, but he still attributes the cause of sin to the carnal in man. It is man's *desire* that is responsible for sin.

> Now *want* unsatisfied is an evil; and unsatisfied want is the first movement to action or volition. The motives which invite to action, owe their strength to the nature and strength of desire which want creates, and the moral character of the action depends on the character of the motive.[27]

But he does not abandon man to materialism. Although man was not, after all, created in Christ before being formed in the dust, he still is basically of heavenly extraction. For man possesses a "law of moral, or spiritual life." [28]

This alteration in Ballou's thought was caused by a more basic change. He had come to the belief that Christ was not a pre-existent being. He admits that there are passages of Scripture which seem to favor the idea of Christ's pre-existence, but these do not appear strong enough to make such a belief irresistible. To hold such an opinion would be "mere speculation." [29]

To bring the body of the *Treatise* into conformity with this new belief, Ballou finds it necessary to delete passages which represent Jesus as the eternal spirit of love, or *logos*, which was with God and was hidden "behind the letter of the law, and in the cabalistical allegories of the prophets, until it brake forth in the official character of Jesus." [30] But despite this change of heart, Ballou does not revere Christ any less. He still believes that Christ was invested by God with majestic power, so that he was capable of performing the great task of atonement.

This change in Ballou's view of Christ's pre-existence may have been due to the influence of the writings of Joseph Priestley. He had published Priestley's treatise—*A General View of the Arguments for the Unity of God. From Reason, from the Scriptures, and from History*—in several installments in *The Universalist Magazine* in 1819.[31] He would probably not have devoted so much space to this material if he had not tended to accept Priestley's arguments against the Arian view of Christ and against the idea of his pre-existence.

In one other important area, the 1832 edition differs strikingly from the earlier editions. This is the doctrinal question of punishment for sin. Formerly he had explained that the coming of the Son of man with fire was a figurative way of saying that the chaff of man's nature would be consumed by the fire, or love, of God. Now he interprets these passages as referring to the judgment which came on the generation of Jesus. Since Jesus said these things would happen in the lifetime of his disciples, he must have been referring to the destruction of Jerusalem in 70 A.D.

The whole question of future punishment was the subject of a separate book which appeared two years later. In *An Examination of the Doctrine of Future Retribution*,[32] Ballou set forth his views so that

when the time shall come, as he believes it will, when people in general will number the tenet of future punishment among those corruptions of Christianity, which will then be abandoned, it may be known that the writer disbelieved it in his day; and also that the arguments with which he opposed it may then be known.

He knows that he will be accused of harassing the Restorationists by publishing such a book, but he feels that each man has the right to think his own thoughts and publish them to the world. He will not hold his brethren less warmly in his affections if they do not agree with his position.[33] It is a great virtue of the Universalist denomination that each member is free to think and speak for himself.[34]

Ballou argues his case against future punishment on the basis of morals, analogy and the Scriptures. The moral argument is directed against those who would promote morals by "depending on a belief in a future state of rewards and punishment"; it supports those who would promote morals by "teaching that all the reward we ought to expect, for a faithful discharge of our duty to God and our fellow-creatures, is found in the enjoyments which are necessarily connected with religion and duty" in the here and now.[35]

Ballou effectively repeats an argument which he used in the *Treatise* to show that men are motivated to act by the hope of present happiness. The wicked person is such because he expects the reward of his actions here and now. The great bulk of sinners in this world have been taught to believe in the reality of future rewards and punishments, but the threat of future punishment has been no deterrent to sin:

> . . . The expectation of enjoyment in the present state, has carried them on in the strong current of sin, which has broken down every barrier, and furnished conclusive proof that no motive is so sure of inducing to action, as the expectation of immediate happiness.[36]

The wicked person obviously does not have a true picture of religion and morality; he needs to be persuaded "that righteousness brings an ample reward, in the present life." [37]

Love for the good cannot be induced by fear. Man cannot be made to love even his Creator by the threat of punishment.[38] The preaching of future rewards and punishments in order to persuade people to love God "is not only *useless*, but *pernicious*," for it implies that God and morality are inherently "unlovely, and unworthy of being loved." [39]

It is the task of the divines to instill in man a fear of sin, but they have fallen into the error of believing "that the evil of sin is not in sin, but in a punishment" of a future state. If man realized that sin is *inherently* unpleasant, he would attempt to avoid sin. As it is, he is intent on avoiding not sin but punishment—both here and hereafter.[40]

As in the *Treatise,* Ballou contends here that a man's idea of God affects his own character. The "human heart is capable of becoming soft, or hard; kind, or unkind; merciful or unmerciful, by education and habit." The orthodox picture of infernal torment has so hardened the hearts of believers that they act toward their fellow mortals in the same wrathful manner that they expect of the heavenly Father.[41]

Ballou next turns to the arguments of analogy used by the proponents of future punishment. He claims that he is hesitant to discuss this subject for fear of misrepresenting its proponents, since they have not as yet come forth with a systematic presentation of their point of view. He feels it safe, however, to define the minimum essential of their position thus:

. . . In all respects . . . the future state . . . will be analogous to this mode of being. So that, reasoning from analogy, as moral agents sin, and thereby render themselves miserable in this world, the same moral agents may continue to do the same in the world to come. In connexion with this argument it is urged, that as it is evident to our senses that sin often escapes a just retribution in this world, it must be recompensed in another state, or divine justice must forever be deprived of its claims.[42]

The divines who use this argument of analogy are basically inconsistent. They assert that, in this world, sin not only procures for "its agents the riches and honors" of life but also escapes detection and punishment. By analogy, the same conditions would persist in a future state, and the sinner would be as successful there as here. Furthermore, by analogy, if divine justice is never fully satisfied in this world, it would be no better served in the next![43]

In this way we might proceed and make the future state precisely like the present; for we have no more authority for carrying sin and its miseries into a future world, than we have for carrying all other things into that state which we find in this.[44]

Reason leads us to believe that sin is the result of temptation. If sin is to exist in a future world, then temptation must exist there also; for to argue that sin will exist there without temptation is altogether arbitrary—and contrary to analogy.[45] But if temptation exists in the future world, the good and pious will be subject to a falling away from the good life there, as they are on earth. Then for whom is heaven secure?

Furthermore, the righteous in the next world will suffer vicariously for the unrighteous, just as they do on earth:[46]

If the pious in this world are so distressed, as they profess to be, with the apprehensions which they entertain of the future sufferings of their wicked fellow-creatures, what must be their anguish hereafter, when they shall see, in awful reality, the sufferings which they now have only in prospect![47]

Finally, according to the principle of analogy, if punishment for sin is relegated to a future life, virtue and vice must continue from state to state endlessly in the future, with the evil person in each state being threatened with punishment in the next.[48]

As might be expected, Ballou devotes the greater part of the *Examination* to arguments from the Scriptures; he raises the cogent question: why, if the doctrine of future punishment is true and necessary to piety, was the information not given to Adam? He cites Genesis 2:16-17:

And the Lord God commanded the man, saying, of every tree or the garden thou mayest freely eat: but of the tree of the knowledge of good and evil, thou shalt not eat of it; for in the day that thou eatest thereof, thou shalt surely die.

There is no indication that Adam was threatened with the "intolerable pains of hell in an eternal state, about which there is so much preached in our times." He was warned only about punishment in this world: "In the day thou eatest thereof, thou shalt surely die." [49] And the progeny of Adam were at no time warned of a future retribution.[50]

When they sinned, Adam and Eve were not simply docketed for a trial in eternity in which they would be judged for their earthly transgressions. The Lord God took action immediately. The tempter he condemned to a life of degradation as the lowest of beasts and the enemy of mankind. The woman he sentenced to a life of multiplied sorrow, pain in childbirth and subjection to man. Adam he sentenced to a life of hard labor on a land made difficult on his account.[51]

Ballou then rehearses the long catalogue of the sins recorded in the Old Testament—sins which grew worse as time passed. Nowhere does he find a future retribution threatened; rather, punishment is imposed in this world.[52] He takes his readers to Mount Sinai with Moses and his Israelites.

We shall now learn, no doubt, the mind of God respecting the demerit of sin and the severity of its just punishment. We can hardly expect to go from this mountain ignorant of those divine sanctions which will best serve the cause of piety, religion, and moral virtue. The lightnings have flashed! the thunders have rolled! God has spoken! the verdict of heaven is registered! Come, ye doctors, who insist that neither judgment nor punishment is in this world—and who, without hesitation, doom your fellow-sinners to endless wo [sic],—come and read the following verdict: "Life for life, eye for eye, tooth for tooth, hand for hand, foot for foot, burning for burning, wound for wound, stripe for stripe."—(Exodus xxi. 23-25.) All this is evidently in this world, where life can be taken, where eyes can be destroyed, where teeth can be extracted, where hands and feet can be amputated, where burnings, wounds, and stripes can be inflicted.[53]

Jesus himself followed the prophets in expecting retribution in his own time, not in a future state.[54] He said that his disciples would not die before the Son of man came on the clouds of heaven.[55] And there is no basis for believing that his references to "hell fire" (literally, a "Gehenna of fire") should be taken to mean a future state. Rather, Jesus used this allusion to Gehenna, the town dump in the valley of Hinnom, "symbolically" to indicate "spiritual punishment in this world." (This interpretation, Ballou points out, is supported by the testimony of the respected scholars Dr. Adam Clarke and John Parkhurst, who were themselves believers in future punishment.[56]) In speaking of the "damnation of Gehenna," Jesus was clearly referring to the coming destruction of Jerusalem, an earthly event.[57]

Ballou then incorrectly interprets the many references to the Second Coming in the New Testament (in the letters of Paul and "Peter," and in the Revelation) as predictions of the destruction of Jerusalem in 70 A.D. He interprets these in the light of the various apocalyptic sayings of Jesus in the gospels.[58] Mistaken though he may have been in this detail, he at least recognized that these passages refer not to a judgment in an afterlife but to an earthly event.

Having considered the doctrine of future retribution from the points of view of morals, analogy and the Scriptures, Ballou concludes his work by reprinting several of his letters and articles on the subject which had appeared in periodicals. The most interesting of these is a letter "To a Friend Who Had Written Him on the Subject of 'Death and Glory.'" Ballou here accepts the implications of a term which was to become one of disrepute in Universalist circles. He does not know whether there is a period of unconsciousness between death and the "resurrection state," as Priestley contended; but he does know that there is no scriptural basis for belief in a transitional "moral state." It is therefore

immaterial whether we enter, immediately, after the dissolution of body, on the resurrection state, or sleep in unconscious quietude any given time before that glorious event shall take place. In either case, it is what you call "death and glory;" for it makes no difference as to the

length of time during an unconscious state. In such a state there can
be effected no moral preparations.[59]

It was possible for Ballou to accept the idea of "death and
glory" because of his very exalted view of man. Man is the offspring of the heavenly Father, and once rid of carnal desire—at the
dissolution of the body—he would return to that heavenly state
from which he came. But, as has been wisely pointed out, Ballou's
"main contention was not the one which linked death and glory, but
one which bound together life and judgment." [60]

CHAPTER XVII

"SALVATION IRRESPECTIVE OF CHARACTER"

Ballou's Second Universalist Society in Boston now meets with the Unitarian Arlington Street Church, which in Ballou's day stood on Federal Street and was led by the distinguished liberal minister William Ellery Channing. The two parent denominations of these churches have consolidated to become the Unitarian Universalist Association. Similarities of belief have created a continuing rapprochement and fellowship which has culminated in an organizational merger. But it was not always so. . . .

The seeds of antitrinitarian liberalism had been sprouting in America from late Colonial days, but not until 1805 can Unitarianism be said to have been clearly defined. In that year, the election of a liberal to the Hollis Professorship of Divinity at Harvard College precipitated in the Congregational churches the first skirmish of what came to be known as the Unitarian Controversy. Ten years later, most liberals were at last ready to accept the name Unitarian. In 1815 a pamphlet on *American Unitarianism* was published and was reviewed in a biting article in Jedidiah Morse's reactionary magazine, *The Panoplist*. The storm which blew up over this review included the exchange of several "letters" between Channing and Samuel Worcester of Salem. In 1819, Channing delivered his definitive statement of *Unitarian Christianity* in a sermon in Baltimore. By then, the Unitarians can be said to have become a distinctive group, although the American Unitarian Association was not actually chartered until 1825.

Ballou had been unitarian in belief a decade before the Unitarian movement began to take formal shape. He delivered his first unitarian sermon as early as 1795; by 1805 he had converted the Universalists as a whole to the new position. *A Treatise on Atonement,* published in that year, contained a forthright, hard-hitting attack on the doctrine of the trinity and advocated a unitarian doctrine of God.

It would be logical to assume that, when Ballou came to the School Street Church in 1817, he would have been welcomed by the Unitarians as an ally. In fact, he and his denomination were snubbed. The Unitarians did not wish to be classed as Universalists by their orthodox brethren. They were anxious to conciliate, whenever possible, the conservative wing of Congregationalism. Their heresy regarding the nature of Christ was radical enough; to embrace universal salvation was unthinkable. When a New York preacher charged them with holding universalist beliefs, Henry Ware, Junior, called it an "unfounded" and "cruel accusation." [1] Very few would take the position of James Walker, later president of Harvard, but in 1823 minister of the Unitarian church in Charlestown:

> If by "everlasting punishment" is meant "the proper eternity of hell-torments," it is a doctrine which *most Unitarians of the present day concur in rejecting; some* understanding, by that "everlasting destruction" to which the wicked are to be consigned, an absolute annihilation; *others* conceiving of their sufferings as *consequential,* and *indefinite* as to their duration; and *others,* that *all punishment will be remedial, and will end at last in a universal restoration to goodness and happiness.*[2]

(Some of the Unitarians were obviously tending toward restorationism. Indeed, the Restorationist secessionists from the Universalist denomination were eventually welcomed into the Unitarian fold.[3])

A second reason that the Unitarians avoided association with Universalists was social. The Unitarians generally were of the higher social class in New England; their ministers were Harvard literati, who were contemptuous of the unlearned Universalist clergy.[4] While the Unitarians as a whole were a homogeneous group in the established church, the Universalists were "come-outers" from all denominations—"a motley group." [5] The crudeness, even vulgarity, of some of the Universalist preachers "excited disgust, and assisted in nullifying their influence." [6]

This social cleavage, while not mentioned openly at the time, may explain the refusal of the Unitarian ministers to exchange pulpits with the Universalists. Ballou favored pulpit exchanges among men of all shades of opinion represented in Boston at the time— Calvinist, Arminian and Universalist. He believed this was a way of promoting truth and eliminating error. The Unitarians, however, exchanged pulpits with Congregationalists, Baptists and other orthodox sects, but very seldom with Universalists. Ballou suggested that the Unitarian clergy were not afraid of orthodoxy in their pulpits, for they knew their people rejected it, but that they would not allow Universalism for fear their people might accept it.[7]

In Ballou's "Dialogue between a Universalist and a Limitarian,"[8] which appeared in 1819, those who profess "liberal sentiments"—that is, the Unitarians—are said to be Universalists in disguise. That they were not willing to drop this disguise must have pained Ballou deeply. But he never castigated them; he seems to have had a love for them similar to that of a father for an erring child. He praised the Unitarians for the great advance they had made in theology—their recovery of the great biblical teaching of the unity of God.[9] Moreover, because they recognized the fatherly love of God for His children, they rejected such partial doctrines as those of election and reprobation.[10] And they believed that the doctrines of total depravity and regeneration are untrue,[11] that man is capable of moral improvement in this life and does not need the power of irresistible grace to pull him upward.

Ballou commended them for these beliefs, as well as for their insistence on the right of the individual conscience to interpret the Scriptures by the light of reason. He was troubled only by their inconsistency. Why, in view of their other liberal beliefs, did they not advocate belief in universal salvation?

To avoid the charge of being universalists, Unitarian preachers would frequently quote the scriptural passages which were mistakenly interpreted by their congregations as referring to everlasting misery in the future life. They themselves, Ballou was sure, knew that these passages were not opposed to universalism, but they did not explain this to their hearers. Many a time he heard with excitement an uplifting sermon by a Unitarian minister. The preacher would paint vividly the picture of an infinitely benevolent Father, Who loves all His children and Whose purpose in creation is to make them happy. And then, "when the cheering light of this blessed doctrine shone about us, and in us, to such a degree as to lead us to think the preacher was about to remove the veil from his congregation at once, all of a sudden a deep wound was inflicted by the artful preacher" as he would quote one of the usual passages erroneously taken to signify endless punishment.[12]

This problem of the inconsistency of the Unitarians faced Ballou shortly after he arrived in Boston. In the third and fourth issues of *The Universalist Magazine*[13] in 1819, he printed long excerpts from Channing's Baltimore Sermon. Commenting on it, he observes that there is no doubt that Channing means to state a universalist position.[14] He cites passages which illustrate Channing's position, such as:

> We believe that God is infinitely good, kind, benevolent, in the proper sense of these words; good in disposition, as well as in act; good, not to a few, but to all; good to every individual, as well as the general system.[15]

Ballou points out that, since it is "impossible for God to be more than infinitely good to any, he must mean, that God is as good to every individual as he is to any." He also calls attention to passages in which Channing rejects "the false and dishonourable views of God" conceived by the orthodox.[16]

But then Ballou has the painful task of exposing serious inconsistencies in Channing's statements concerning God. How can his faith in the God of love—Who is, Channing says, "originally, essentially, and eternally placable, and disposed to forgive," a God who punishes only to correct—be reconciled with his belief that Jesus uses, among other means, "threatenings against incorrigible guilt"? Does Channing mean what he says? "Incorrigible means bad beyond amendment; and to talk of benevolently punishing the individuals who cannot be reclaimed really appears absurd." Such serious inconsistencies expose Channing to the criticism of the orthodox, and Ballou hopes that Channing will present a clarification of "these mysterious statements."[17] So far as is known, Channing never did.

On two occasions, Ballou took it upon himself publicly to reprove Channing. The first of these was in December 1820, when he opposed Channing on the question of continuing the establishment of the Congregational Church in Massachusetts. The question had come before the Constitutional Convention, which met during late 1820 and early 1821.[18] At this period, Channing's Federal Street Church was still Congregational in name and stood to benefit by the religious tax. The dissenting churches did not; and while the dissenter could divert his own share to the church of his choice, the taxes of the large numbers of non-church members went to support the established church.

In December 1820, Channing preached in favor of establishment,[19] giving a glowing description of the importance of religion to society. Religion is a social principle, not just a personal matter between man and his God.[20] The individual gains his religion in society; he does not bring it into the world with him.[21] ". . . Therefore Society ought, through its great organ and representative, which is government, as well as by other methods, to pay homage to God, and express its obligation."[22] Elected officials should have the "power of providing religious instruction" in order to safeguard public morals.[23] Since religion is essential to society, it is entitled to "any grateful offering from the state which it upholds."[24]

Within ten days,[25] Ballou had rushed into print a pamphlet of "strictures" on Channing's sermon.[26] His reply is quite restrained. He praises Channing's exalted sentiments regarding "the foundation of pure and undefiled religion"[27] and commends his ideas on the social nature of religion.[28] But then, in his usual thorough manner, he examines Channing's views in favor of establishment.[29] He points out cogently that a glance at history will prove that legislation on religious matters has always corrupted Christianity.[30] And Channing's own logic invites religious oppression:

> If one set of religious sentiments ought to be supported by law, because they are of a social and salutary nature in society, there surely is the same reason for preventing by law the propagation of principles which are subversive of them.[31]

Furthermore, Channing should know that it is impossible to make men religious by law.[32] ". . . The internal principles of religion cannot be controled [sic] by legislation, and therefore stand in no need of its aid."[33]

There is no way of knowing whether Ballou's comments had any effect on Channing's mind. That he thought better of his stand on established religion is sure. When *Religion a Social Principle* appeared in his *Works* in 1841, all mention of state support of religion was excluded. He retained only the section on the "Importance of Religion to Society."[34] But Ballou's strictures clearly had no great impact on the Constitutional Convention. This body kept the religious provision, which was not repealed until 1833.

A much more serious difference between Ballou and Channing arose over the question of ultra-universalism, the no-future-punishment school. In 1832, Channing delivered a discourse on *The Evil of Sin.*[35] Sin, he maintains, sometimes prospers in this world; it is not always punished here. It is obvious, therefore, that retribution must be made in the future life, and the idea of retribution "finds a response now in every mind not perverted by sophistry."[36] Channing was much too polite to name names, but there is no doubt that he was alluding to Ballou when he criticized "some among us" who maintain "that punishment is confined to the present state" and claim that "in changing worlds we shall change our characters; that moral evil is to be buried with the body in the grave." The Doctor notices this particular opinion because it "spreads industriously" and "tends to diminish the dread of sin."[37] So Ballou found himself attacked even by the great Doctor Channing!

A "more irrational doctrine" than ultra-universalism, says Channing, he has never seen. It is plain from analogy (an argument which Ballou later laughed to scorn) that such a "sudden revolution" as the death-and-glory doctrine proposes would destroy a man's identity. There could be no on-goingness of man's mind from this state to the next if such a system were true.[38] Channing does not see how the dissolution of the body can purify the mind. "Why should the last grow pure from the dissolution of the first?"[39]

Regarding the future state, Channing is noncommittal. Whether the evil soul will suffer complete extinction or will be reformed and made happy, he is not sure. On this question the Bible "throws no clear light." But the sacred writings do impress upon the mind the terrible suffering that awaits the wicked soul.[40]

Ballou subjected this sermon to a "candid examination."[41] In his reply, he admits that he was shocked at this sermon by Channing, whose talents and labors he has always esteemed so highly. As he became aware that Channing was attacking himself and the doctrine "which is now so rapidly prevailing," he "felt a sinking, a momentary enervation of mind, and a morbid gloom seemed to obscure mental vision."[42] But he soon recovered and decided to defend the goodness of God by pointing out Channing's contradictions.[43]

The doctor does not present one jot or tittle from the Scriptures to prove his assertions that there is to be a greater misery after this life.[44] And Ballou regrets that Channing has not taken the opportunity to understand the doctrine he is seeking to disprove. Channing had summarized the views of "some of us" very inaccurately.

> . . . If he had been rightly informed, he would have said, It is maintained by some among us that as neither scripture nor reason show to us that sin will continue beyond this state of flesh and blood, so neither do they prove that punishment for sin will so continue; that when we exchange worlds, and this corruptible puts on incorruption, our constitutions will be essentially changed, as is particularly described by St. Paul in his first Epistle to the Corinthians; and that we shall be equal unto the angels, and shall die no more, as Jesus testified to the Sadducees.[45]

Channing had implied that, according to the Ultra-Universalists, moral evil resides in the body rather than in the soul. With the dissolution of the body, the evil would inevitably vanish, leaving the soul pure and free—with no need for a special divine act of grace. But this implication, says Ballou, is a misrepresentation. Channing "has no reason to believe this, and . . . it has too much the appearance of a canting throw at what he was not disposed to treat with his usual candor."[46] Channing certainly has never read him to the effect that the death of the body has power to change the mind. This power is God's. "We never ascribed the power to change us from this state to another, to anything but God who raised our Lord Jesus Christ from the dead."[47]

Ballou exposes at length every inconsistency in Channing's sermon. He would like the doctor to explain some of his statements but does not expect him to "condescend" to do so.[48]

There is no evidence that Channing was personally acquainted with Ballou. He held himself aristocratically aloof from such a common person. One of the doctor's better biographers has acknowledged that this "aloofness cost him a good deal": he "had not that personal knowledge . . . that could qualify him for a just understanding" of Ballou.[49] Ballou, in turn, may have resented this lack of personal relationship, and he certainly found Channing very inconsistent in his religious thinking. Yet he always respected Channing and spoke highly—at times reverently—of the "impassioned little saint."[50]

The basic difference between Ballou and the Unitarians such as Channing was on the question of salvation. Arminian from the beginning, Unitarian thought always presupposed that man is free to accept or reject God's proferred grace. As it developed, it placed greater and greater responsibility on man. Its rallying cry became "salvation by character"; its credo, that man comes closer to the possibility of salvation as he develops his character. Nothing could have been further from the thought of Ballou, who considered a rigid determinism not only logical but *necessary* to insure the salvation of *every* individual.

This basic difference in attitude is vividly illustrated by an undated anecdote about Ballou. He had gone to an inland town on a preaching engagement and had made arrangements to stay with a lady who, as it turned out, believed that men are to be saved only if they are good. Arriving at the house on Saturday afternoon, Ballou found her in the kitchen, mop in hand. Looking up, the woman said:

"This is Mr. Ballou, I suppose?"

"Yes, madam, my name is Ballou."

"Well, Mr. Ballou, they say you hold that all men will be saved. Do you really believe that doctrine?"

"Yes, madam, I really believe it."

"Why, sir! Do you really believe that all men are going to be saved just such creatures *as they are?*"

Seeing that she did not understand the nature of salvation, Ballou asked:

"What is that you have in your hand, dear woman?"

"Why," she replied, laughing, "it is my mop."

"Your mop? Well, what are you going to do with it?"

"I am going to mop up my floor. I always do it on Saturday afternoon."

"Well, sister, I understand you. Are you going to mop it up *just as it is?*"

"Mop it up just as it is?"

"Yes; you wished to know if I hold that all men will be saved *just as they are.* Do you intend to mop up the floor *just as it is?*"

"Why," she replied, "I mop it up to clean it."

"True," said Ballou. "You do not require it to be made clean before you will consent to mop it up. God saves men to purify them; that's what salvation is designed for. God does not require men to be pure in order that he may save them." [51]

As if to accent this difference between himself and the Unitarians, Ballou published in the *Trumpet* in 1849 an article titled "Salvation Irrespective of Character." [52] He announces:

There is, at this time, no objection to the doctrine of Universal Salvation more pertinaciously insisted on by its opposers, than that the doctrine teaches that all men are to be saved irrespective of moral character, and in violation of the freedom of man's will. The objection supposes that Universalists believe and teach, that God has decreed the happiness of all men, and that he will make them thus happy and forever blessed, be their moral characters what they may; holy or unholy; clean or unclean; righteous or wicked. The amount of the objection is, that the doctrine contends that as God will have all men to be saved, he will save them whether they will or not; whether they repent of their sins or not;—whether they reform or remain sinful.

Such an objection comes from those who are ignorant not only of Universalist doctrine but also of the nature of salvation. Salvation is not salvation from hell, or from the wrath of God, or from punishment. Salvation, as seen in the Bible, is salvation from sin. Jesus said, "I came not to call the righteous, but sinners to repentance" (Luke 5:32). Did anyone ask whether he would "call sinners to repentance irrespective of moral character"? Jesus told men that he was—and Ballou paraphrases John 6:33—"the bread of God which came down from heaven to give life to the world." Imagine his reaction if someone had asked whether he would "give life to the world irrespective of moral character"! And does Jesus the shepherd save the lost sheep irrespective of moral character? ". . . The question proves either the ignorance or insincerity of him who asks it."

As was his custom, Ballou cites many scriptural passages to drive home his point—that Christ will lead all men to salvation and that it is ridiculous to raise the questions of moral character and freedom of the will.

The whole subject is seen in this simple question: Was Saul fit to become a Christian? Is a sinner fit to be saved from sin? Is a sick person fit to be cured? Is a blind man fit to have his eyes opened? Are such as are dead in sin fit to be quickened into a life of holiness? [53]

If the opponent of universalism would face these questions candidly, less would be heard regarding the licentiousness of the doctrine of the salvation of sinners.

Many of our Unitarian brethren have lately manifested a disposition to show some favor to Universalism, if it be so modified as to teach the certainty of a future state of rewards and punishments. This they contend is indispensable; and that it is licentious not to believe it.[54]

Unitarians should see that an intricate question is involved: if man is to be recompensed in a future state for his actions in this life, where will he be recompensed for his actions in the afterlife? "According to such a theory, recompense will forever be one state of existence in arrear."

Opposed to the Unitarian position is divine truth: "Behold, the righteous shall be recompensed in the earth: much more the wicked and the sinner" (Proverbs 11:31). To say that sin is not fully punished in this state of existence is "the most licentious doctrine ever invented; and is, in the very nature of things, the only deception which leads into sin." [55]

To the end of his life, Ballou stressed this difference between himself and the Unitarians—or, as he might have put it, between the true and false understanding of salvation. At the General Convention held in Boston in September 1851, he explained the difference in that homely language in which he expressed himself best:

Your child has fallen into the mire, and its body and its garments are defiled. You cleanse it, and array it in clean robes. The query is, Do you love your child because you have washed it? or, Did you wash it because you loved it? [56]

How much more, the Father in heaven!

CHAPTER XVIII

"A FATHER IN ISRAEL"

In his old age, Ballou was like a father to the Universalist denomination. He was universally respected and loved by his brethren as the patriarch of the movement; indeed, they found it natural to call him "Father" Ballou. Outside of the movement, he was known by a somewhat less respectful title. As he walked the streets of Boston rapt in thought, he was pointed out—by those who knew him only by sight—as "Old Ballou." [1]

Some humorous stories are told of strangers who took it upon themselves to question his religion in public. One day he boarded an omnibus to travel from one end of town to the other. As he sat down, an elderly woman addressed him from the next seat:

"Mr. Ballou, do you not constantly preach to your congregation, 'O ye generation of vipers! how can ye escape the damnation of hell?'"

The old woman was obviously picking a quarrel, but Ballou replied in his most polite manner:

"No, madam; that class do not attend my church!" [2]

But, on the whole, there was less opposition to Universalism when Ballou was in his seventies than when he was a young man just beginning to preach. Numbers often bring respectability, and the Universalists were now numerous. In Boston alone, there were four societies; and in August 1838 a cornerstone-laying ceremony was held for the meetinghouse of the Fifth Universalist Society, which since January 1836 had been gathering at Boylston Hall.[3] Nor was the denomination localized in New England. By 1840 the faith was prospering in all the states and territories of the young nation. There were almost seven hundred societies, with 311 preachers—and these figures were almost to double in the remaining dozen years of Ballou's life. At his death there would be more than 800,000 adherents to the faith.[4] How things had changed since his young manhood, when a handful of preachers served the few faithful!

His home, on Myrtle Street in the west end of town, was a

happy one.[5] All of the children had married by 1839, and there were many grandchildren to brighten his last years. Two of his sons were preaching the gospel of universal salvation—Hosea Faxon in Vermont and Massena in not-very distant Stoughton—while the youngest, Maturin, was beginning a distinguished career as a journalist.[6] All six girls had married capable young men, two of them preachers. Only one cloud darkened the family sky: poor Mandana was going through many trials with the early death of several of her children.[7]

Cassandana and her husband, Joseph Wing, and their children had come to live with Hosea and Ruth. Cassandana took on the responsibility of managing the household, thus fulfilling Ballou's desire to free his wife of care in their old age.[8] It was a large and happy household which, with bowed heads, heard the old patriarch in "a most impressive manner" ask the blessing of the throne of grace before the Sunday meal.[9]

Ballou had financial security throughout his years in Boston. Gone were the days of relentless struggle. The salary paid by his church was adequate, and his sermons and other publications sold so well that a profit accrued to both him and his publisher. These earnings, plus wise investment, provided a comfortable existence.[10] But he had not lost his early habit of frugality. He lived a simple life, believing that extravagance was contrary to the preaching of the gospel.

It always appeared to me inconsistent, with the profession of a minister of the gospel, to live expensively; that is, far beyond what is required for the necessities and comforts of life. As the minister is supported by the people of his charge, the propriety of his living beyond the income of his parishioners in general, seems questionable. Moreover, it has best suited my natural taste to avoid extravagances and superfluities.[11]

He was as meticulous in these matters as he was in his thinking. He would not be underpaid, nor—as his contemporaries testified—would he accept more than was due him. This exactness, said his son Maturin, gave some the impression that he was tight-fisted, but he was generous where it counted.[12] In several instances he sent money to help churches in financial need; in at least one such case, the pastor was far from friendly to Ballou.[13] But he always insisted on knowing that his gifts to various causes would be spent wisely.[14]

Ballou saw the erratic career of his old friend Abner Kneeland come to an end in 1838. Although Kneeland had supposedly been convinced of the authenticity of divine revelation after his correspondence with Ballou[15] in 1814, his conviction was built on a foundation of sand. Because of newly risen doubts on the subject of Christianity, he had asked to be suspended from membership in the Southern Association in 1829, possibly on Ballou's advice.[16] In September of that year, the long struggle with his soul was resolved; and he announced to the world, via the press, that he had embraced atheism.[17] In a caustic letter to Thomas Whittemore, Ballou called attention to Kneeland's announcement:

. . . He informs the public that he does not believe in the existence of God, nor in man's conscious existence in a future state. After having stated his unbelief in these two propositions, he has thought it necessary to inform the public that he does not believe in the crucifixion and resurrection of Jesus.[18]

Kneeland gathered a congregation of freethinkers at the Federal Street Theatre and, at the same time, started a paper, the *Investigator*.[19] His performances at the theatre must have been something to behold. An eyewitness has left this brief account:

Mr. Kneeland would read portions of the Old Testament, not designed for public reading in a non-Jewish assembly; he would dramatically cast the Bible across the hall as a book not fit to be kept in decent company.[20]

Kneeland's writings in the *Investigator* soon got him into trouble with the authorities. Early in 1834 he was indicted by the grand jury of Suffolk County on charges of blasphemy and obscenity.[21] In June 1838, after prolonged legal action, he was finally convicted of blasphemy and was sentenced to sixty days' imprisonment.[22]

Ballou pitied his old friend but had little sympathy for his infidelity. Others raised a cry that Kneeland was being persecuted, but Ballou disagreed:

. . . Whoever will read with candor the arguments in the case in behalf of the government will come to the conclusion that the learned attorney, so far from manifesting the spirit of persecution for honest sentiments, has ably vindicated the rights of conscience, the rational liberty of the press, and has in no instance overleaped the bounds of his duty.[23]

He would not champion Kneeland's right to "blasphemy" (though Universalism itself had once been so named by its enemies), but he often walked to the jail to visit Kneeland, counsel him and attempt to comfort him in his misfortune.[24]

After his release from jail, Kneeland stayed in Boston for a while. He still preached to his congregation of freethinkers—but now in smaller quarters, for his misfortune had diminished their numbers. Soon he decided to give up the struggle and move to Iowa to start his life anew. His parting advice to his congregation was to stay together as long as possible and then to join the Unitarians!

The Unitarians are nothing more than a fashionable kind of deists, believing, perhaps, more in "the God of the statute," than in any other God distinct from nature; but they have little to say in their preaching about heaven or hell, God or devil, in a way by which anybody can tell what they mean, while, as I am told, they deliver many good moral lectures.[25]

No matter how popular and vigorous a preacher Ballou had been and still was, no matter how he was honored and revered, the time came when a group of his parishioners began to wish for an associate pastor who would appeal to the younger generation. Agitation for this change began in 1841—Ballou was then seventy—and continued for about four years.[26] But no agreement could be reached on a man to succeed "Father" Ballou in the pulpit. From May 1842 to the following January, T. C. Adam candidated,[27] but he was obviously not capable of replacing the old lion. The society next tried the young, sensitive H. B. Soule, who candidated for a full year beginning in May 1844.[28] His letters of this period suggest that he had not acquired full self-confidence, and he was surprised when he was first asked to be "a sort of colleague" with Ballou.[29] He was genuinely impressed with his senior, as is clear from this letter written in 1844:

You will want to hear a word of our Father in Israel. He continues in good health for a man seventy-three years old; he preaches yet as strong as most men at forty. Nothing but death will ever bring rest to his labors:—most men at his age would sit down, and in dreamy idleness or mere social converse, wait their call. Not so with him—his God-given mission will not be finished till his lips are sealed forever,—he will preach as long as he can stand.[30]

But Soule proved incapable of filling the patriarch's shoes.

In the fall of 1845, the agitation came to a head. A few gentlemen who owned a substantial number of pews called on the proprietors to sell the meetinghouse and dissolve the society. Some other members claimed that their primary motivation was the monetary profit they expected from such a transaction. After an acrimonious debate, the proposal was rejected by a vote of two to one, with an impressive one hundred votes cast.[31]

The difficulties over calling an associate finally resulted in a schism in the church. A group of dissatisfied members withdrew, took their children out of the Sunday school and began holding services on Chardon Street.[32] This incident was probably responsible for Ballou's next—and generous—action. Knowing that the church could not afford to pay his salary and still call a top-notch preacher, he offered to give up all financial compensation and retain only the title of senior pastor. On September 28, 1845,[33] the society voted to accept his offer and extended a call to the rising star among the younger generation of Universalist preachers, Edwin H. Chapin of the Charlestown church.[34] His salary was set at $2,000.[35] Ballou preached the sermon at Chapin's installation service on January 28, 1846.[36]

The conservative School Street Church, used to sermons on theological subjects, was not prepared for the sermonizing of a "new-born reformer." Chapin pounded home the evils of slavery, intemperance and war.[37] And he preached a different brand of Universalism: he was outspoken in his disagreement with Ballou's position on future punishment.[38] Nor was he a Bible preacher.[39] He was one of the younger generation that Ballou, in these years, constantly criticized for straying from the Bible and preaching sermons of nondoctrinal subjects.

It is much to Ballou's credit that he remained fond of the young man, though Chapin's preaching was now overshadowing his own great accomplishments and their ideas were at odds on many points. On just one subject was he was willing to criticize the meteoric young pulpiteer—the subject of money. The frugal "Father" Ballou was shocked at Chapin's extravagance, and he was frank in saying so.[40]

It was the problem of money which finally caused Chapin to resign from the School Street Church in February 1848.[41] As a result of his extravagance, he had piled up a sizable number of debts. The Fourth Universalist Society in New York City managed to attract Chapin to their pulpit by offering a higher salary and agreeing "to assume certain debts which he had incurred with characteristic prodigal generosity and openhandedness." [42] In their letter to Chapin, the committee of the New York church offered him $3,000 a year—$1,000 more than his salary at School Street. They also mentioned "a small amount of ready money" ($1,100) that he might have need of if he were to decide to move, and pointed out that he could have this money as soon as he made his decision. [43]

Chapin was succeeded by the young pastor of the church at Lowell, Alonzo Ames Miner, who assumed his new duties on May 1, 1848. [44] He was installed at the end of May, with both Ballou and Chapin taking part in the service. [45] This young man was more to Ballou's liking: he was an "exact logician" and thoroughly versed in the Scriptures. [46] But he also had a touch of the reformer in him. He accepted the call to School Street only after it was fully understood that he would champion the cause of temperance in rum-making Boston. [47]

Ballou and Miner had a father-son type of relationship. When Ballou was not off preaching on the Sabbath, he would sit in the pulpit with the young man. He often encouraged him with such comments as "Brother Miner, the devil will never thank you for that sermon." [48] Miner, like Chapin, hammered away at the evil of slavery; and despite the difference of approach, Ballou approved his efforts, often vocally. As Miner pursued the antislavery cause more and more sharply, Ballou remarked, "You know, Brother Miner, that Demosthenes kept up warning the Athenians to beware of Philip, and when asked why he did so since the Athenians continued listless, said: 'I mean that Athenian ears shall get familiar with warnings against Philip.'" [49]

Chapin's great pulpit oratory had brought some of the dissenters back to the School Street Church, but it was the capable Miner who accomplished the delicate task of healing the wounds. [50]

It is to be expected that an old man will cling to the past and the old ways of doing things. During the last dozen years or so of

Ballou's life, he often objected to what he considered bad trends in his beloved denomination. He had finally yielded on the subject of Sunday schools, after having opposed them for years on the ground that young minds are warped by the teaching given in such institutions. The School Street Church started its Sunday school in 1835,[51] and occasionally the venerable pastor himself was "present and addressed the School." [52] To further "right views of Christianity," [53] he wrote a new catechism, designed especially for use in Sunday schools, which was published in 1841.

To the new trend in Universalist preaching he was never reconciled. He had the good sense to realize that his complaints might be those of a man grown old, but he still did not approve. The younger men were replacing sermons on straight biblical truth with eloquent, even poetical, sermons on moral themes. Ballou protested: "For one, I am willing to confess that I have no relish for golden goblets which contain no wine, nor for costly dishes which contain no food." [54] He said in 1839 that he had not time in his remaining years to bring his preaching up to the polished standards of the theological schools, so he would just attempt to live up to the standard set by Jesus.[55]

He wrote articles and letters on this subject until shortly before his death. In October 1850, for example, he attended a prayer meeting and heard the orthodox minister frighten the young people with terrible descriptions of God's wrath in hell. This reinforced his belief that Universalists needed to preach doctrine more forcefully than ever, and he wrote a letter to Whittemore (as editor of the *Trumpet*) to express his concern.[56] The time has not gone by, as many of his colleagues think, for doctrinal preaching. Universalists must continue to expose error in the doctrines "of the Roman, the Episcopal, the Presbyterian, the Congregationalist, the Baptist, the Methodist and other sects," for these errors persist.

> . . . I feel it a duty to add, that within six months I have travelled in five of our States, and preached in as many as fifteen towns to Universalist Societies; and it has been a very general complaint, made known to me, that the Societies were favored with but a very little doctrinal preaching, and heard scarcely any sermons designed to make people understand the Scriptures, or the great truths they teach. But sermons suitable for moral and scientific lectures were nearly all the food the pastors gave their flocks.[57]

All his life, Ballou had opposed theological schools, and he kept this animosity to the very end. He was not opposed to education in general; indeed, he had served as a trustee of the Nichols Academy, founded by Universalists.[58] He believed in literary attainments—but not in theological schools, which he said were "employed in teaching youth how to evade the plain testimony of Jesus, and how to keep the people from receiving it." [59] This prejudice, of course, went back to his boyhood: his father, like other early Baptists, had had no theological education, and Ballou himself was a self-trained preacher.

In 1840, several men in the denomination began a concerted drive to found a theological school for the training of their ministers. The Massachusetts Convention in that year voted to establish a seminary for "the preparation of young men for the gospel ministry." [60] Despite Ballou's known opposition to theological schools, he was appointed to the committee—possibly because he was too influential to be ignored and possibly in hopes of converting him to the proposal. After several meetings, the committee accepted an offer of ten acres of land on Walnut Hill in Medford, donated by Charles Tufts, and named the proposed school the Walnut Hill Evangelical Seminary.[61]

Ballou was one of the trustees chosen to raise the money and establish the school,[62] but he seems not to have been converted. On the contrary, he carried on a lengthy debate in the columns of the *Trumpet* with a proponent of the plan.[63] He pointed out that Universalism had originally thrived under such unlettered men as Rich, the Elder Streeters, Barnes, Laithe and Young, as well as among men of higher education in later years. "The question here comes up, what evidence have we that the course which has thus succeeded, and the means which divine wisdom has used hitherto and blessed, are not suitable to be continued?" [64] Theological schools will inculcate prejudice and train unfit men who, under the present system, never seek to preach. He challenges the committee to show that theological schools have extended "unadulterated Christianity." The present system of having young men read divinity under a settled minister is better than a school where all the graduates will be stamped with the mentality of its head.[65]

Despite Ballou's opposition, the friends of the Walnut Hill

Seminary proceeded with their plans.[66] Their failure to raise the necessary funds was due not so much to Ballou as to the lack of foresight on the part of Universalists generally.[67]

In the late 1840s, transcendentalism and the new rationalistic views of the Bible began to infiltrate the Universalist denomination. This "German philosophy," as it was called at the time, was zealously propagated among the Unitarians by such men as the fiery transcendentalist Theodore Parker. It was bound to be felt in Universalist circles. The older men of the denomination resisted the new influence, believing that there could be no confidence in Christianity if the scriptural accounts of the miracles were to be questioned. But a small group of preachers began to express their doubts publicly.

The first overt act occurred in 1846, when a young preacher aired this latest form of infidelity at an installation.[68] Hosea Ballou, 2d, who was present for the occasion was extremely upset by the new views. At the conclusion of the sermon, he rose to his feet and publicly dissociated himself from the young man's statements. Universalists, he said, should not be held accountable for them.[69] The new views were also opposed by Alonzo Miner when the Massachusetts Convention met at Hingham that year. In a sermon entitled "Seal of Christ's Messiahship," he reasserted his own faith in the miracles.

The crisis came to a head at the Boston Association meeting at Lynn in November 1847. One of the brethren raised the issue in three questions:

[1] What constitutes a Christian minister in full fellowship with the Boston Association? [2] How far does this tie bind one brother to exchange pulpit services with another? [3] What should be believed by one who calls himself a Christian? [70]

After some discussion, a committee, including both Hosea Ballous, was appointed to study the matter. The elder Ballou was elected chairman. From the committee came the following resolution, in the chairman's handwriting:

Resolved, That this Association express its solemn conviction, that in order for one to be regarded as a Christian minister with respect to faith, he must believe in the Bible account of the life, teachings, miracles, death, and resurrection of the Lord Jesus Christ.[71]

The debate which followed was so heated and prolonged that it became necessary to recess the meeting and set an extraordinary session of the Association for a later date. This session was held on December 1, 1847, at Cambridgeport.[72] It was marked by a lengthy debate, in which many members charged that the proposed resolution would, in effect, impose a creed on the Boston Association.[73] Finally, Ballou rose from his seat, amid much applause, and gave his views in support of the resolution.[74] It was not a creed, as the opponents of the measure had claimed; it was simply a definition of a *Christian* minister:

. . . The report supposes that no man can justly be regarded as a Christian minister, who does not believe the Bible account of the life, teachings, miracles, death and resurrection of the Lord Jesus. I give my vote for the report because I am satisfied that the condition of our ministry, and, that of our Societies, and, in a word of the Christian cause, demands such an expression.[75]

Ballou was obviously afraid that the new rationalistic spirit would weaken the Universalist church. He was defending both his church and the book he loved so well. He had overcome his doubts many, many years before and now had complete confidence that the Bible contained the true account of Jesus' life and ministry.

The resolution was overwhelmingly accepted,[76] and the Association's action was commended by the Massachusetts Convention the following June.[77] The rationalists thereafter lost their influence in the denomination; some left the church, and others appeared to come around to the more conservative position. Thomas Whittemore observed a few years later: "Quiet was restored, and the Bible lives in the hearts of our people." [78]

In the summer of 1847, the people of the School Street Church commissioned the artist H. C. Pratt to paint a portrait of Ballou to be hung in Murray Hall, the vestry of the meetinghouse.[79] The result was a life-size portrait to the waist, picturing Ballou in the pulpit, his right hand fingering the pages of the Bible, his left arm extended. This portrait, in which Ballou appears suspiciously young for a man of seventy-six, is the most attractive and best known of the several portraits in existence.

Although Ballou contributed many reviews, articles and letters to various Universalist publications, he had not undertaken any extended publication since his work on future retribution in 1834. He probably would not have undertaken another book, had not the publisher J. M. Usher persuaded him to write "A General Epistle to Universalists," a sort of farewell address. With this in hand, he talked Ballou into adding several other pieces,[80] all of which, along with bits of earlier writings and many poems, were published as *A Voice to Universalists* in September 1849. These articles serve as an index of the subjects which kept him preoccupied in his late years.

Ballou complains that the young Universalist ministers are more concerned with "what is called science" than with biblical preaching:[81]

> Under pretence [*sic*] of progress, it seems that some have come to the conclusion, that they must leave the Scriptures, Christ and his apostles, all which only served for their times, and go on to perfection, adopting as a motto, *Upward and Onward!* [82]

His advice to young men who plan to enter the ministry reflects the struggle over the influx of German rationalism.[83] He praises the "Sabbath schools," their superintendents and teachers, and compares these new advantages to the state of things fifty years earlier. Parents should take advantage of this progress so "that all Zion's children shall be taught of the Lord." [84]

The poetry which composes the bulk of the book is an embarrassing collection of mediocrity. In the brief preface to this section, Ballou admits that he "makes no pretensions of being a poet, having never studied the art for a single hour; and it was with great reluctance that he consented that this volume should be presented to the public." [85] The subject of Ballou's verse was to be a sore point with thinking Universalists for years to come. The Reverend E. G. Brooks later attested:

> The grossest unkindness ever done to him, or to us in him, and that which many of us have never yet been able to forgive, was done when one of our publishers gathered up these rhymes and published them as part of his "Voice to Universalists." He never had such terrible occasion to say, "Save me from my friends." [86]

On November 10, 1850, Ballou conducted the morning service at the School Street Church. At the close of the service, he announced that he would preach again that afternoon—and that it would be a valedictory sermon. Feeling that his life might end soon without warning, he desired to preach as if it were the last

sermon he would ever deliver to his beloved congregation.[87] It
can be imagined that the congregation that afternoon was even
more attentive than usual to the words of "Father" Ballou.

In his *Valedictory Discourse*, Ballou reviews and once again
refutes the long catalogue of errors in the orthodox Christian
church, the refutation of which had consumed much of his life.
But the most interesting part of the valedictory is that which deals
with the state of Universalism at that time.

At the time, there were Universalists who saw a swing in the
denomination away from Ballou's theory of no future judgment and
toward restorationism. In a biographical sketch of Ballou in 1846,
Otis Skinner had noted that "a very large proportion of our ministers" did not agree with Ballou on the subject of future punishment.[88] And Hosea, 2d, wrote in 1848 that he thought he could
discern the beginning of a new period in Universalist history. He
felt that current opinion was "strongly in favor of a moral connection of the present life with the future." [89]

In the light of this trend, the disgruntlement expressed in
Ballou's valedictory can be understood. He blames the trend toward
restorationism on those Universalists who are attempting to in-
gratiate themselves with the Unitarians by adopting opinions peculiar to that denomination—that is,

the opinion that men carry into the next world the imperfections of
this; so that their moral condition, hereafter, will depend on the characters they form while here in the flesh; but that they may and will
improve, and progress in virtue and holiness, in the spirit world.[90]

Once again he marshals his favorite texts to show that such reasoning is contrary to the words of that great universalist, St. Paul. He
cites I Corinthians 15:42-44 and 15:22:

It is sown in corruption; it is raised in incorruption: it is sown
in dishonour; it is raised in glory: it is sown in weakness; it is raised in
power: it is sown a natural body; it is raised a spiritual body.

As in Adam all die, even so in Christ shall all be made alive.

Those who indulge in speculation respecting the future state rather
than trust the Scriptures are saying, in effect, that divine revelation
is "not only incomplete, but also inaccurate." [91]

This was the last sermon Ballou put on paper.[92] But he was
to live to say much more.

CHAPTER XIX

THE LAST DAYS

It is perhaps symbolic that, in the last year of Ballou's life, the old School Street Church underwent a complete remodeling. It was modernized, and the building was raised and moved back from the street to provide more adequate space in the basement and a better, more attractive frontage. The work began in April 1851.[1]

Although Ballou approved of the change, it must have pained him to see the old, plain building altered. Here he had declared war on the orthodoxy of Boston almost thirty-five years before, and here he had steadfastly proclaimed the love of God for His children and their immediate salvation and transformation at the dissolution of the body. But times had changed; and, like the old-fashioned sermon, the old School Street Church was no longer considered beautiful. The work of remodeling continued through the summer and fall, and the building was ready for occupancy by early December. The venerable senior pastor offered the prayer at the service of rededication.[2]

In his later years, Ballou often returned to his birthplace at Richmond, New Hampshire.[3] One of the most delightful of these visits occurred in October 1851, just eight months before his death, when he spent eleven days[4] there with his friends, new and old. He was met at the depot at Fitzwilliam by a good friend; from there they drove down the narrow road which winds through the wooded hills and, in Richmond, passes through the farm on which he had been born.[5]

During his stay, he spent much time with Joshua Britton, Jr., the Universalist minister of Winchester and Richmond. Together they visited acquaintances, and on Sunday Ballou entered the pulpit and preached to a congregation which had come in his honor from all the surrounding towns—Swanzey, Fitzwilliam, Troy, Warwick, Royalston, Orange and Winchester. He visited the old hillside burial ground which held the dust of his beloved parents. And, of course, he exulted in the clear, beautiful vista of Ballou's Dell. The old homestead was gone, and a new house, inhabited by strangers, had been built near the spot where the log cabin once stood—the cabin in which he had been born.

As the two men stood in the Dell looking up at the hills, which were still the same, Britton suggested that Ballou recite the poem he had written telling of his love for this scene. Ballou acquiesced and, with a sense of exhilaration, spoke the words of "My Native Richmond":

> There are no hills in Hampshire New,
>   Nor valleys half so fair,
> As those outspread before our view,
>   In merry Richmond, where
>
> I first my mortal race began,
>   And spent my youthful days;
> Where first I saw the golden sun,
>   And felt his 'livening rays. . . .[6]

When his friends asked Ballou if he planned to visit soon again, he said he couldn't be sure. After almost two weeks of preaching and visiting, he headed home by way of Lancaster, Massachusetts, where he had left Ruth visiting their daughter Mandana.[7]

Although he was eighty, Ballou did a remarkable amount of preaching. Since he rarely preached at School Street, he was off to the inland towns practically every weekend.[8] Itinerating was a little easier than it had been in his early years—there were now railroads to many points—but it still left much to be desired in the way of comfort. On New Year's Day, 1852, he was in New York preaching. The growth of Universalism in that area delighted him: there were five congregations in New York City, one in Brooklyn and one in Williamsburg.[9]

April 30, Ballou's birthday, saw him in good health. An eighty-first birthday is an important occasion, and he felt that it warranted a poem. "My Labors Last Year" was better than most of his other efforts in verse. It is easy to imagine him penning the lines and then reading them to Ruth for her approval. Perhaps they would cheer her up, for she had not been well lately and spent much of her time in bed.

> How swiftly on the wheel of time
>   Twelve months have past away!
> And, by a Providence divine,
>   Brought this my natal day!

And O, how kind to me has been
    My heavenly Father's care,
Thus to sustain, and me to bring
    To this, to me, new year!

In many vineyards of our Lord
    My labors have been spent,
To plant the doctrine of his word,
    By skill which He has lent.

And large has been the sweet reward
    My soul has garner'd up,
While drinking deeply of the word,
    From an o'erflowing cup.

Who would not live a thousand years
    To feed the lambs of Him,
Who died to banish all our fears,
    And save the world from sin?

But God will many laborers send,
    When I am called away;
His cause and doctrine to defend:
    For their success I pray.[10]

"Father" Ballou was honored as a celebrity at the Reform Festival that May. The General Reform Association, a confederation of specialized reform groups, had been created in 1849 to meet the need to apply the ethics of Universalism to the social problems of the day.[11] Ballou was a little too old and conservative to take the stump for such causes as antislavery and temperance, but he was appreciated as a reformer in his own right. He had told the Association meeting in 1850:

Why, this work of *reform* has gone on so effectually that even the old partial god himself, in whom the theologians used to believe, has got *reformed.* He is so changed that the old clergy, if they were to hear him described now, would not know him.[12]

Now, in 1852, he was called upon to give his yearly message and blessing to the brethren. He said he was not sure why such compliments were paid to an old man. He knew he was old, and he intended to avail himself of the privilege of age. What was that privilege? To be a child: "Once a man and twice a child." He remembered that, when he was a child, he had been fond of praise and loved to be patted and called a good boy. Now, as an old man, he found himself a child again. He was the same boy: he loved to be praised now.[13]

Ballou then spoke a few words on the progress of Universalism in his lifetime:

> I have lived to see and to realize, and to be confident, that there is not an opposer of Universalism in the world who is not at heart a Universalist. And how long do you suppose they can keep out of their heads [that] which is in their hearts? [14]

None present realized that this was the last time Ballou would hear the praise of his Universalist brothers. On Sunday, May 30, he spent the day at Woonsocket, Rhode Island,[15] where he preached at both the morning and the afternoon services. The afternoon service was based on Titus 2:11-12, an ideal text for the last sermon by this greatest preacher of modern Universalism:

> For the grace of God that bringeth salvation hath appeared to all men, teaching us that, denying ungodliness and worldly lusts, we should live soberly, righteously, and godly, in this present world.

The next day Ballou returned to Boston. Tuesday night his sleep was disturbed, and he coughed frequently; but he rose early on Wednesday morning, June 2, for this was an important day. He was to travel to Plymouth for the sessions of the Massachusetts Convention. Ruth had been in bed for several weeks.[16] When it was time to go, he entered her room, gave her a tender kiss and then made ready to depart.

As he was passing through the parlor, he suddenly grew faint and fell on the sofa. His daughter Cassandana came to his aid. He was suffering from chills, which continued all day; all night he lay in a delirium. The next day he was much better, and his mind was as bright as usual; but as the day wore on, fever set in. He remained in this condition Friday, Saturday and Sunday. He was failing fast.

On Monday morning, his old friend and disciple Thomas Whittemore came to see him. Ballou seemed to recognize him and tried to speak, but in vain.[17] Hosea, 2d, and Miner also came, anxious to see their master before the end.[18] Ballou's old friend Dr. A. R. Thompson of Charlestown was at his side when he spoke his last words. The doctor addressed him, and the old man replied, "I do not think I *understood* what the doctor said." [19] The end had come. With most of the family, including Hosea, 2d, at his side, Ballou met his death and glory at 10:15 on the morning of June 7, 1852.

The School Street Church, decked in black crepe, was filled long before the time set for the funeral.[20] At the Ballou home, prayers were said in the hearing of Ruth Ballou, who was still not able to leave her bed. Then the body was taken across Beacon Hill to School Street. It was brought into the church by the pallbearers, all close friends: his Universalist colleagues Sylvanus Cobb, Lucius R. Paige, Sebastian Streeter, Josiah Gilman and Thomas Whittemore; his Baptist friend, the Reverend Doctor Daniel Sharp; the Reverend Doctor Samuel Barrett of the Twelfth Congregational Church (Unitarian) on Chambers Street; and Edward Turner, now reconciled.[21]

The funeral tribute was spoken by Ballou's associate, Alonzo Ames Miner: "Our Father has fallen! Loved, venerated, full of years, as he was, he has passed from the places of his love to the home of his hope." [22]

The funeral procession passed up School Street, down Tremont and along Boylston Street to the graveyard at the foot of Boston Common. The procession, which included nearly one hundred Universalist clergymen, extended from the head of School Street to the corner of Boylston Street—a distance of half a mile. The body was laid in a temporary resting place, until arrangements could be made for an appropriate tomb.[23]

In the days that followed, many tributes were offered to Ballou, both written and spoken. Probably none was as truthful as that of the great soul Theodore Parker. He told his Twenty-Eighth Congregational Society at the Melodeon:

There died in this city recently, a man, who a little more than half a century ago, arose in our midst, a man not remarkable for extensive culture or acquirements, but certainly remarkable for great energy, who received the sentiment that God is the Father and Friend of the whole race of man, that it was the will of our Heavenly Father that "not one of his little ones would perish." I refer to Rev. Hosea Ballou. He went through the land proclaiming this great truth, and he has wrought a revolution in the thoughts and minds of men more mighty than any which has been accomplished during the same time by all the politicians in the nation. At the commencement of his labors there probably were not five thousand persons who would give heed to his teachings; now there are probably five millions! an illustration of the great results which may be attained without the use of extraordinary means, by the persevering energy of a single mind.[24] ‑

Ballou provided well for his wife in his will.[25] Ruth was to receive $300-a-year annuity from a fund set up for that purpose; the rest of his estate was to be divided equally among their nine children. But Ruth was not to enjoy this generous provision. Nine months after Hosea passed on, she followed in his steps.[26]

The remains of Hosea and Ruth Ballou were laid side by side in the beautiful Mount Auburn Cemetery in Cambridge. The soaring monument, with the figure of Hosea in preaching posture, was the tribute of grateful Universalists to their "Father" Ballou.[27]

CHAPTER XX

EPILOGUE

Several years after Ballou's death, the Universalist minister Dr. Theodore Clapp of New Orleans was present at a gathering of Unitarian ministers in Boston. The conversation eventually turned to the great changes that had taken place in American theology and the contributions of several great theologians. The reverend gentlemen ventured their opinions as to who, among the New England theologians, had made the greatest contribution. Most of them suggested William Ellery Channing, but more orthodox names were also mentioned—Edwards, Emmons and Hopkins. At this point, Dr. Clapp, who had not entered the discussion, spoke up.

"Gentlemen, you have not yet named the man!"

"What," said the company in amazement, "not named him!"

"No, gentlemen, you have not yet named him."

"Why, who can it be? We have named every preacher of eminence in New England."

"And yet, gentlemen, you have not named *the* man."

"Well, who do you say he is?"

"Hosea Ballou," said Dr. Clapp impressively, " has effected more and greater changes in the theological opinions of the people of New England than any man dead or living."

There was a long, cold silence. Then the conversation started up again—along different lines.[1]

Ballou's contribution to liberal religion has been overshadowed by that of other divines with more polished literary accomplishments. The rough—in places, crude—writing in which Ballou expressed much of his thought has not found its way into the libraries of the cultured. His language was that of the lower social classes of New England. It could not be expected to compete with the polished, rich expression of a man such as the great Channing. The contrast is made vivid when Ballou takes occasion to quote Channing in his own works.[2]

As his style failed to please the literary Brahmins of New England, so two essential tenets of his thought were soon rejected even by the liberal churches, which thus tended to ignore all his work. During the latter years of his life, restorationism was already gaining a clear ascendancy over his theory of no future punishment. By 1871, Adin Ballou could write with satisfaction that nine-tenths of the Universalist denomination had rejected ultra-universalism and had embraced the theory of a limited future punishment.[3] In 1878 the Universalist ministers of Boston and the surrounding area accepted a platform which specifically denounced the "death and glory" theory which, they said, was "repudiated by all." [4] And by 1917, John Coleman Adams could assert:

> . . . Today the entire Universalist church is frankly of the con-
> viction that not only do we "get our punishment as we go along"—to
> revive a theological colloquialism of the former days—but that it may go
> a long way with us into the future.[5]

The second element in Ballou's thought which was unpalatable to the liberal churches of succeeding generations was his determined determinism. He insisted that if God is infinite, all-gracious, all-loving and all-wise, He must have complete control of His creation—and that it was shoddy thinking to believe otherwise. Universalists tended to shy away from this theory of "necessity" and to adopt the Arminianism of the Unitarians, which gave all men the choice of accepting or rejecting God's proffered grace. They ignored the implication, which Ballou was quick to expose, that Arminianism empowers an individual to resist through all eternity the love of God—in short, to be more powerful than God.

The essentials of Ballou's thought resulted from a compromise between Deism and the Bible. The deistic influence came close to destroying his Christian faith, but he was able to overcome the pangs of doubt and to construct a theology which combined the finest of Enlightenment thought with a biblical view of God and man. The result was a supernatural rationalism. He believed firmly in the biblical account of the life, miracles and resurrection of Christ; he had faith that the Bible contains a revelation of the Deity, and so is at the center of the Christian faith. But he believed also that God has given to man a faculty that distinguishes him from the beasts—the faculty of reason. With reason, man is capable of studying God's Word and finding there both the true purpose of creation and what God expects of him.

Ballou assumed that all parts of the Scriptures could be understood in the light of the central truth of God's love for His children. This led to many strained interpretations of biblical texts, especially in his early years of preaching, when he freely indulged in allegorization and cabalistic interpretations of irreconcilable texts. That he made many serious errors is to be expected; but he was not alone in this.

In his later years, Ballou tended to outgrow this approach and to interpret the Scriptures in a more natural manner. Abandoning the allegorization of the New Testament passages which speak of a second coming of Christ, he interpreted these in the context of the apocalyptic sayings in the gospels, which refer to the destruction of Jerusalem in 70 A.D. Mistaken though he may have been in this pinpointing of time, he at least recognized that these passages do not refer to hell-fire and damnation in a future state of existence. He was thus not far from the present-day understanding of the eschatological element in the preaching of Jesus.

In his interpretation of the Old Testament, he was definitely ahead of his time. Almost alone among biblical scholars, he recognized the belief of the ancient Israelites that man receives just recompense for his actions in this life. They had no conception of a future state of rewards and punishment.

Ballou's greatest contribution was that he translated these issues into language that the people could understand. He would brook no retreat into the obscure regions of metaphysics. If a doctrine was reasonable—and reason was God-given—it was true. If not, it was to be discarded. Such was the duty of the truly religious man: to accept no belief which could not be rationally defended.

Since Ballou was primarily a controversialist, much of his writing is cast in the form of debate. This material is often of no interest, except to the student of religious history. But of lasting value is the truly great *Treatise on Atonement.* Its brilliant examination of the varieties of theological thought, though expressed in the language of rural, early nineteenth-century New England, is still instructive. Its theory of atonement should be considered seriously by all who place Christ, as a revelation of God, at the center of their faith. Throughout—despite its sharp criticism and, at times, irreverent wit—it breathes the piety of a great soul who is utterly committed to the faith that religion can be reasonable.

Ballou's contributions to American religious history were great, although not generally recognized or appreciated. He had fought the battle against the trinity, the traditional theories of atonement and the Calvinistic view of man, and he had carried the day in the Universalist denomination long before the Unitarians were willing to take a stand within the Congregational establishment. He was truly a unitarian before the Unitarians. And whereas Unitarianism was more or less restricted to the higher social classes, unitarian Universalism was a movement among the people. The stern grip of Calvinism was broken by the efforts of simple, unlearned men, whose foremost champion was Ballou.

It was a humane theology that Ballou vigorously preached for so many years. Rejecting the theories of the infinity of sin and a vicarious atonement, he substituted for them theories more in line with man's highest insight of God. The Father is not angry at His children; rather, man misunderstands God and must be reconciled to Him. God does not need to be reconciled; for He is unchangeable love and will remain so through all eternity. Christ was sent to man as an expression of the Father's love, God's gift for the reconciliation of His children.

Unlike the later liberals, Ballou did not take an overly optimistic view of man in his life on earth. He looked on man as misguided and, in many cases, degraded. But he did not consider him utterly depraved. It was his great faith in man's potentiality which led him to see man as akin to the nature of God and Christ. Because man is a "heavenly extraction," he can be guided back to the path of the true life of virtue and love. It is not necessary to threaten eternal or even limited punishment in a future world. Man will respond to his higher nature if he is shown that sin cannot produce happiness, that holiness and happiness are inseparably connected.

Hosea Ballou was indisputably the foremost man and the greatest influence in the Universalist denomination of his day. As a denomination, Universalism has failed to capture the world; but as an outlook on life it has made great strides. Few Protestants today believe in endless future punishment; many believe in no future punishment whatsoever. And few now believe that God is partial toward His creatures. Ballou's thought has had a great liberalizing effect on American religion. His life and teachings, so long neglected, should at last be given the recognition they deserve.

CHRONOLOGY

1771   *April 30.* Born in Richmond, New Hampshire.

1773   *December 21.* Mother dies.

1778   Caleb Rich begins preaching Universalism in the Richmond area.

1789   *January.* Baptized (Baptist).

       Summer. Converted to Universalism.

       Fall. Excommunicated by Baptist Church.

1790   Attends Quaker school.

1791(?)   Attends Chesterfield Academy.

       Fall. Begins preaching.

       September. Meets John Murray at General Convention of Universalists at Oxford, Massachusetts.

1792   Begins itinerant preaching. Teaches school.

1794   *September.* Ordained by Elhanan Winchester at General Convention at Oxford.

       Moves to Dana, Massachusetts.

1795   Preaches first unitarian sermon.

1796   *September 15.* Marries Ruth Washburn.

1797   *October.* Begins correspondence with Joel Foster.

1798   *October.* Begins ten-week engagement at Murray's First Universalist Church in Boston.

1803   *February.* Moves to Barnard, Vermont.

       September 22. Universalist Profession of Faith adopted at General Convention at Winchester, New Hampshire.

       September 27. Reordained at Barnard, Vermont.

1804   Publishes *Notes on the Parables.*

1805   *June.* Disputes with Lemuel Haynes of West Rutland, Vermont.

       Publishes *A Treatise on Atonement.*

1808   Publishes *A Doctrinal Controversy* with Reed Page and Isaac Robinson.

1809   *October.* Moves to Portsmouth, New Hampshire.

       Enters on controversy with Joseph Buckminster and Joseph Walton.

1812   Publishes enlarged edition of *Notes on the Parables*.
        Publishes second edition of *A Treatise on Atonement*.
        Publishes reply to an attack by George Forrester.
        Preaches in favor of "Mr. Madison's War" and encounters
           controversy within his own church.
1815   *June*. Moves to Salem, Massachusetts.
        Engages in controversy with Brown Emerson and Benjamin
           Dole.
        Publishes reply to attack by John Kelly.
1816   Enters on correspondence with Abner Kneeland about divine
           revelation.
1817   Enters on debate with Edward Turner about doctrine of fu-
           ture punishment.
        December 25. Installed as minister of Second Universalist
           Society in Boston.
1818   *January*. Enters on controversy with Timothy Merritt.
        August. Begins series of *Lecture Sermons*.
1819   *July 3*. Begins *The Universalist Magazine*.
1821   With Edward Turner, publishes *The Universalists' Hymn-
           Book*.
        July. Restorationist Controversy begins.
1821-22 *December-January*. Goes on preaching tour to Philadel-
           phia; delivers *Eleven Sermons*.
1828   *June*. Goes on preaching tour to New York and Philadelphia.
1830   *July*. Becomes co-editor with Hosea Ballou, 2d, of *The Uni-
           versalist Expositor*.
1831   *August*. Restorationists secede.
1832   Publishes his *Works*.
1834   Publishes *An Examination of the Doctrine of Future Retri-
           bution*.
        November. Goes on preaching tour to Philadelphia; delivers
           Nine Sermons.
1846   *January 28*. E. H. Chapin installed as associate.
1848   *May 1*. A. A. Miner installed as associate.
1849   *November*. Publishes *A Voice to Universalists*.
1850   *November 10*. Delivers *Valedictory Discourse*.
1851-52 *December-January*. Goes on preaching tour to New
           York.
1852   *June 7*. Dies in Boston.

BIBLIOGRAPHY

Three full-length biographies of Ballou have appeared in the past. The first was the work of his youngest son, Maturin Murray Ballou.[1] This biography appeared three months after Ballou's death,[2] and was obviously rushed into print to capture the ready market. Indeed, Maturin Ballou and Thomas Whittemore, Ballou's closest disciple, had a brief misunderstanding on the subject. Whittemore was preparing his biography when the son proposed that he give way to the family and defer publication.[3]

Maturin Ballou's book is a filial eulogy. Much of it is devoted to long extracts from tributes by well-known Universalists. It was hastily prepared and suffers from a lack of orderly arrangement. But despite its faults, it is valuable for the historian and biographer. Many of the stories and the anecdotes which fill its pages must have come directly from Hosea Ballou himself. This material, which otherwise might have been lost, is invaluable not only as information but also for the insight it affords into Ballou's character.

One other feature of this biography is helpful. Hosea Ballou never kept a journal[4] and was reluctant to write an autobiography, but Maturin had prevailed upon him to record some reminiscences,[5] which are scattered throughout the book. These give Ballou's own interpretation of some of the events of his life.

Thomas Whittemore's biography of Ballou appeared in 1854-55. It is a long, rambling account of everything—no matter how trivial—that Whittemore could collect concerning his master.[6] Much of it, Whittemore himself claimed, was prepared before Ballou's death.[7] Whittemore uses largely the annalistic method; to trace the development of specific incidents, it is necessary to skip from section to section in his work.

Whittemore's four volumes suffer from his attempt to record everything Ballou ever did. He obviously kept a file of newspaper clippings and articles, and used all of them. He tells of every convention Ballou attended in his more than fifty years of preaching. He also seems to have had a file of old ordination and installation programs, for he dutifully lists every one in which Ballou took part, along with the names of the other participants. While these features give the historian much raw material, they are far from interesting to the general reader.

Both these biographies, having been written immediately after Ballou's death, are naturally lacking in perspective. The authors were too close to the events to form any clear judgment; they were too personally involved to be able to see Ballou's weaknesses and failings. Most serious of all, their work nourished the myth that Ballou was purely an original thinker. They believed that he had arrived at his theory of atonement, his unitarian conception of God, his Arian conception of Christ and many aspects of his thought simply through an independent study of the Bible.

Thirty-seven years after Ballou's death, a third full-length biography appeared. This was the work of the Universalist divine Oscar Safford.[8] He had not known Ballou; and, writing almost two generations later, he should have had more perspective on his subject. But his book is little more than a denominational eulogy of a past leader. He fails to realize Ballou's indebtedness to other thinkers, and he propagates the myth that Ballou was completely original. Moreover, writing at a time when Ballou's theory of no future punishment had come into discredit in his denomination, Safford attempts to minimize Ballou's devotion to this belief. As a result, he seriously distorts Ballou's opinions.

Safford's treatment, on the whole, is light; he makes no serious attempt at an exposition of Ballou's thought. He writes more in the style of a Victorian novelist than of a serious biographer; but, because of the inadequacies of his two predecessors, his work has been influential.

Since Safford's day there has appeared a scattering of periodical articles and addresses on Ballou's life and work. These are primarily indebted to the three biographies for their material. The most notable exceptions are two articles of E. G. Brooks[9] and A. St. John Chambré.[10] Brooks, who appears to have known Ballou intimately, presents a refreshingly frank portrayal of him —his weaknesses as well as his virtues. Chambré presents a series of letters between Ballou and Edward Turner, a documentary report which has added much to our knowledge of these men and the relations between them during the Restorationist Controversy.

Two lectures published in 1903 also deserve mention. They were both written by the Universalist minister John Coleman Adams. "Hosea Ballou and the Larger Hope"[11] and *Hosea Ballou and the Gospel Renaissance of the Nineteenth Century* point out Ballou's contributions to the rise of American religious liberalism, but they offer little or no new material.

Of equal importance with this biographical material for an understanding of Ballou are his own writings—the many books and sermons; the periodicals of which he was editor or co-editor over the years; and the many letters and articles he contributed to newspapers and periodicals when he was without editorial duties.

The biographies and autobiographies of several of Ballou's friends and acquaintances supply much detail which helps fill in the more obscure areas of his life. These are also helpful, of course, in elucidating his relationship to his contemporaries.

The present study has made use of much material never before consulted. Ballou's sermon workbook is extant and gives an indication of his approach to sermon preparation. His last will and testament is also available. Many letters exchanged between Ballou and his friends have been found in the files of the various churches he served. These provide many details not known before. In addition, the records of these Universalist societies contain most revealing information concerning Ballou's relationship with his parishes.

Finally, the impressions gathered in many an hour spent at the places familiar to Ballou have helped to breathe a feeling of reality into the recorded incidents of his life. Visits to his birthplace in Ballou's Dell at Richmond, New Hampshire; travels over the Vermont roads on which he rode horseback; views of the harbor at Portsmouth as he looked on it for several years —these and many other first-hand experiences have, I trust, brought to this biography an appreciation of the man which books alone could not give.

WORKS OF HOSEA BALLOU

Published Material:

An Attempt with a Soft Answer to Turn Away Wrath, in Letters addressed to Mr. George Forrester, Calvinist-Baptist Preacher. In Reply to His Strictures on works entitled "A Treatise on Atonement," and "Notes and Illustrations on Parables." Portsmouth, New Hampshire, 1813.

Ballou's Miscellaneous Poems. Boston, 1852.

A Brief Reply to a Pamphlet entitled Strictures on Mr. Ballou's Sermon, delivered in the Second Universalist Meeting in Boston, on the evening of the First Sabbath of January, 1818, by T. Merritt. By the Author of the Sermon. Boston, n.d. [1818].

A Brief Reply to a Pamphlet entitled a Vindication of the Common Opinion Relative to the Last Judgment and End of the World, in answer to Mr. Ballou's Reply. By Timothy Merritt. Boston, n.d. [1818].

"A Candid Examination and Scriptural Trial of a Sermon entitled God a Rewarder—delivered at the Tabernacle in Salem, Lord's Day, January 27, 1811. By Samuel Worcester, A.M. Text, Heb. xi. 6.," *The Gospel Visitant,* I, (September 1811), 65-99.

A Candid Examination of Dr. Channing's Discourse on the Evil of Sin. Boston, 1833.

A Candid Review of a Pamphlet entitled A Candid Reply; the Whole being a Doctrinal Controversy between the Hopkintonian and the Universalist by E. Paine and H. Ballou. *And Continued on the part of the Hopkintonian by the Rev. Isaac Robinson, A.M., of Stoddard, N. H., and now further continued on the part of the Universalist.* Portsmouth, New Hampshire, n.d. [1809].

The Child's Scriptural Catechism. Boston, 1837. [1st ed., Portsmouth, New Hampshire, 1810.]

The Christian Catechism, designed for the use of Sabbath Schools. Boston, 1841.

A Collection of Valuables, consisting of Pieces on Doctrinal, Practical and Experimental Subjects, originally published in the Universalist Expositor and Universalist Magazine. Compiled by John E. Palmer. Montpelier, 1836.

Commendation and Reproof of Unitarianism. A Sermon delivered in the Second Universalist Church in Boston, on Sabbath Evening, Nov. 29. Boston, 1829.

[with Edward Turner], "Correspondence on the Doctrine of Future Punishment," *The Gospel Visitant,* II (July 1817), 115-25; (October 1817), 186-91; (January 1818), 206-11; III (April 1818), 296-317; (July 1818), 269-79.

"Discourse at Mr. Kneeland's Re-installation, Sept. 5th.," *The Gospel Visitant,* I (September 1811), 114-26.

A Discourse delivered at Salem, June 22nd, 1809, at the Installation of the Rev. Edward Turner over the First Universal Society in Said Place. Salem, 1809.

A Discourse delivered at the Universalist Church in Lombard Street, Philadelphia, on Monday Evening, June 2, at the Ordination of T. Fisk. Philadelphia, 1828.

Divine Benevolence: being a Reply to a Pamphlet, entitled, Solemn and Important Reasons against becoming a Universalist. By John Kelly, A.M. Boston, 1815.

Divine Benevolence further Vindicated: In a Reply to a Pamphlet entitled "Additional Reasons Against Universalism" &c. "By John Kelly, A.M., Author of Solemn and Important Reasons against becoming an Universalist." Salem, 1816.

A Doctrinal Controversy, between the Hopkintonian and the Universalist: begun on the part of the Universalist by Brother Ebenezer Paine, of Washington, N. H., and Brother Hosea Ballou, of Barnard, Vt., to be continued by the Rev. Reed Page, of Hancock, and the Rev. Isaac Robinson, of Stoddard, N. H., on the part of the Hopkintonian. Randolph, Vermont, 1808.

The Eleven Sermons, which were Preached during a Visit to Philadelphia in the Months of December and January, 1821-22 . . . to which are added Critical and Explanatory Notes, by the Rev. Abner Kneeland. Philadelphia, 1822. [Reissued as *Sermons on Important Doctrinal Subjects,* 1832.]

The End of the World. A Lecture Sermon, delivered in the Second Uni-

180   BIBLIOGRAPHY

versalist Meeting House, in Boston, on the Evening of the Fourth Sabbath in February. Boston, 1820.

Epistle to Lemuel Haynes. Reply to His Sermon. 1806. [Reprinted in The Universalist Magazine, III, 29-30.]

[with Walter Balfour], Everlasting Destruction: A Discourse by Rev. Walter Balfour, to Which is Added, A Letter from Rev. Hosea Ballou to Rev. Dr. Beecher. New York, 1829.

"The Evils of Striving Against the Government of God," Original Sermons on Various Subjects: by Living Universalist Ministers. Vol. II. Gardiner, Maine, 1832.

An Examination of the Doctrine of Future Retribution, on the Principles of Morals, Analogy, and the Scriptures. Boston, 1834.

Feast of Knowledge. A Lecture Sermon, delivered in the Second Universalist Meeting House in Boston, on the Evening of the Second Sabbath in March, 1822 . . . . Boston, 1822.

Five Sermons . . . by the Late Walter Ferriss, Pastor of the Universalian Church in Charlotte and Monkton, Vt., to which is subjoined a Festival Sermon, by Brother Hosea Ballou. Randolph, Vermont, 1807.

God Shall Send Them Strong Delusion. A Lecture Sermon, delivered in the Second Universalist Meeting House in Boston, on the Second Sabbath in February. Boston, 1820.

God the Author of All Things. A Sermon delivered in the Second Universalist Church in Boston, Sabbath Morning, July 5th. Boston, 1829.

The Golden Calf. A Sermon Delivered in the Second Universalist Meeting House, in Boston, on the Evening of the Fourth Sabbath in February. Boston, 1822.

Husbands, Love Your Wives. A Lecture Sermon, delivered in the Second Universalist Meeting House in Boston, on the Evening of the Second Sabbath in March. Boston, 1820.

Hymns Composed by Different Authors, at the Request of the General Convention of Universalists of the New England States and Others, adapted to Public and Private Devotion. Compiled by Rev. Messrs. Hosea Ballou, Abner Kneeland, and Edward Turner. Charlestown, 1810. [1st ed., Walpole, 1808.]

[with Lemuel Haynes], An Interesting Controversy . . . Consisting First, of a Sermon by Mr. Haynes, delivered at West Rutland, in the Year 1805, entitled, "Universal Salvation, a Very Ancient Doctrine: with some account of the Life and Character of its Author," immediately after Hearing Mr. Ballou Exhibit His Sentiments in Support of that Doctrine. Second, an Epistle from Mr. Ballou to Mr. Haynes, being a Reply to His Sermon delivered at West Rutland. Third, A Letter of Mr. Haynes to Mr. Ballou, in Reply to the Epistle. Rutland, 1807.

Jacob's Ladder. A Sermon delivered at the Dedication of the Universalist Chapel, in Providence, R. I., November 20. Boston, 1822.

A Lecture Sermon, delivered in the Second Universalist Meeting House, in Boston, on the Evening of the First Sabbath in December. Boston, 1819.

A Lecture Sermon, delivered in the Second Universalist Meeting House, in Boston, on the Evening of the Third Sabbath in December, 1819. Boston, 1819.

A Letter from Hosea Ballou to Dr. Lyman Beecher. Boston, 1828.

A Letter to the Rev. Brown Emerson, Pastor of a Congregational Church and Society in Salem. Salem, 1816.

[with Joel Foster] A Literary Correspondence, between Joel Foster, A.M., Minister of the Congregational Society in New-Salem, and Hosea Ballou, an Itinerant Preacher of the Sect called Universalists, in which the Question concerning Future Punishment, and the Reasons for and against It, are Considered. Northampton, 1799.

"The Ministry of Reconciliation" [A Sermon delivered in Orchard Street Church, Wednesday Evening, September 15, 1841], *The Occasional Sermon delivered before the Universalist General Convention, at its session in the City of New-York, Sept. 1841; together with Thirteen Other Sermons, delivered on the Same Occasion.* New York, 1841.

The New Birth. A Lecture Sermon, delivered in the Second Universalist Meeting House in Boston, on the Evening of the Third Sabbath in January. Boston, 1820.

Nine Sermons on Important Doctrinal and Practical Subjects, delivered in Philadelphia, November, 1834, with a Brief Memoir of the Author, and an Appendix. Philadelphia, 1835.

Notes on the Parables of the New Testament. Randolph, Vermont, 1804; 2d ed., enlarged, Portsmouth, New Hampshire, 1812; 3d ed., Hallowell, Maine, 1822; 5th ed., revised [actually 4th ed.], Boston, 1832.

Orthodoxy Unmasked. A Sermon delivered in the Second Universalist Meeting in Boston on Sabbath Morning, June 24, 1827, in which Some Notice is taken of Professor Stuart's Election Sermon. Boston, 1827.

[Anonymous], *A Plain Answer to "A Sermon, delivered at Rutland West-Parish, in the Year 1805," entitled "Universal Salvation a Very Ancient Doctrine: with Some Account of the Life and Character of its Author, by Lemuel Haynes, A.M.," in Prose and Poetic Composition.* Weathersfield, Vermont, 1815.

A Review of Dr. Church's Two Sermons on the Final Condition of All Men, published in the National Preacher, No. 3, Vol. 3. Boston, 1828.

A Review of some of Professor Stuart's Arguments in Defence of Endless Misery, published in the American Biblical Repository, July, 1840. Boston, 1840.

St. Paul a Universalist. A Sermon delivered in the Second Universalist Meeting House in Boston, on the Afternoon of the First Sabbath in September. Boston, 1822.

Select Sermons, delivered on Various Occasions from Important Passages of Scripture. Boston, 1832.

A Series of Lecture Sermons, delivered at the Second Universalist Meeting, in Boston. Boston, 1819.

[with Joseph Buckminster and Joseph Walton] *A Series of Letters between the Rev. Joseph Buckminster, D.D., the Rev. Joseph Walton, A.M., Pastors of Congregational Churches in Portsmouth, N. H., and the Rev. Hosea Ballou.* Windsor, 1811.

A Series of Letters in Defence of Divine Revelation; in Reply to Rev. Abner Kneeland's Serious Inquiry into the Authenticity of the Same, to which is added a Religious Correspondence between the Rev. Hosea Ballou and the Rev. Dr. Joseph Buckminster and Rev. Joseph Walton, Pastors of Congregational Churches in Portsmouth, N. H. Boston, 1820.

"Sermon I," *The Universalist Preacher*, I (January 1829), 1-7.

A Sermon delivered in Bleecker Street Church, New York, at the Session of the General Convention of Universalists. September 16th. Boston, 1847.

A Sermon delivered at the Second Universalist Meeting in Boston, on the Evening of the First Sabbath in January. Boston, 1818.

A Sermon delivered at the Second Universalist Meeting in Boston, in the Afternoon of the Second Sabbath of February, 1818. Boston, 1818.

A Sermon delivered at the Second Universalist Meeting in Boston, on the Afternoon of the Fourth Sabbath in July, 1818. Boston, 1818.

A Sermon, delivered at the Second Universalist Meeting House, in Boston, on the Morning of the Third Sabbath in November. [The "Fox" Sermon] Boston, 1819.

A Sermon, delivered at the Second Universalist Meeting House, in Boston. Boston, 1819.

A Sermon delivered in the Second Universalist Meeting in Boston on Fast Day Morning, April 3, 1828. Boston, 1828.

A Sermon, delivered in the Second Universalist Meeting House, in Boston, March 3, 1839, occasioned by the Recent Decease of Several of its Members. Boston, 1839.

A Sermon, delivered in the Second Universalist Meetinghouse, Sabbath Afternoon, January 12th, 1840. Boston, 1840.

A Sermon delivered at the Dedication of the Universalist Meeting-House, in Cambridge Port, on Wednesday, Dec. 18. Boston, 1822.

A Sermon, delivered at the Ordination of the Rev. John Samuel Thompson, as Pastor of the First Universalist Society in Charlestown, Mass., on Wednesday, July 11. Boston, 1827.

A Sermon on the Nature and Tendency of the Opposition to the True Doctrine of Jesus Christ: delivered at Dedham, on the Evening of August 14. Dedham, n.d. [1822].

A Sermon delivered at the Dedication of the New Universalist Meeting House in Duxbury, on Wednesday, Oct. 18. Boston, 1826.

A Sermon, delivered at Hartford, Conn., on Wednesday, August 18, at the Dedication of the New Universalist Meeting-House. Boston, 1824.

Sermon delivered in Hingham at the Funeral of Mrs. Mary Gardner. Boston, 1832.

A Sermon delivered at the Dedication of the First Universalist Meeting House, in Milford, Mass., Wednesday, January 10, 1821. Boston, 1821.

"Sermon 5," *Six Sermons delivered at the General Convention of Universalists at its Annual Session in Concord, N. H., on the Nineteenth and Twentieth, September, 1832.* Portland, 1833.

A Sermon, delivered at Portsmouth, N. H., appropriate to the Occasion of a Day of Humiliation and Prayer, recommended by the President of the United States on the 20th of August, 1812. Published by request of the Wardens. Portsmouth, n.d. [1812].

A Sermon, delivered in the Universalist Meeting-House in Portsmouth, N. H., on the Day of the National Thanksgiving and State Fast, April 13. Portsmouth, 1815.

A Sermon delivered at Langdon (N. H.), on the 30th Oct., 1805, at the Ordination of the Rev. Abner Kneeland to the Pastoral Care and Charge of the Universalian Church and Society in Said Town. Randolph, Vermont, 1806.

A Sermon, delivered at the Dedication of the First Universalist Meeting House, in Roxbury, Thursday, January 4, 1821. Boston, 1821.

A Sermon, delivered at the Dedication of the Universalist Meeting-House at Shirley, Mass., January 9, 1817. Salem, 1817.

"A Sermon, delivered at Salem, on the 2d Sabbath in February, 1816—St. Luke xvi. 19-31," *The Gospel Visitant,* II (April 1817), 3-16.

"A Sermon, delivered at the Dedication of the Universalist Meeting-House in Stafford, Conn., on the 14th of November last." *The Gospel Visitant,* II (October 1817), 149-60.

A Sermon designed to Notice in a Religious Manner the Death of the Rev. George Richards of Philadelphia, formerly of this Town, delivered in the Universalist Meeting-House in Portsmouth on the Evening of the 4th Sabbath in March, 1814. Portsmouth, n.d. [1814].

Sermons on Important Doctrinal Subjects, to which are added Critical and Explanatory Notes, together with a Brief Memoir of the Author, written by Himself. Boston, 1832. [Reissue of *Eleven Sermons,* 1822.]

Speech of the Dead. A Sermon, occasioned by the Death of Deacon Moses

Hall, delivered in Charlestown, the First Sabbath in August, 1826. Boston, 1826.

Strictures on a Sermon entitled "Religion a Social Principle"; delivered in the Church in Federal Street, Boston, Dec. 10, by William Ellery Channing. Boston, 1820.

A Treatise on Atonement; in which the Finite Nature of Sin is Argued, its Causes and Consequences as Such; the Necessity and Nature of Atonement, and its Glorious Consequences in the Final Reconciliation of All Men to Holiness and Happiness. Randolph, Vermont, 1805; Pirated ed., Bennington, Vermont, 1811; 2d ed., Portsmouth, New Hampshire, 1812; 3d ed., Gardiner, Maine, 1827; 4th ed., Boston, 1832.

[with Edward Turner], *The Universalists' Hymn-Book: a New Collection of Psalms and Hymns, for the use of Universalist Societies*. Boston, 1821.

Valedictory Discourse (No. 1. January, of the Series *The Universalist Pulpit*). Boston, 1851.

A Voice to Universalists. Boston, 1849.

"A Word on God's Behalf," *Universalist Expositor*, II (November 1831), 146-61.

Unpublished Material:

Last Will and Testament of Hosea Ballou. Whitingham, Vermont, September 24, 1844.

Workbook (in possession of the Universalist Historical Society Library, Crane Theological School, Tufts University).

Letters:

To Henry Archer, Clerk of the Universalist Society in Salem. Boston, July 3, 1818 (in the files of the First Universalist Church, Salem).

To Nathaniel Frothingham and the Committee of the Universalist Society in Salem. Salem, September 6, 1815 (in the files of the First Universalist Church, Salem).

To Joseph Newel [sic], Salem. Boston, May 15, 1819 (in the files of the First Universalist Church, Salem).

To Joseph Newhall, Salem. Boston, February 1, 1820 (in the files of the First Universalist Church, Salem).

To Joseph Newhall, Salem. Boston, February 19, 1820 (in the files of the First Universalist Church, Salem).

To Joseph Newhall, Salem. Boston, April 12, 1820 (in the files of the First Universalist Church, Salem).

To Joseph Newhall, Salem. Boston, May 10, 1820 (in the files of the First Universalist Church, Salem).

To Joseph Newhall, Salem. Boston, May 14, 1820 (in the files of the First Universalist Church, Salem).

To Joseph Newhall, Salem. Boston, May 24, 1820 (in the files of the First Universalist Church, Salem).

To Samuel H. Putnam, Clerk of the Universalist Society of Salem. Portsmouth, May 23, 1815 (in the files of the First Universalist Church, Salem).

To the Committee of the Universalist Society of Salem: Ebenezer Burrill, Nathaniel Frothingham, Joseph Newhall, Benjamin Goodridge, Israel Putnam; Samuel H. Putnam, Clerk. Portsmouth, April 28, 1815 (in the files of the First Universalist Church, Salem).

To the Committee of the Universalist Society of Salem: Nathaniel Frothingham, Joseph Newhall, Benjamin Goodridge, Israel Putnam; Samuel Putnam, Clerk. Portsmouth, May 13, 1815 (in the files of the First Universalist Church, Salem).

To the Committee of the Universalist Society of Salem. Salem, May 21, 1816 (in the files of the First Universalist Church, Salem).

To the Committee of the Universalist Society of Salem. Salem, June 15, 1816 (in the files of the First Universalist Church, Salem).

To the Standing Committee of the Universalist Society of Salem. Salem, May 22, 1817 (in the files of the First Universalist Church, Salem).

To the Committee of the Universalist Society of Salem. Salem, October 22, 1817 (copy of letter of resignation in Ballou's handwriting; in possession of the Universalist Historical Society Library, Crane Theological School, Tufts University).

BOOKS AND ARTICLES

An Account of the Celebration of the Seventy-Fifth Anniversary of the Second Society of the Universalists, Boston, December 18, 1892. Boston: Universalist Publishing House, 1893.

Adams, John Coleman, *Hosea Ballou and the Gospel Renaissance of the Nineteenth Century.* Boston: Universalist Publishing House, 1903.

———. "Hosea Ballou and the Larger Hope," *Pioneers of Religious Liberty in America, being the Great and Thursday Lectures delivered in Boston in Nineteen Hundred and Three.* Boston: American Unitarian Association, 1903.

———. "The Universalists," *The Religious History of New England.* Cambridge: Harvard University Press, 1917.

Adams, John G., *Fifty Notable Years. Views of the Ministry of Christian Universalism during the Last Half-Century, with Biographical Sketches.* Boston: Universalist Publishing House, 1882.

———. *Memoir of Thomas Whittemore, D.D.* Boston: Universalist Publishing House, 1878.

Allen, Ethan, *Reason the Only Oracle of Man, or a Compenduous [sic] System of Natural Religion, alternately Adorned with Confutations of a Variety of Doctrines incompatible to It; deduced from the Most Exalted Ideas which We are able to Form of the Divine and Human Characters, and from the Universe in General.* Bennington, Vermont, 1784.

Anderson, George Pomeroy, "Who Wrote 'Ethan Allen's Bible'?" *The New England Quarterly,* X (December 1937), 685-96.

Balch, W. S., "Caleb Rich," *The Universalist Quarterly and General Review,* New Series IX (January 1872), 58-78.

Balfour, Walter, *Letters on the Immortality of the Soul, the Intermediate State of the Dead, and a Future Retribution, in reply to Mr. Charles Hudson, Westminster, Mass.* Charlestown, 1829.

———. *Three Essays: on the Intermediate State of the Dead, the Resurrection from the Dead, and on the Greek Terms rendered Judge, Judgment, Condemned, Condemnation, Damned, Damnation, etc., in the New Testament, with Remarks on Mr. Hudson's Letters in Vindication of a Future Retribution, addressed to Mr. Hosea Ballou of Boston.* Charlestown, 1828.

Ballou, Adin, *An Elaborate History and Genealogy of the Ballous in America; carefully compiled and edited by Adin Ballou; with Numerous Artistic Illustrations.* Providence, 1888.

———. *Autobiography,* completed and edited by His Son-in-law, William S. Heywood. Lowell, 1896.

Ballou, Hosea, 2d, "Dogmatic and Religious History of Universalism in America," *The Universalist Quarterly and General Review,* V (January 1848), 79-103.

————. "Rev. Hosea Ballou; His Parentage and Early Life," *The Universalist Quarterly and General Review*, XI (April 1854), 174-94.

————. "Rise and Prevalence of Unitarian Views Among the Universalists," *The Universalist Quarterly and General Review*, V (October 1848), 370-95.

Ballou, Hosea Starr, *Hosea Ballou, 2d, D.D., First President of Tufts College: His Origin, Life, and Letters.* Boston, 1896.

Ballou, Maturin M., *Biography of Rev. Hosea Ballou, by His Youngest Son, Maturin M. Ballou.* Boston, 1852.

————. *Life-Story of Hosea Ballou, for the Young.* Boston, 1854.

Bassett, William, *History of the Town of Richmond, Cheshire County, New Hampshire, from Its First Settlement, to 1882.* Boston, 1884.

Brooks, E. G., "Edward Turner," *The Universalist Quarterly and General Review*, New Series VIII (April 1871), 151-80; (July 1871), 261-289.

————. "Rev. Hosea Ballou," *The Universalist Quarterly and General Review*, New Series VII (October 1870), 389-420.

Brown, Arthur W., *Always Young for Liberty, a Biography of William Ellery Channing.* Syracuse: Syracuse University Press, 1956.

Brownson, Orestes A., *The Convert: or, Leaves from My Experience.* New York, 1857.

Canfield, Mary Grace, "Early Universalism in Vermont and the Connecticut Valley." Woodstock, Vermont, 1941 (unpublished manuscript in possession of the Universalist Historical Society).

Cassara, Ernest, *Hosea Ballou and the Rise of American Religious Liberalism.* Boston: Universalist Historical Society, 1958.

Chadwick, John White, *William Ellery Channing, Minister of Religion.* Boston: Houghton, Mifflin Co., 1903.

Chambré, A. St. John, "Hosea Ballou and Edward Turner.—A Contribution to the 'Truth of History,'" *The Universalist Quarterly and General Review*, New Series X (January 1873), 40-49.

Channing, William Ellery, *Religion a Social Principle. A Sermon delivered in the Church in Federal Street, Boston, Dec. 10, 1820.* Boston, 1820.

————. *The Works of William Ellery Channing, D.D., to which is added the Perfect Life.* 1 vol., "Complete." Boston: American Unitarian Association, 1886.

Chauncy, Charles, *The Mystery Hid from Ages and Generations, Made Manifest by the Gospel-Revelation: or, the Salvation of All Men the Grand Thing Aimed at in the Scheme of God, as Opened in the New-Testament Writings, and Entrusted with Jesus Christ to Bring into Effect.* London, 1784.

Church Harmonies New and Old, a Book of Spiritual Song for Christian Worshippers. Boston: Universalist Publishing House, 1900.

Cooley, Timothy Mather, *Sketches of the Life and Character of the Rev. Lemuel Haynes, A.M., for many years Pastor of a Church in Rutland, Vt., and late in Granville, New-York.* Introduction by William B. Sprague. New York: Harper, 1837.

Dana, Henry Swan, *History of Woodstock, Vermont.* Boston: Houghton, Mifflin Co., 1889.

Darling, Nancy, *A Brief History of the Universalist Society of Hartland, Vermont, during its First Century with Biographical Sketches.* Castleton, Vermont, 1902.

Dean, Paul, "A Sermon, delivered at the Re-Installation of the Rev. Hosea Ballou to the Pastoral Care and Charge of the Second Universalist Church and Congregation, in School Street, Boston, Dec. 25," *The Gospel Visitant*, II (January 1818), 232-49.

Dole, Benjamin, *A Letter to Mr. Hosea Ballou, Pastor of the Society of*

Universalists in Salem, occasioned by His Letter to Rev. Brown Emerson. Andover, 1816.

Doten, Dana, "Ethan Allen's 'Original Something,'" *The New England Quarterly,* XI (June 1938), 361-66.

Eddy, Richard, *Universalism in America, A History.* 2 vols. Boston: Universalist Publishing House, 1884-86.

Edwards, Jonathan, *A Careful and Strict Enquiry into the Modern prevailing Notions of that Freedom of Will which is supposed to be essential to Moral Agency, Vertue and Vice, Reward and Punishment, Praise and Blame.* New Haven: Yale University Press, 1957. [1st ed. 1754.]

Ellis, Sumner, *Life of Edwin H. Chapin, D.D.* Boston: Universalist Publishing House, 1882.

Emerson, George H., *Life of Alonzo Ames Miner, S.T.D., LL.D.* Boston: Universalist Publishing House, 1896.

Fisher, Lewis B., *Which Way? A Study of Universalists and Universalism.* Boston: Universalist Publishing House, 1921.

Forrester, George, *Remarks suggested by Mr. Ballou's late Publication.* Portsmouth, New Hampshire, 1813.

———. *Strictures on Works entitled 'Treatise on Atonement,' and 'Notes on the Parables.'* Portsmouth, New Hampshire, 1812.

Foster, Frank Hugh, *A Genetic History of the New England Theology.* Chicago: University of Chicago Press, 1907.

Guild, Rev. E. E., *The Universalist's Book of Reference, containing all the Principal Facts and Arguments, and Scripture Texts, Pro and Con, on the Great Controversy between Limitarians and Universalists.* Boston, 1844.

Haynes, Lemuel, *A Letter to Rev. Hosea Ballou, being a Reply to His Epistle to the Author; or, His Attempt to Vindicate the Old Universal Preacher.* Rutland, Vermont, 1807. [Reprinted in Cooley, Timothy Mather, *Sketches of the Life and Character of the Rev. Lemuel Haynes, A.M., for many years Pastor of a Church in Rutland, Vt., and late in Granville, New-York.* Introduction by William B. Sprague. New York: Harper, 1837.]

———. *Universal Salvation, a Very Ancient Doctrine: with some account of the Life and Character of Its Author. A Sermon Delivered at Rutland, West Parish, in the Year 1805.* 9th ed. Boston, 1806. [1st ed. New Haven, 1806.]

Hudson, Charles, *A Reply to Mr. Balfour's Essays touching the State of the Dead and a Future Retribution.* Woodstock, Vermont, 1829.

———. *A Series of Letters, addressed to Rev. Hosea Ballou, of Boston, being a Vindication of the Doctrine of a Future Retribution, against the Principal Arguments used by Him, Mr. Balfour, and Others.* Woodstock, Vermont, 1827.

Hymns of the Spirit for use in the Free Churches of America. Boston: Beacon Press, 1953. [1st ed. 1937.]

Hymns of the Church with Services and Chants. Boston: The Murray Press, 1917.

Inventory of Universalist Archives in Massachusetts. Boston: The Historical Records Survey, Division of Community Service Program, Work Projects Administration, 1942.

Jones, Thomas, *Dedication Sermon, delivered at the New Brick Meeting House, of the Second Society of Universalists in Boston, October 16th, 1817.* Boston, 1817.

Journal of Debates and Proceedings in the Convention of Delegates, chosen to Revise the Constitution of Massachusetts, begun and holden at Boston, November 15, 1820, and continued by adjournment to January 9,

1821, reported for the Boston Daily Advertiser. New ed., Boston: published at the Office of the Daily Advertiser, 1853.

Kelly, John, A. M., *Additional Reasons against Universalism; or Divine Benevolence Vindicated in the Distribution of Future Everlasting Rewards and Punishments, containing Strictures on the Writings of Hosea Ballou, Pastor of the Universalist Church Congregation in Salem, Mass.* Haverhill, 1815.

———. *Solemn and Important Reasons against becoming a Universalist.* Haverhill, 1815.

Lalone, Emerson Hugh, *And Thy Neighbor As Thyself, a Story of Universalist Social Action.* Boston: Universalist Publishing House, 1939.

Merritt, Timothy, *Strictures on Mr. Ballou's Sermon, delivered at the Second Universalist Meeting in Boston, on the Evening of the First Sabbath in January, 1818.* Boston, 1818.

———. *A Vindication of the Common Opinion relative to the Last Judgment and End of the World, in Answer to Mr. Ballou's Reply.* Boston, 1818.

Miner, A. A., "Ballou and Universalism," *The Universalist Quarterly and General Review*, XIX (October 1862), 379-400.

———. *Choosing Death Rather Than Life. A Discourse, delivered in the Universalist Church, School-Street, March 6, Being the Sunday after the Funeral of Mrs. Ruth Ballou, Relict of the Late Rev. Hosea Ballou.* Boston, 1853.

———. *A Discourse, delivered in School-Street Church, Boston, June 9, 1852, at the Funeral of the Rev. Hosea Ballou, Senior Pastor.* Boston, 1852.

Murray, John, *Records of the Life of the Rev. John Murray; Late Minister of the Reconciliation, and Senior Pastor of the Universalists, congregated in Boston, written by Himself, to which is added, a Brief Continuation to the Closing Scene, by a Friend* [Mrs. Judith Murray]. Boston, 1816.

Newton, William Monroe, *History of Barnard, Vermont, with Family Genealogies, 1761-1927.* 2 vols. n.p.: The Vermont Historical Society, 1928.

Paine, Thomas, *The Complete Writings of Thomas Paine*, edited by Philip S. Foner. 2 vols. New York: Citadel Press, 1945.

Paley, William, D. D., *A View of the Evidences of Christianity in Three Parts.* New York, 1817. [1st English ed. 1794.]

Petitpierre, Ferdinand Olivier, *Thoughts on the Divine Goodness, relative to the Government of Moral Agents, particularly displayed in Future Rewards and Punishments.* [Trans. from the French: *Le Plan de Dieu envers les Hommes tel qu'il l'a manifesté dans la Nature et dans la Grace.*] Preface by Thomas J. Sawyer. Philadelphia, 1843. [First published Amsterdam, 1786. English trans., 1788; American eds. Hartford, 1794; Walpole, New Hampshire, 1801.]

Pioneers of Religious Liberty in America, being the Great and Thursday Lectures Delivered in Boston in Nineteen Hundred and Three. Boston: American Unitarian Association, 1903.

The Religious History of New England. Cambridge: Harvard University Press, 1917.

Relly, James, *Union: or a Treatise of the Consanguinity and Affinity between Christ and His Church.* Philadelphia: 1843. [Original London ed. 1759. Among the early American eds. Boston, 1779; Providence, 1782.]

Robinson, Isaac, A. M., *A Candid Reply to a Late Publication entitled "A Doctrinal Controversy between the Hopkintonian and the Universalist. . . ."* Keene, New Hampshire, 1809.

Rusterholtz, Wallace P., *American Heretics and Saints.* Boston: Manthorne and Burack, Inc., 1938.

Safford, Oscar, *Hosea Ballou: A Marvellous Life Story.* Boston: Universalist Publishing House, 1889.

Skinner, O. A., "Biographical Sketch of Rev. Hosea Ballou," *The Universalist Miscellany: A Monthly Magazine*, III (May 1846), 430-35.
Smith, S. R., *Historical Sketches and Incidents, illustrative of the Establishment and Progress of Universalism in the State of New York.* 2 vols. Buffalo, 1843-48.
Soule, Caroline A., *Memoir of Rev. H. B. Soule.* 2d ed. New York, 1852. [1st ed. same year.]
Stacy, Nathaniel, *Memoirs of the Life of Nathaniel Stacy, Preacher of the Gospel of Universal Grace.* Columbus, Pennsylvania, 1850.
Stuart, Moses, *A Sermon delivered before His Excellency Levi Lincoln, Esq., Governor, His Honor Thomas L. Winthrop Lieutenant Governor, the Hon. Council, the Senate, and House of Representatives of the Commonwealth of Massachusetts, May 30, 1827, being the Day of General Election.* Boston, 1827.
Thomas, Rev. Abel C., *Autobiography.* Boston, 1852.
———. *A Century of Universalism in Philadelphia and New York with Sketches of its History in Reading, Hightstown, Brooklyn and elsewhere.* Philadelphia, 1872.
Turner, Edward, "Changes in the Religious Views of Universalists," *The Universalist Quarterly and General Review*, VI (January 1849), 1-15.
———. *A Discourse delivered at the Universal Meeting-House in Portsmouth, N. H., November 8, 1809, at the Installation of the Rev. Hosea Ballou to the Pastoral Charge of the Society in that Place.* Portsmouth, New Hampshire, n.d. [1809].
Whittemore, Thomas, *The Early Days of Thomas Whittemore, an Autobiography: extending from A.D. 1800 to A.D. 1825.* Boston, 1859.
———. *Life of Rev. Hosea Ballou; with accounts of His Writings, and Biographical Sketches of His Seniors and Contemporaries in the Universalist Ministry.* 4 vols. Boston, 1854-55.
———. *Memoir of the Rev. Walter Balfour, Author of Letters to Prof. Stuart, and Various Other Publications.* Boston, 1852.
———. *The Modern History of Universalism from the Era of the Reformation to the Present Time.* Boston, 1830.
Winchester, Elhanan, *An Attempt to Collect the Scripture Passages in Favour of the Universal Restoration, as connected with the Doctrine of Rewards and Punishments, all Tending to Prove, the Universal Empire of Christ, the Total Destruction of Evil, and the Final Re-establishment of Lapsed Intelligences.* Providence, 1786.
———. *A Course of Lectures on the Prophecies that Remain to be Fulfilled, delivered in the Borough of Southwark—as Also at the Chapel in Glass House Yard, in the Years, 1788, '9, '90.* 2 vols. London, 1790-91. [American ed. Walpole, New Hampshire, 1800.]
———. *The Universal Restoration: exhibited in Four Dialogues between a Minister and His Friend; comprehending the substance of Several Real Conversations which the Author had with Various Persons both in America and Europe on that Interesting Subject: chiefly designed fully to State and Fairly to Answer the Most Common Objections that are brought against It, from the Scriptures.* Philadelphia, 1843. [1st ed. Philadelphia, 1792.]
The Winchester Centennial, 1803-1903. Historical Sketch of the Universalist Profession of Belief adopted at Winchester, N. H., September 22, 1803. Boston: Universalist Publishing House, 1903.
Wright, Conrad, *The Beginnings of Unitarianism in America.* Boston: Starr King Press, 1955.

IMPORTANT UNIVERSALIST PERIODICALS

The Gospel Visitant, being principally Original Tracts on Moral and Religious Subjects: in which an Illustration of the Gospel of God Our Saviour is attempted by Arguments drawn from Reason, the whole directed to the Promotion of Piety and Morality. [Vols. I (by the Gloucester Conference), Charlestown, 1811-12; II-III (by Edward Turner and Hosea Ballou), Boston, 1817-18.]

The Universalist Expositor. 2 vols. Boston, 1830-32. [I, ed. Hosea Ballou, Hosea Ballou, 2d; II, ed. Hosea Ballou, Hosea Ballou, 2d, L. S. Everett.]

The Universalist Magazine. 9 vols. Boston, 1819-28. [I-II, ed. Hosea Ballou; 10 months of III, ed. Foster; IV-VII, ed. Hosea Ballou, Hosea Ballou, 2d, Thomas Whittemore; VIII-IX, ed. Hosea Ballou, Thomas Whittemore.]

The Universalist Miscellany: A Monthly Magazine, devoted to Biblical Literature, Explanations of Scripture, Doctrinal and Moral Discussions, and the Promotion of Practical Piety. 6 vols. Boston, 1844-49.

The Universalist Quarterly and General Review. 42 vols. Boston, 1844-86.

Trumpet and Universalist Magazine. 34 vols. Boston, 1828-62. [Ed. Thomas Whittemore until his death in 1861.]

RECORDS

Choir Record Book, Second Society of Universalists in the Town of Boston, January 29, 1843—December 26, 1847.

Collector's Annual Report of the Universalist Society at Portsmouth, New Hampshire, 1809-15.

Financial Receipts of the Universalist Society at Portsmouth, New Hampshire, June, 1812; June, 1813.

Miscellaneous Papers in the Files of the First Universalist Society in Salem, Massachusetts.

Miscellaneous Papers in the Files of the Second Society of Universalists in the Town of Boston.

Perley Putnam's Book which contains some of the Earley [sic] Votes and Records of the First Proprietors of the First Universalist Society in Salem Massachusetts, 1806 (in possession of the First Universalist Church, Salem).

Records of the Universalist Society at Portsmouth, New Hampshire. Book One, 1793-1852.

Sunday School Minute Book, Second Society of Universalists in the Town of Boston. 2 vols. May 31, 1835—July 14, 1839; July 21, 1839—August 20, 1843.

Treasurer's Account Book with various other items, Second Universalist Society in the Town of Boston, 1844-69.

Warden's Accounts of the Universalist Society at Portsmouth, New Hampshire, 1809-15.

Walnut Hill Evangelical Seminary Trustees Record Book, 1840-41 (in possession of the Universalist Historical Society Library, Crane Theological School, Tufts University).

LETTERS

See also "Letters" under Works of Hosea Ballou.

Chapin, E. H., [Letter of Resignation] to the Second Society of Universalists in the Town of Boston. Boston, February 5, 1848 (in the files of the Second Society of Universalists, Boston).

Flagg, Joshua, to the Universalist Society of Salem. Salem, August 29, 1818 (in the files of the First Universalist Church, Salem).

Flagg, Joshua, to the Universalist Society of Salem. Salem, October 10, 1819 (in the files of the First Universalist Church, Salem).

Flagg, Joshua, to the Universalist Society of Salem. Salem, November 13, 1819 (in the files of the First Universalist Church, Salem).

Flagg, Joshua, to the Universalist Society of Salem. Salem, November 21, 1819 (in the files of the First Universalist Church, Salem).

Flagg, Joshua, to the Universalist Society of Salem. Salem, December 28, 1819 (in the files of the First Universalist Church, Salem).

Committee of the Fourth Universalist Society, New York, to E. H. Chapin. Boston, January 12, 1848 (in the files of the Second Society of Universalists, Boston).

Frothingham, Nathaniel, to Samuel H. Reed. Salem, November 15, 1820 (copy in the files of the First Universalist Church, Salem).

Frothingham, Nathaniel, to Samuel H. Reed. Salem, July 2, 1821 (copy in the files of the First Universalist Church, Salem).

Miner, A. A., to George W. Gage. Boston, November 18, 1850 (in the files of the Second Society of Universalists, Boston).

Miner, A. A., to Deacon Daniel E. Powers, John M. Wright, and George W. Gage. Lowell, March 15, 1848 (in the files of the Second Society of Universalists, Boston).

Miner, A. A., to Newton Talbot, Clerk of the Second Society of Universalists in the Town of Boston. Lowell, April 12, 1848 (in the files of the Second Society of Universalists, Boston).

Committee of the Universalist Society at Portsmouth: A. Greenleaf, Samuel Mudge, and Thomas S. Bowles, to "the wardens or other officers who may represent the Universalist Society in Salem." Portsmouth, June 5, 1815 (in the files of the First Universalist Church, Salem).

Committee of the Universalist Society of Salem: Ebenezer Burrill, Joseph Newhall, Nathaniel Frothingham, Benjamin Goodridge, Israel Putnam, and Samuel Putnam, Clerk, to Hosea Ballou. Salem, April 26, 1815 (copy in the files of the First Universalist Church, Salem).

Committee of the Universalist Society of Salem: Ebenezer Burrill, Nathaniel Frothingham, Joseph Newhall, Benjamin Goodridge, Israel Putnam, Samuel Putnam, Clerk, to Hosea Ballou. Salem, May 10, 1815 (copy in the files of the First Universalist Church, Salem).

Committee of the Universalist Society of Salem: Nathaniel Frothingham, Joseph Newhall, to the Universalist Society at Portsmouth. Salem, July 1, 1815 (copy in the files of the First Universalist Church, Salem).

Universalist Society of Salem to Edward Turner [letter of dismissal]. Salem, May 16, 1814 (copy in the files of the First Universalist Church, Salem).

Universalist Society of Salem to Edward Turner, Thomas Jones, Paul Dean [invitation to participate in installation of Hosea Ballou]. June 21, 1815 (copy in the files of the First Universalist Church, Salem).

Streeter, Barzillai, to William Mansfield, Clerk of the Universalist Society of Salem. Salem, n.d. [1821] (in the files of the First Universalist Church, Salem).

Turner, Edward, to Joseph Newhall. Salem, April 5, 1813 (in the files of the First Universalist Church, Salem).

Turner, Edward, to Joseph Newhall. Salem, January 5, 1814 (in the files of the First Universalist Church, Salem).

Turner, Edward, to the Committee of the Universalist Society of Salem. Salem, February 18, 1814 (in the files of the First Universalist Church, Salem)

NOTES

Detailed information about the sources mentioned in the notes, as well as complete title references, will be found in the bibliography, which begins on page 177.

CHAPTER I. RICHMOND, 1770

1. A. Ballou, *Ballous in America*, p. 67.
2. Whittemore, *Life of Ballou*, I, 18.
3. A. Ballou, *Ballous in America*, p. v.
4. *Ibid.*
5. *Ibid.*, p. 66.
6. Whittemore, *Life of Ballou*, I, 19.
7. M. M. Ballou, *Biography of Ballou*, p. 24.
8. A. Ballou, *Ballous in America*, p. 65.
9. *Ibid.*
10. M. M. Ballou, *Biography of Ballou*, p. 18.
11. A. Ballou, *Ballous in America*, p. 125.
12. Statistics drawn from *ibid.*, pp. 124-30, *passim;* the interpretation is mine.
13. Whittemore, *Life of Ballou*, I, 19.
14. Bassett, *op. cit.*, pp. 1, 10.
15. *Ibid.*, pp. 27, 31.
16. *Ibid.*, pp. 2, 6.
17. *Ibid.*, p. 244.
18. *Ibid.*, p. 222.
19. *Ibid.*, p. 223.
20. *Ibid.*
21. A. Ballou, *Ballous in America*, p. 68.
22. M. M. Ballou, *Biography of Ballou*, p. 16.
23. Safford, *op. cit.*, p. 18.
24. Bassett, *op. cit.*, p. 223.
25. Statistics derived from A. Ballou, *Ballous in America*, p. 124. The interpretation is mine.

CHAPTER II. THE EARLY YEARS

1. The spot in Ballou's Dell where the log cabin stood is marked by a granite stone with the inscription:

> Birthplace of
> Hosea Ballou
> 1771
> Erected 1903

It was erected through the efforts of Hosea Starr Ballou as part of the centennial celebration of the Winchester Profession of Faith. See *Winchester Centennial*, pp. 210, 212.
2. M. M. Ballou, *Biography of Ballou*, pp. 24-25.
3. A. Ballou, *Ballous in America*, p. 66.
4. M. M. Ballou, *Biography of Ballou*, p. 22.
5. A. Ballou, *Ballous in America*, p. 66. There is disagreement regarding her name. Bassett, *History of Richmond*, p. 280, gives it as Lydia Blois.

6. A. Ballou, *Ballous in America,* p. 66.
7. *Ibid.,* p. 125.
8. Statistics in *ibid.,* pp. 125-26, 296. Interpretation is mine.
9. *Ibid.,* p. 124.
10. Quoted by M. M. Ballou, *Biography of Ballou,* p. 299.
11. Bassett, *op. cit.,* p. 59.
12. *Ibid.,* pp. 84ff.
13. *Ibid.,* p. 85.
14. *Ibid.,* p. 88.
15. *Ibid.,* pp. 223-24.
16. *Ibid.,* p. 227.
17. *Ibid.*
18. Whittemore, *Life of Ballou,* I, 21.
19. Hosea Ballou, *A Treatise on Atonement* (1805 ed.), p. 51.
20. A. Ballou, *Ballous in America,* p. 124.
21. *Ibid.,* p. 126.
22. *Ibid.,* p. 129.
23. M. M. Ballou, *Biography of Ballou,* p. 30.
24. *Ibid.,* pp. 29-30.
25. Safford, *op. cit.,* p. 21.
26. *Ibid.,* p. 44; M. M. Ballou, *Biography of Ballou,* p. 34.
27. M. M. Ballou, *Biography of Ballou,* p. 34.
28. Whittemore, *Life of Ballou,* I, 41.
29. *Ibid.,* p. 42.
30. Letter from Hosea Ballou to Thomas Whittemore, November 25, 1829, in Whittemore, *Modern History of Universalism,* p. 433n.
31. Hosea Ballou quoted in M. M. Ballou, *Biography of Ballou,* p. 23.
32. Letter from Hosea Ballou to Thomas Whittemore, November 25, 1829, in Whittemore, *Modern History of Universalism,* p. 434n.
33. Autobiographical sketch of Hosea Ballou quoted by M. M. Ballou, *Biography of Ballou,* p. 36.

CHAPTER III. THE GREAT REFORMATION

1. Eddy, *op. cit.,* I, 168.
2. *Ibid.,* pp. 168-69.
3. *Ibid.,* p. 171.
4. *Ibid.*
5. Whittemore, *Life of Ballou,* I, 28.
6. H. Ballou, *Examination of the Doctrine of Future Retribution,* p. 172.
7. *Ibid.*
8. Safford, *op. cit.,* p. 32.
9. M. M. Ballou, *Biography of Ballou,* p. 32.
10. H. S. Ballou, *Hosea Ballou, 2d,* p. 16.
11. A. Ballou, *Ballous in America,* p. 128.
12. Letter from Hosea Ballou to Thomas Whittemore, November 25, 1829, in Whittemore, *Modern History of Universalism,* p. 434n.
13. Bassett, *History of Richmond,* p. 227, gives the date as January 1790. Other sources, including Whittemore, favor 1789.
14. Whittemore, *Life of Ballou,* I, 49.
15. Letter of Hosea Ballou to Thomas Whittemore, November 25, 1829, in Whittemore, *Modern History of Universalism,* p. 434n.
16. *Ibid.*
17. Safford, *op. cit.,* p. 25.
18. Quoted by M. M. Ballou, *Biography of Ballou,* p. 39. See Hosea Ballou, *A Treatise on Atonement* (1805 ed.), p. 124: "That multitudes have been in great fear of being rejected by the Almighty, at last, I

have no doubt; for I confess those torments have been mine, in no small degree."

19. M. M. Ballou, *Biography of Ballou*, pp. 39-40.
20. Safford, *op. cit.*, p. 39.
21. Letter of Hosea Ballou to Thomas Whittemore, November 25, 1829, in Whittemore, *Modern History of Universalism*, p. 435n.
22. *Ibid.*, pp. 435-36n.
23. *Ibid.*, p. 436n.
24. *Ibid.*
25. Writing fifteen years later, Ballou shows great sympathy for those who, despite all his arguments, are still not convinced. "The time has been, when I believed as little of the doctrine as you now do; I never adopted the belief of universal holiness and happiness out of *choice*, but from the *force* of *real* or *supposed evidence*." See *A Treatise on Atonement* (1805 ed.), p. 214.
26. Whittemore, *Life of Ballou*, I, 65.
27. *Ibid.*, pp. 60-61.
28. Letter of Hosea Ballou to Thomas Whittemore, November 25, 1829, in Whittemore, *Modern History of Universalism*, p. 436n.
29. Although Ballou was forced to leave the Baptist Church, he always had a tender spot in his heart for the church of his childhood: "I have always felt towards this people as one feels towards his family, and though the religion of Christ consists in love to all men, I have a peculiar feeling for the Baptists." Quoted by M. M. Ballou, *Biography of Ballou*, p. 39.
30. A. Ballou, *Ballous in America*, p. 126.
31. Safford, *op. cit.*, p. 38.
32. H. Ballou, 2d, "Hosea Ballou," *Universalist Quarterly*, XI (April 1854), 186n.

CHAPTER IV. "THE WRITTEN JEHOVAH"

1. A. Ballou, *Ballous in America*, p. 124.
2. Statistic from *ibid.*, p. 126. Interpretation is mine.
3. Bassett, *op. cit.*, p. 128.
4. The meetinghouse, now a private dwelling, with the plain Quaker graveyard at the rear, is still standing at Richmond Four Corners.
5. See his own description in M. M. Ballou, *Biography of Ballou*, p. 48.
6. *Ibid.*, pp. 49-50.
7. *Ibid.*, p. 49.
8. *Ibid.*, p. 50.
9. Whittemore, *Life of Ballou*, I, 72.
10. *Ibid.*, p. 53.
11. *Ibid.*, p. 54.
12. Quoted by M. M. Ballou, *Biography of Ballou*, pp. 315-16.
13. Quoted in *ibid.*, p. 54.
14. *Ibid.*, pp. 317-19.
15. *Ibid.*, p. 53.
16. Whittemore, *Life of Ballou*, I, 80.
17. See Relly, *op. cit.*
18. Letter of Hosea Ballou to Thomas Whittemore, February 25, 1829, in Whittemore, *Modern History of Universalism*, p. 436n.
19. *Ibid.* It should be added, however, that Ballou was not wholly untouched by the influence of Relly's thought. See Chap. 8.
20. *Ibid.*
21. M. M. Ballou, *Biography of Ballou*, p. 58.
22. Whittemore, *Life of Ballou*, I, 92.

23. Safford, *op. cit.*, p. 183.
24. Whittemore, *Life of Ballou*, I, 106.
25. H. Ballou, 2d, "Hosea Ballou," *Universalist Quarterly*, XI (April 1854), 188.
26. M. M. Ballou, *Biography of Ballou*, p. 59.
27. *Ibid.*, p. 60.
28. Hosea Ballou, quoted in *ibid*.
29. *Ibid*.

CHAPTER V. ORACLES OF REASON

1. The preface is dated July 2, 1782. Allen's claim to sole authorship of the work has been challenged. An attempt has been made to demonstrate that most of it was written several years earlier by Allen's old friend Dr. Thomas Young (1732-77). See George Pomeroy Anderson, "Who Wrote 'Ethan Allen's Bible'?" *New England Quarterly*, X (December 1937), 685-96. The topic is pursued further, in a most delightful manner, by Dana Doten, "Ethan Allen's 'Original Something,'" *ibid.*, XI (June 1938), 361-66.
2. Anderson, *op. cit.*, p. 696.
3. *Reason the Only Oracle*, p. vii.
4. *Ibid.*, p. 34.
5. For example, he claims that Moses on Sinai must have seen the "BACK-PARTS" of God, since the Bible states that no man can view God's face and live. *Ibid.*, p. 278.
6. Several years after I first propounded the theory of Ballou's debt to Ethan Allen's book (in the monograph *Hosea Ballou and the Rise of American Religious Liberalism*), I received corroboration from an unexpected source. Orestes A. Brownson, in his long religious evolution to Roman Catholicism, went through a Universalist stage. During this period he was well acquainted with Ballou (then an elderly man). In answer to an inquiry by Brownson concerning his *Treatise*, Ballou said, "My only aids in writing my Treatise on the [*sic*] Atonement were the Bible, Ethan Allen's Oracles of Reason, and my own reflections." See Brownson's autobiography, *The Convert*, p. 51.
7. Letter to Thomas Whittemore, November 25, 1829, in Whittemore, *Modern History of Universalism*, pp. 436-37n. Past writers have apparently shown no inclination to look into the "deistical writings" referred to by Ballou. It is true that Safford speculates that Ballou was referring to Thomas Paine's *Age of Reason* (*Hosea Ballou*, p. 74), but both the date and the contents of Paine militate against this suggestion. As will be noted later, Ballou preached his first unitarian sermon in 1795, whereas Paine's book was published only a year before. Furthermore, no influence of Paine is obvious in the *Treatise*, although Ballou had probably read Paine by the time of its publication in 1805. Investigation would have shown that Allen's book was the one referred to, but Safford and others have propagated the myth that Ballou was a completely original thinker, indebted to no man but to reason and Holy Writ for his theological position. That Ballou was a powerful logician cannot be denied; but all men owe a great debt to the past and to their contemporaries for much of their thought.
8. Allen, *Reason the Only Oracle*, pp. 34-46.
9. *Ibid.*, pp. 352ff.
10. *Ibid.*, p. 363.
11. *Ibid.*, p. 405.
12. *Ibid.*, p. 112.
13. *Ibid.*, p. 111.

14. *Ibid.*, p. 112.
15. *Ibid.*, pp. 142ff.
16. *Ibid.*, p. 466.
17. *Ibid.*, p. 334.
18. *Ibid.*, p. 118.
19. *Ibid.*
20. *Ibid.*, pp. 118-119.
21. H. Ballou, *Series of Letters in Defence of Divine Revelation.*
22. *Ibid.*, p. 25.
23. *Ibid.*, p. 111. See also his laudatory comments on the Deists in *Strictures on a Sermon entitled "Religion a Social Principle," by William Ellery Channing*, pp. 12-14.
24. It should be stressed that he did not accept many of Allen's views; these have not been included in the present work.
25. *The Mystery Hid from Ages and Generations, or, the Salvation of All Men.* For an excellent discussion of the events accompanying the publication of Chauncy's book, see Wright, *Beginnings of Unitarianism in America*, pp. 187ff
26. Foster and H. Ballou, *Literary Correspondence*, p. 62.
27. Chauncy, *op. cit.*, pp. 260ff.
28. *Ibid.*, pp. xiff, 242.
29. *Ibid.*, pp. 319-20.
30. *Ibid.*, p. 327.
31. *Ibid.*, pp. 11, 322.
32. *Ibid.*, p. 11.
33. *Ibid.*, pp. 170-237.
34. *Ibid.*, p. 127ff.
35. *Le Plan de Dieu envers les Hommes, tel qu'il l'a manifesté dans la Nature et dans la Grace* was the original title. The title was rendered in English as *Thoughts on the Divine Goodness, relative to the Government of Moral Agents, particularly displayed in Future Rewards and Punishments.*
36. *Ibid.*, p. 4.
37. For these and other editions see "Bibliography" in Eddy, *op. cit.*, II, 490.
38. Stacy, *Memoirs*, p. 71
39. *On Divine Goodness*, p. 39.
40. *Ibid.*, p. 38.
41. *Ibid.*
42. *Ibid.*, pp. 39-41.
43. *Ibid.*, pp. 38-39.
44. Turner, "Changes in the Religious Views of Universalists," *Universalist Quarterly*, VI (January 1849), 14.
45. H. Ballou, 2d, "Rise and Prevalence of Unitarian Views among the Universalists," *Universalist Quarterly*, V (October 1848), 374.
46. Quoted by Whittemore, *Life of Ballou*, I, 119.
47. Hosea Ballou in *Trumpet*, XVI, 116; quoted by Whittemore, *Life of Ballou*, I, 118.
48. H. Ballou, 2d, "Dogmatic and Religious History of Universalism in America," *Universalist Quarterly*, V (October 1848), 102.

CHAPTER VI. RUTH

1. Dana, incorporated in 1801, was made up of land from Greenwich, Petersham and Hardwick. In 1926-27, the Commonwealth of Massachusetts voted to inundate Dana and much of the surrounding area as part of the Quabbin Reservoir. Roland D. Sawyer, "Where the

Universalist Denomination was Born," *The Christian Leader*, CXXVII (August 4, 1945), 346-47.

2. *Inventory of Universalist Archives in Massachusetts*, p. 175.
3. M. M. Ballou, *Biography of Ballou*, p. 64.
4. Whittemore, *Life of Ballou*, I, 121.
5. *Ibid.*, p. 156.
6. M. B. Ballou, *Biography of Ballou*, p. 64.
7. *Ibid.*, p. 68.
8. Safford, *op. cit.*, p. 59.
9. Stacy, *op. cit.*, p. 57.
10. Whittemore, *Life of Ballou*, III, 226.
11. As later told to Thomas Whittemore. *Ibid.*, I, 120.
12. A. Ballou, *Ballous in America*, p. 131.
13. Safford, *op. cit.*, p. 220.
14. M. M. Ballou, *Life-Story of Hosea Ballou, for the Young*, p. 48.
15. M. M. Ballou, *Biography of Ballou*, p. 198.
16. Whittemore, *Life of Ballou*, I, 120.
17. H. Ballou, 2d, "Hosea Ballou," *Universalist Quarterly*, XI (April 1854), 190.
18. M. M. Ballou, *Life-Story of Hosea Ballou, for the Young*, p. 48.
19. H. S. Ballou, *Hosea Ballou, 2d*, p. 5.
20. Eddy, *op. cit.*, I, 479.
21. H. Ballou in *Universalist Magazine*, II (June 9, 1821), 198.
22. Whittemore, *Life of Ballou*, I, 127.
23. Foster and H. Ballou, *Literary Correspondence*, p. 6.
24. *Ibid.*
25. *Ibid.*, p. 12.
26. Statistics from A. Ballou, *Ballous in America*, p. 131. It is difficult to determine how many children were born to Hosea and Ruth. Safford, *op. cit.*, pp. 221-22n., gives the total as eleven; A. Ballou, *Ballous in America*, p. 131, gives the figure as thirteen. Only nine survived infancy.
27. That Foster is aware of Ballou's indebtedness to Chauncy is obvious. See *Literary Correspondence*, p. 62.
28. *Ibid.*, p. 19.
29. *Ibid.*, p. 20.
30. *Ibid.*, p. 23.
31. *Ibid.*, p. 24.
32. *Ibid.*, p. 56.
33. *Ibid.*, p. 36.
34. *Ibid.*, p. 41.
35. *Ibid.*, pp. 55-56.
36. *Ibid.*, p. 3.
37. *Ibid.*, p. 58.
38. *Ibid.*, p. 56.
39. *Ibid.*, p. 61.
40. *Ibid.*, pp. 60-61.
41. Quoted by Eddy, *op. cit.*, I, 506-7.
42. *Trumpet*, XX (March 4, 1848), 150; Whittemore, *Life of Ballou*, I, 147-48.
43. Whittemore, *Life of Ballou*, I, 148.
44. *Ibid.*, pp. 160-61.
45. *Ibid.*, p. 162.
46. A. Ballou, *Ballous in America*, p. 131.
47. Whittemore, *Life of Ballou*, I, 149.
48. Stacy, *op. cit.*, p. 57.
49. Dana, *op. cit.*, p. 399.
50. Stacy, *op. cit.*, p. 62.

51. *Ibid.*, pp. 67-68.
52. *Ibid.*, p. 71.
53. *The Universal Restoration: exhibited in Four Dialogues.*
54. *A Course of Lectures on the Prophecies that remain to be Fulfilled.*
55. Stacy, *op. cit.*, p. 69.
56. *Ibid.*, p. 70.
57. *Ibid.*, pp. 71-73.
58. A. Ballou, *Ballous in America*, p. 131.
59. Massena B. Ballou, quoted by Safford, *op. cit.*, p. 205.
60. A. Ballou, *Ballous in America*, p. 131.

CHAPTER VII. THE SISTER SOCIETIES

1. Dana, *op. cit.*, pp. 397-98.
2. Newton, *op. cit.*, I, 130f.
3. *Vermont Standard*, January 12, 1939.
4. *Ibid.*, p. 148.
5. Darling, *op. cit.*, p. 5.
6. *Ibid.*, pp. 9-10.
7. Canfield, *op. cit.*, p. 202.
8. *Ibid.*
9. Darling, *op. cit.*, p. 9.
10. Whittemore, *Life of Ballou*, I, 257.
11. Canfield, *op. cit.*, p. 214.
12. *Ibid.*, p. 202.
13. *Ibid.*, p. 191.
14. Darling, *op. cit.*, pp. 9, 11.
15. *Ibid.*, p. 12.
16. Newton, *op. cit.*, I, 148
17. Dana, *op. cit.*, p. 80.
18. Darling, *op. cit.*, p. 11.
19. Canfield, *op. cit.*, p. 196.
20. Quoted by *Vermont Standard*, January 12, 1939.
21. Whittemore, *Life of Ballou*, I, 164-65.
22. *Ibid.*, p. 165.
23. Eddy, *op. cit.*, I, 297ff.
24. *Ibid.*, p. 164.
25. Whittemore, *Life of Ballou*, I, 174.
26. *Ibid.*
27. Stacy, *op. cit.*; quoted in *ibid.*, I, 179.
28. Whittemore, *Life of Ballou*, I, 172n.
29. Quoted in *ibid.*, p. 173n.
30. *Ibid.*, p. 305.
31. Haynes, *Universal Salvation*, p. 3.
32. Whittemore, *Life of Ballou*, I, 239.
33. *Ibid.*
34. Haynes, *Universal Salvation*, p. 5.
35. *Ibid.*, p. 10.
36. *Ibid.*, pp. 10-11.
37. Whittemore, *Life of Ballou*, I, 241.
38. *Universal Salvation.*
39. H. Ballou, *Epistle to Lemuel Haynes. Reply to his Sermon.* Reprinted in *The Universalist Magazine*, III (August 18, 1821), 28. Also reprinted in Whittemore, *Life of Ballou*, I, 241-51.
40. *The Universalist Magazine*, III, 28.
41. *Letter to Reverend Hosea Ballou*; reprinted in Cooley, *op. cit.*
42. Haynes' biographer stated: "This discourse has been printed and re-

printed, both in America and in Great Britain, till no one pretends to give any account of the number of editions." Cooley, *op. cit.*, p. 96. Ballou, in *The Universalist Magazine*, took note of various reprints and editions and took occasion to refute Haynes again. See II (March 10, 1821), 146-47; V (September 20, 1823), 48. The entire controversy was published, probably through the efforts of Haynes, in *An Interesting Controversy between Lemuel Haynes and Hosea Ballou*. Some years later an anonymous pamphlet appeared taking the side of Ballou: *A Plain Answer* (1815). Since this pamphlet is not available, I have not been able to determine its authorship by internal evidence. Eddy, *op. cit.*, II, 498, speculates that Ballou was the author, but it was not his habit to choose anonymity.

43. H. Ballou, *Nine Sermons*, pp. 94ff.
44. Whittemore, *Life of Ballou*, I, 271n.
45. Ferriss and H. Ballou, *Five Sermons*, pp. 90-104.
46. Whittemore, *Life of Ballou*, I, 271n.
47. *Ibid.*, pp. 257-58.
48. *Ibid.*, p. 260.
49. A. Ballou, *Ballous in America*, p. 69.
50. *Ibid.*, p. 131.
51. Newton, *op. cit.*, II, 38.
52. *Ibid.*
53. The stone can be seen in the Central Cemetery, Barnard, Vermont. *Vermont Standard*, January 12, 1939.

CHAPTER VIII. "OF MAKING MANY BOOKS . . ."

1. H. Ballou, *Notes on the Parables* (1804 ed.), p. iv.
2. Whittemore, *Life of Ballou*, I, 186.
3. H. Ballou, *Notes on the Parables* (1804 ed.), p. iv.
4. H. Ballou, *Notes on the Parables* (1832 ed.), p. 7.
5. *Notes on the Parables* (1804 ed.), p. iii.
6. Cf. Relly, *op. cit.*
7. *Notes on the Parables* (1804 ed.), p. 10.
8. *Ibid.*
9. Exposition of Matthew 13:33. *Ibid.*, pp. 27-28.
10. *Ibid.*, p. 49.
11. *Notes on the Parables* (1804 ed.), p. 49.
12. H. Ballou, *Voice to Universalists*, p. 127.
13. Whittemore, *Life of Ballou*, I, 252, 256, 267.
14. *Hymns Composed by Different Authors*, p. iii.
15. Whittemore, *Life of Ballou*, I, 270, 270n.
16. *Hymns Composed by Different Authors*, p. iii.
17. *Ibid.*
18. *Ibid.*, p. iv.
19. Whittemore, *Life of Ballou*, I, 275.
20. *Ibid.*, pp. 270-71.
21. *Church Harmonies New and Old.*
22. *Hymns of the Church.*
23. *Hymns of the Spirit.*
24. He is not completely neglected by others, however. The current *Christian Science Hymnal* (Boston: Christian Science Publishing Society, 1937) contains his hymn, "When God is seen with men to dwell."
25. H. Ballou and E. Paine, *Doctrinal Controversy.*
26. Whittemore, *Life of Ballou*, I, 282.
27. Robinson, *op. cit.*,

28. H. Ballou, *Candid Review.*
29. *Ibid.*, p. 205.
30. *A Treatise on Atonement,* p. 93.
31. H. Ballou, 2d, "Rise and Prevalence of Unitarian Views among the Universalists," *Universalist Quarterly,* V (October 1848), 375.
32. *Ibid.*
33. Letter from George Richards to Edward Turner, May 4, 1807, quoted in *Universalist Quarterly,* New Series VIII (July 1871), 272n.
34. H. Ballou, *A Treatise on Atonement* (1811 ed.).
35. Quoted by Whittemore, *Life of Ballou,* I, 235.

CHAPTER IX. THE GREAT TREATISE

1. *A Treatise on Atonement,* p. iv.
2. *Ibid.*
3. *Ibid.*
4. *Ibid.*
5. *Ibid.*, p. 15.
6. *Ibid.*
7. *Ibid.*, p. 16.
8. *Ibid.*, pp. 16-17.
9. *Ibid.*, p. 17.
10. *Ibid.*, p. 18.
11. *Ibid.*
12. *Ibid.*, p. 19.
13. *Ibid.*
14. *Ibid.*, p. 20.
15. *Ibid.*
16. *Ibid.*, p. 21.
17. *Ibid.*
18. *Ibid.*, p. 59.
19. *Ibid.*, p. 24.
20. *Ibid.*, p. 29.
21. *Ibid.*, pp. 29-34.
22. *Ibid.*, pp. 30-31.
23. Ballou may have received the distinction between the creation and formation of man from Ethan Allen, *Reason the Only Oracle of Man,* pp. 61-71. If so, he translated it into biblical terms lacking in the original. This distinction has also been attributed to Caleb Rich, from whom, it is supposed, Ballou derived it. See W. S. Balch, "Caleb Rich," *Universalist Quarterly,* New Series IX (January 1872), 62. Balch quotes Russell Streeter to the effect that Zephaniah Laithe told him that Caleb Rich claimed to be responsible for the leading ideas in the *Treatise.* It is not to be doubted that Rich was very influential in Ballou's life and thought. But, in the light of Chap. V of this study, it is safe to say that Ballou's main indebtedness lay elsewhere.
24. H. Ballou, *A Treatise on Atonement,* pp. 33-34.
25. *Ibid.*, pp. 34-35.
26. *Ibid.*, pp. 36ff. His arguments at this point are reminiscent of the approach used by Jonathan Edwards in his *Freedom of the Will.* He may have been influenced by it.
27. H. Ballou, *A Treatise on Atonement,* p. 36.
28. *Ibid.*, p. 39.
29. *Ibid.*, p. 41.
30. In his introduction, "A Letter to the Reader," he states that he is not contending against any particular denomination or sect and so will not quote specific books or name any group. His only object is to strive against

error and to set forth and defend the truth as he understands it. *Ibid.*, p. vi.

31. *Ibid.*, p. 42.
32. *Ibid.*, p. 43.
33. *Ibid.*, pp. 43-44.
34. *Ibid.*, p. 54.
35. *Ibid.*, p. 45.
36. *Ibid.*, pp. 46-47.
37. *Ibid.*, pp. 48-49.
38. *Ibid.*, pp. 65-66.
39. *Ibid.*, p. 66.
40. *Ibid.*, p. 64.
41. *Ibid.*, p. 67.
42. *Ibid.*
43. Frank Hugh Foster, in his famous work on New England theology, accuses Ballou of transgressing "the proprieties of a sober discussion by the bitterness of his expressions against orthodox theories." At the least, Foster feels, Ballou has little sympathy for or understanding of the positions of his opponents. Certainly Ballou's treatment of their theories is vigorous, in places witty. Yet if he is bitter, it is because of the reflections he believed were cast on his loving Father by the current theories of atonement. It should also be noted that, at this stage of Foster's development, he had little sympathy with Ballou. See Foster, *op. cit.*, p. 321.
44. H. Ballou, *A Treatise on Atonement*, pp. 67-68.
45. *Ibid.*, p. 67.
46. *Ibid.*, p. 68.
47. *Ibid.*, pp. 68-69.
48. *Ibid.*, p. 69.
49. *Ibid.*, p. 71.
50. *Ibid.*, p. 72.
51. *Ibid.*
52. Isaiah 53:5-6; I Timothy 2:5-6; I John 2:1-2; Hebrews 2:9.
53. *A Treatise on Atonement*, p. 74.
54. *Ibid.*, pp. 76-77.
55. *Ibid.*, pp. 81-82.
56. *Ibid.*, p. 83.
57. *Ibid.*, p. 87.
58. *Ibid.*, p. 91.
59. *Ibid.*, p. 92.
60. *Ibid.*, p. 94.
61. *Ibid.*, p. 96.
62. *Ibid.*, p. 98.
63. *Ibid.*
64. *Ibid.*, p. 102.
65. *Ibid.*, p. 98.
66. *Ibid.*, p. 99.
67. *Ibid.*, p. 100.
68. *Ibid.*, p. 99.
69. *Ibid.*
70. E.g. Romans 5:8 and I John 4:9, 10, 19.
71. *A Treatise on Atonement*, p. 102.
72. *Ibid.*, pp. 103-4.
73. Ballou's views on the trinity will be treated here as a unit. In the Treatise, however, he included them in his discussion of the various "erroneous" theories of atonement.
74. *A Treatise on Atonement*, p. vii.
75. *Ibid.*

76. *Ibid.*, p. 93.
77. *Ibid.*, p. 108.
78. He says that Mark 13:32 is still more explicit on this point. *Ibid.*
79. *Ibid.*, p. 109.
80. *Ibid.*, p. 110.
81. *Ibid.*, p. 112.
82. *Ibid.*, p. 109.
83. *Ibid.*, p. 112.
84. See Philippians 2:9. *Ibid.*, p. 110.
85. *Ibid.*
86. *Ibid.*
87. *Ibid.*
88. *Ibid.*, p. 111.
89. *Ibid.*, p. 113. It is interesting to read the exalted picture of Christ in the sermon Ballou preached this same year (1805) at the ordination of his friend Abner Kneeland. Although he stresses Christ's subordination to the Father, he still calls him "the true God and eternal life" and makes a strong scriptural case for Christ as the "head" of mankind. "Could it be proved, that a single individual of the human family did not belong to Christ, there could be no propriety in persuading such a person to believe in Christ as Redeemer, or of exhorting him to yield obedience to his commands." See *Sermon delivered at the Ordination of Abner Kneeland*, pp. 9-11, 13.
90. *A Treatise on Atonement*, p. 113.
91. *Ibid.*, p. 117.
92. *Ibid.*, p. 118.
93. *Ibid.*
94. *Ibid.*, p. 115.
95. *Ibid.*
96. *Ibid.*, p. 119.
97. *Ibid.*, pp. 119-20.
98. *Ibid.*, p. 120.
99. *Ibid.*, pp. 126-27.
100. *Ibid.*, p. 127.
101. *Ibid.*, p. 129.
102. *Ibid.*, p. 130.
103. *Ibid.*, pp. 130-31.
104. *Ibid.*, pp. 125-26.
105. *Ibid.*, p. 126.
106. "If sin and guilt had never been introduced into our system, the plan of grace, by atonement, could never have been exhibited." *Ibid.*, p. 61.
107. *Ibid.*, pp. 130-32.
108. *Ibid.*, p. 134.
109. *Ibid.*, p. 171. Foster, *op. cit.*, p. 323, believes that Ballou misrepresents the Hopkinsians in his discussion of the "supposition that eternal punishment is necessary to the greatest amount of happiness." He finds Ballou's statement of the Hopkinsian positions "very objectionable." Foster probably did not take into consideration the fact that Ballou is answering, not only the arguments of the eminent theologians of that school, but also those of the general-store Hopkinsians, who no doubt stated the case quite differently from the masters.
110. *A Treatise on Atonement*, p. 137.
111. *Ibid.*, pp. 137-38.
112. *Ibid.*, p. 153.
113. *Ibid.*, pp. 140ff. He feels that it is not necessary to "labor this point largely, for it has been done faithfully by an able author, whose works are among us." If by "among us" Ballou means Universalists, he is re-

ferring to Elhanan Winchester, who discusses "unlimited words" in *The Universal Restoration*. See especially "Dialogue One," pp. 5-17. Ballou may be referring, however, to Charles Chauncy, *op. cit.*
114. *A Treatise on Atonement*, pp. 142ff.
115. *Ibid.*, pp. 148-49.
116. *Ibid.*, p. 148.
117. *Ibid.*, p. 169.
118. *Ibid.*, p. 176.
119. *Ibid.*, p. 171.
120. *Ibid.*, p. 214.
121. *Ibid.*, p. 204.
122. *Ibid.*, p. 216.

CHAPTER X. PORTSMOUTH

1. Whittemore, *Life of Ballou*, I, 311.
2. Records of the Universalist Society at Portsmouth. Bk. I (1793-1852), pp. 1-4.
3. *Ibid.*, pp. 13-14.
4. Minutes of Meeting, January 26, 1807. *Ibid.*, p. 71.
5. *Ibid.*, pp. 78, 83.
6. Minutes of Meeting, April 26, 1809. *Ibid.*, p. 85.
7. *Ibid.*
8. H. Ballou, *Discourse delivered at the Installation of Edward Turner*.
9. Records of the Universalist Society at Portsmouth. Bk. I (1793-1852), p. 87.
10. Minutes of Meeting, October 9, 1809. *Ibid.*, pp. 89-90.
11. Letter from Hosea Ballou to the Wardens and Committee of the Universalist Society in Portsmouth. *Ibid.*, pp. 90-91.
12. The moving expense was $36.82. Warden's Account, July 14, 1810, Universalist Society of Portsmouth.
13. Turner, *Discourse delivered at the Installation of Hosea Ballou*.
14. Whittemore, *Life of Ballou*, I, 315.
15. *Series of Letters between Buckminster, Walton and Ballou*, p. 56.
16. Buckminster was the father of Joseph Stevens Buckminster, minister of the Brattle Street Church in Boston and one of the circle of liberal ministers who inclined toward Unitarianism. The younger Buckminster died in 1812 (one day before his father) before the outbreak of the Unitarian controversy. Whittemore, *Life of Ballou*, I, 317.
17. *Series of Letters between Buckminster, Walton and Ballou*, p. 3.
18. *Ibid.*, pp. 4-5.
19. *Ibid.*, pp. 6-7.
20. *Ibid.*, p. 7.
21. *Ibid.*, pp. 11-16.
22. *Ibid.*, p. 19.
23. *Ibid.*, p. 23.
24. *Ibid.*, p. 24.
25. *Ibid.*, p. 29.
26. *Ibid.*, pp. 31-32.
27. *Ibid.*, pp. 36-37.
28. *Ibid.*, pp. 41-43.
29. *Ibid.*, p. 56.
30. *Ibid.*, p. 44.
31. *Ibid.*
32. *Ibid.*, pp. 44-46.
33. *Ibid.*, p. 46.
34. *Ibid.*, p. 47.

35. *Ibid.*, p. 53.
36. *Ibid.*, p. 61.
37. *Ibid.*, p. 64.
38. *Ibid.*, p. 67.
39. *Ibid.*, pp. 67-68.
40. He justifies this position on the basis of Acts 5:31 and 11:18. *Ibid.*, p. 69.
41. *Ibid.*, pp. 75-76.
42. Eddy, *op. cit.*, II, 132.
43. Letter, November 5, 1810. Quoted in *Universalist Quarterly*, New Series VIII (July 1871), 272n.
44. Whittemore, *Life of Ballou*, I, 353.
45. *Gospel Visitant*, I, 220-23.
46. *Ibid.*
47. *Child's Scriptural Catechism.*
48. Whittemore, *Life of Ballou*, I, 316.
49. *Child's Catechism*, pp. 5f., 7f.
50. See especially *ibid.*, pp. 15-18.
51. Whittemore, *Life of Ballou*, I, 316. Whittemore comments that, because of this difficulty of comprehension on the part of the child, the booklet was never widely used. Yet the seventh edition of the catechism was published in Boston twenty-seven years later!
52. *Notes on the Parables* (enlarged ed., 1812), pp. 198-200.
53. Forrester, *Strictures.*
54. H. Ballou, *Attempt with a Soft Answer to Turn Away Wrath*, p. 15.
55. Forrester, *Remarks.*
56. Whittemore, *Life of Ballou*, I, 376.
57. "His Universalism and his faith in American Democracy in many points coincided." Safford, *Hosea Ballou*, p. 107.
58. M. M. Ballou, *Biography of Ballou*, p. 219.
59. An unfortunate but, at this distance, humorous incident happened at an ordination service at the General Convention of 1829. The ordination prayer was assigned to the Reverend Joshua Flagg, "a man of strong feelings on political matters. . . ." Flagg was a supporter of General Andrew Jackson, who, the previous March, had been inaugurated as President of the United States. Near the close of his ordination prayer, Flagg raised his voice in "ardent supplication" in behalf of Jackson: "And, O Lord, wilt thou remember thy servant, the President of these United States, elevated to his high position by the free-will suffrages of his grateful fellow-citizens. Wilt thou bless him, O Lord, and crown him with success; and may he be enabled to put down all his political foes, as he put down the British hosts at the battle of New Orleans." Thomas Whittemore records that "such a petition, so out of place at any time in public worship, but more especially as a part of an *ordaining* prayer, sent a shudder over the assembly, especially the preachers; and Mr. Ballou felt it his duty to administer a faithful rebuke to Mr. Flagg, as they walked away from the church at the close of the service." Whittemore, *Life of Ballou*, III, 58.
60. H. Ballou, *A Sermon appropriate to the Occasion of a Day of Humiliation and Prayer.*
61. *Ibid.*, p. 1. (Pagination used here is that of a typed copy to be found in the collection of the Universalist Historical Society and at the Unitarian-Universalist Church of Portsmouth.)
62. *Ibid.*, p. 2.
63. *Ibid.*, pp. 2-5.
64. *Ibid.*, pp. 6-7.
65. *Ibid.*, p. 7.

66. *Ibid.*, p. 10.
67. *Ibid.*, p. 1.
68. Whittemore, *Life of Ballou*, I, 379.
69. *Ibid.*, pp. 379-80.
70. Minutes of Meeting, June 21, 1813. Records of the Universalist Society at Portsmouth. Bk. I (1793-1852), pp. 104-5.
71. *Ibid.*, p. 105.
72. *Ibid.*
73. *Ibid.*
74. *Ibid.*, p. 104.
75. *Ibid.*, p. 105.
76. Financial Receipts of the Universalist Society at Portsmouth, June 1812.
77. Whittemore, *Life of Ballou*, I, 403.
78. H. S. Ballou, *Hosea Ballou, 2d*, pp. 55, 56, 63.
79. *Ibid.*, p. 55.
80. *Ibid.*, p. 56.

CHAPTER XI. SALEM

1. Letter from Committee of the Universalist Society in Salem to Hosea Ballou, April 26, 1815.
2. Letter from Hosea Ballou to Committee of the Universalist Society in Salem. Portsmouth, April 28, 1815.
3. Letter from Committee of the Universalist Society in Salem to Hosea Ballou, May 10, 1815.
4. Minutes of Meeting, May 22, 1815. Records of the Universalist Society at Portsmouth. Bk. I (1793-1852), p. 112.
5. Minutes of Meeting, June 5, 1815. *Ibid.*, p. 114.
6. Letter from Committee of the Universalist Society at Portsmouth to the Universalist Society in Salem, June 5, 1815.
7. Letter from Committee of the Universalist Society in Salem to the Universalist Society at Portsmouth, July 1, 1815.
8. Letters from Edward Turner to Joseph Newhall, April 5, 1813; January 5, 1814; February 18, 1814.
9. Perley Putnam's Book, pp. 1, 6.
10. Record of Proceedings of an Ecclesiastical Council assembled in Salem, Massachusetts, for purpose of examination of the Rev. Edward Turner.—, June 21, 1809.
11. Whittemore, *Life of Ballou*, I, 410.
12. Perley Putnam's Book, p. 58.
13. *Ibid.*, p. 21.
14. Letter from Hosea Ballou to Nathaniel Frothingham, September 6, 1815.
15. $168.20. Warden's Accounts of the Universalist Society at Portsmouth, 1816.
16. Meeting of the Proprietors and Occupants of Pews of the Universalist Society of Salem, April 29, 1816. Perley Putnam's Book, p. 59.
17. Letter from Hosea Ballou to the Committee of the Universalist Society of Salem, May 21, 1816.
18. Minutes of Meeting, May 26, 1816. Perley Putnam's Book, p. 60.
19. Letter from Hosea Ballou to the Committee of the Universalist Society of Salem, June 15, 1816.
20. [Hosea Ballou], "A Candid Examination and Scriptural Trial of a Sermon entitled God a Rewarder,—delivered at the Tabernacle in Salem, Lord's Day, January 27, 1811. By Samuel Worcester, A. M." *Gospel Visitant*, I (September 1811), 65-99.
21. This inference is gained from H. Ballou, *Letter to Brown Emerson*, p. 3.
22. *Ibid.*

23. *Ibid.*
24. *Ibid.*, p. 14.
25. Dole, *Letter to Ballou*, p. 3.
26. *Ibid.*
27. *Ibid.*, p. 4.
28. Whittemore, *Life of Ballou*, I, 412.
29. H. Ballou, *Divine Benevolence*.
30. *Ibid.*, p. 24.
31. Kelly, *Additional Reasons against Universalism*.
32. H. Ballou, *Divine Benevolence Further Vindicated*.
33. Whittemore, *Life of Ballou*, I, 412-13.
34. H. Ballou, *Series of Letters in Defence of Divine Revelation*.
35. *Ibid.*, p. 111.
36. *Ibid.*, p. 23
37. *Ibid.*, pp. 33f.
38. *Ibid.*, p. 174.
39. E.g. *ibid.*, pp. 62, 117, 147.
40. Paley, *Evidences of Christianity*.
41. H. Ballou, *Series of Letters in Defence of Divine Revelation*, pp. 149, 161, 182-84.
42. *Ibid.*, p. 182.
43. Whittemore, *Life of Ballou*, I, 126.
44. [H. Ballou and Turner], "Correspondence on the Doctrine of Future Punishment," *Gospel Visitant*, II, 115-25, 186-91, 206-11; III, 296-311, 269-79. [The pagination of Vol. III is confused. No. 1 continues the pagination of Vol. II and reaches p. 320. But No. 2 then starts with p. 221 and runs to p. 284.]
45. *Ibid.*, II, 116.
46. *Ibid.*
47. *Ibid.*, p. 115.
48. *Ibid.*
49. *Ibid.*, pp. 115-16.
50. *Ibid.*, p. 116.
51. *Ibid.*, I, 65-99.
52. *Ibid.*, pp. 91-92.
53. *Ibid.*, II, 116.
54. *Ibid.*, pp. 188, 189-91.
55. *Ibid.*, pp. 189-91.
56. *Ibid.*, p. 209.
57. Letter from Hosea Ballou to Thomas Whittemore, November 25, 1829. Whittemore, *Modern History of Universalism*, p. 438n.
58. *Gospel Visitant*, III, 297.
59. *Ibid.*, pp. 297ff.
60. Letter from Hosea Ballou to Thomas Whittemore, November 25, 1829. Whittemore, *Modern History of Universalism*, pp. 437-38n.

CHAPTER XII. THE CALL TO BOSTON

1. Eddy, *op. cit.*, II, 179.
2. "He was a *Trinitarian*, of the Sabellian school, and of course had a kind of Calvinistic notion of salvation which I could never comprehend, but on which he was always very sensitive." Charles Hudson, quoted in *Universalist Quarterly*, New Series VIII (April 1871), 178n.
3. *Account of the Celebration of the Seventy-Fifth Anniversary of the Second Society*, p. 13.
4. Whittemore, *Life of Ballou*, I, 419.

5. On the site where the Boston Five Cents Savings Bank stands today: 30-32 School Street, at the corner of Province Street.
6. Safford, *op. cit.*, p. 211.
7. The dedication had originally been scheduled for the previous day but was postponed because it conflicted with the Brighton cattle show! *Account of the Celebration of the Seventy-Fifth Anniversary of the Second Society*, p. 15.
8. Jones, *Dedication Sermon.*
9. *Account of the Celebration of the Seventy-Fifth Anniversary of the Second Society*, p. 18.
10. M. M. Ballou, *Biography of Ballou*, p. 105. Safford gives the figure as $2,000; *op. cit.*, p. 268.
11. According to Perley Putnam, a short while before Ballou left Salem, he asked the society for permission to visit a friend in Vermont. But instead of going to Vermont, he preached for the Second Society in Boston and agreed to become its minister when the new meetinghouse was finished. It was soon rumored about Salem that Ballou was to leave for Boston. When some of his parishioners inquired if the rumor were true, he replied that he understood that the Boston society was to "make overtures to him" but he did not know if he would accept their offer. The persons who asked him had already heard that he had accepted the Boston offer and that a house had been rented there for him. The people of the Salem church would not have minded his moving to Boston "if Mr Ballou had behaved honorable and told the truth." Perley Putnam's Book, p. 18.
12. *Ibid.*, pp. 18, 21.
13. A. Ballou, *Ballous in America*, pp. 131, 325.
14. Letter from Hosea Ballou to Henry Archer, Clerk of the Universalist Society of Salem. Boston, July 3, 1818.
15. Letter from Hosea Ballou to Joseph Newhall, Boston, May 15, 1819.
16. Perley Putnam's Book, pp. 66, 69.
17. List and Amounts of Debts against the Universal Society in Salem, June 1821.
18. It is possible that Ballou transferred the notes to a gentleman by the name of Samuel H. Reed. Copies of two letters from Nathaniel Frothingham of the church to Reed, dated November 15, 1820, and July 2, 1821, are in the files of the Salem Society and appear to indicate that this may have been the case. In both letters Frothingham apologizes for the society's inability to meet his demands. What the transaction between Ballou, Reed and the church involved is not clear.

Perley Putnam recorded in his notebook the following jumbled account, which, if true, does no credit to Ballou: "When Mr Ballou left us the committee Settled with him and for the Balance they then owed him they gave him two Society notes, for the Balance that was then due Which notes He carried to Vermont and there sold them and took a mortgade [*sic*] of the mans farm with a condition that if he the farmer did not pay the amount of the notes at a given time the farm Should be his (Ballous) The man who held the notes Called on the committee to pay the amount of the notes which was not in the power of the committee to do at the time the farmer informed Mr Ballou of the circumstances He says well if you cannot pay me the amount of the morg [rest of word illegible] the farm is mine, Hence he turned the man from his farm and put his disipated Son on to it He (Ballou) than caused the notes to be Sued, Got Judgment against the Society, attached all the Pews in the House belonging to the Corporation and had them Sold at auction The whole of which did not sell for much more than to pay the court

Expenses, after that he Scolded the Sheriff because he did not *attach and Sell the Pulpit*." Perley Putnam's Book, p. 18.

19. *Ibid.*, p. 64.
20. *Ibid.*, p. 76.
21. Letters from Hosea Ballou to Joseph Newhall [for the Committee] of the Universalist Society of Salem, February 1, 1820; February 19, 1820; April 12, 1820; May 10, 1820; May 14, 1820; May 24, 1820.
22. *Account of the Celebration of the Seventy-Fifth Anniversary of the Second Society*, p. 17.
23. M. M. Ballou, *Biography of Ballou*, p. 99.
24. Whittemore, *Life of Ballou*, II, 66-67.
25. Paul Dean, "A Sermon, delivered at the Re-Installation of the Rev. Hosea Ballou to the Pastoral Care and Charge of the Second Universalist Church and Congregation, in School Street, Boston, Dec. 25 [1817]," *Gospel Visitant*, II (January 1818), 232-49.
26. *Ibid.*, pp. 243-44.
27. H. Ballou, *A Sermon delivered at the Second Universalist Meeting in Boston, on the evening of the First Sabbath in January.*
28. *Ibid.*
29. Merritt, *Strictures on Mr. Ballou's Sermon*, p. 4.
30. *Ibid.*, p. 8.
31. [H. Ballou], *Brief Reply to a Pamphlet entitled Strictures on Mr. Ballou's Sermon*; Merritt, *Vindication*; H. Ballou, *Brief Reply to a Pamphlet entitled a Vindication.*
32. Merritt, *Vindication*, p. 31.
33. Safford, *op. cit.*, p. 127.
34. M. M. Ballou, *Biography of Ballou*, p. 105.
35. Sylvanus Cobb. Quoted in *ibid.*, p. 110.
36. H. Ballou, *Series of Lecture Sermons.*
37. *Ibid.*, p. 289.
38. *Ibid.*, p. 131.
39. *Ibid.*, p. 412.
40. *Ibid.*, p. 415.
41. *Ibid.*, p. 387.
42. Whittemore, *Early Days*, pp. 155-56.

CHAPTER XIII. *THE UNIVERSALIST MAGAZINE*

1. Whittemore, *Life of Ballou*, II, 68-69.
2. *Universalist Magazine*, I, 1.
3. *Ibid.*
4. *Ibid.*, p. 58.
5. *Ibid.*, p. 59. See also pp. 146-47.
6. *Ibid.*, p. 117.
7. *Ibid.*, p. 62.
8. *Ibid.*, p. 180.
9. *Ibid.*, pp. 4, 6-7, 10, 16, 24, 28, 46, 60, 76, 80, 84, 86, 94, 100, 108, 116, 128, 134, 144, 152, 168, 180, 184, 188, 192, 196, 204, 208.
10. *Ibid.* p. 208.
11. *Ibid.*, p. 58.
12. *Ibid.*, pp. 73-74, 77-78, 81-82, 85.
13. *Ibid.*, pp. 23, 43, 47, 135.
14. *Ibid.*, pp. 9-10, 13-14. See Chap. XVII of this study.
15. *Ibid.*, II, 89, 93.
16. *Ibid.*, I, 125-26, 129.
17. *Ibid.*, p. 87

18. *Journal of Debates and Proceedings in the Convention to Revise the Constitution of Massachusetts.*
19. *Universalist Magazine,* II, 107, 111.
20. *Ibid.,* p. 107.
21. *Ibid.,* p. 111.
22. Quoted in *ibid.,* I, 11.
23. Quoted in *ibid.,* pp. 14, 22.
24. See *ibid.,* pp. 11, 14-15, 18-19, 22-23, 26-27, 31, 34-35, 38-39, 63.
25. Quoted in *ibid.,* p. 86.
26. Quoted in *ibid.,* p. 90. See also, p. 127.
27. E.g. *ibid.,* pp. 78-79, 83, 126, 130-31, 171.
28. *Ibid.,* p. 163.
29. *Ibid.,* II, 207.

CHAPTER XIV. THE BOSTON YEARS

1. Whittemore, *Life of Ballou,* II, 154.
2. M. M. Ballou, *Biography of Ballou,* p. 124.
3. H. Ballou and Turner, *Universalists' Hymn-Book,* p. iii.
4. *Ibid.,* p. 223.
5. *Universalist Magazine,* II (May 5, 1821), 179.
6. Whittemore, *Life of Ballou,* II, 156.
7. *Ibid.,* p. 157.
8. *Ibid.,* p. 196.
9. H. Ballou, Workbook.
10. H. Ballou, *Eleven Sermons;* H. Ballou, *Nine Sermons.*
11. Quoted by Safford, *op. cit.,* p. 213.
12. Brooks, "Hosea Ballou," *Universalist Quarterly,* New Series VII (October 1870), 406.
13. *Ibid.,* p. 407.
14. H. Ballou, *Select Sermons,* pp. 19-21. This sermon was delivered at the School Street Church on the "Second Sabbath" in February 1818.
15. Otis A. Skinner, quoted by Safford, *Hosea Ballou,* p. 188.
16. Whittemore, *Life of Ballou,* II, 173.
17. Brooks, "Hosea Ballou," *Universalist Quarterly,* New Series VII (October 1870), 408.
18. *Ibid.,* p. 409.
19. Safford, *op. cit.,* p. 210.
20. Thomas Baldwin Thayer quoted in *ibid.,* pp. 213-14.
21. Otis A. Skinner quoted in *ibid.,* p. 190.
22. Whittemore, *Life of Ballou,* II, 200.
23. *Ibid.,* I, 359.
24. Whittemore, *Early Days,* p. 118.
25. *Ibid.,* p. 164.
26. Whittemore, *Life of Ballou,* II, 129.
27. Safford, *op. cit.,* p. 191.
28. Whittemore, *Early Days,* p. 167.
29. *Ibid.,* p. 172.
30. *Universalist Magazine,* I, 184.
31. Whittemore, *Life of Ballou,* II, 130.
32. *Ibid.,* pp. 130-31.
33. *Ibid.,* p. 133.
34. Whittemore, *Early Days,* p. 223.
35. A. Ballou, *Ballous in America,* p. 131.
36. Whittemore, *Life of Ballou,* II, 133, 148.
37. *Ibid.,* p. 154n.

38. Quoted in *Our Paper*, monthly newspaper of the Unitarian Church of Woburn, Massachusetts, I (April 1876), 66.
39. Quoted in *ibid*.
40. H. S. Ballou, *Hosea Ballou*, 2d, p. 76.
41. *Universalist Magazine*, II, 23. See also p. 111.
42. *Ibid.*, IV, 104.
43. M. M. Ballou, *Biography of Ballou*, pp. 112-14.
44. His own account in *Universalist Magazine*, III, 122.
45. *Ibid.*, p. 121.
46. *Ibid*.
47. H. Ballou, *Eleven Sermons*.
48. *Ibid.*, p. v.
49. *Ibid.*, pp. 132-41.
50. *Select Sermons*, p. 183. Cf. *ibid*.
51. Kneeland felt compelled to point out the omission in the critical notes he appended to the Philadelphia collection. *Eleven Sermons*, pp. 157-59.
52. *Ibid.*, p. 7.
53. *Ibid.*, p. 14.
54. *Ibid.*, p. 39.
55. *Ibid.*, pp. 136-37.
56. Whittemore, *Life of Ballou*, II, 332n.
57. *Ibid.*, p. 209.
58. M. M. Ballou, *Biography of Ballou*, pp. 193-94.
59. *Ibid.*, pp. 194-95.
60. Whittemore, *Life of Ballou*, IV, 329.
61. M. M. Ballou, *Biography of Ballou*, p. 145.
62. *Ibid.*, pp. 201-2.

CHAPTER XV. ULTRA-UNIVERSALISM

1. H. Ballou, *A Treatise on Atonement* (1805 ed.), pp. 126-27.
2. Letter from Hosea Ballou to Thomas Whittemore, February 25, 1829. Whittemore, *Modern History of Universalism*, p. 437n.
3. As told to Russell Streeter. Balch, "Caleb Rich," *Universalist Quarterly*, New Series IX (January 1872), p. 76.
4. Eddy, *op. cit.*, II, 266.
5. Quoted in *ibid.*, p. 267.
6. *Ibid*.
7. *Ibid.*, p. 268. The extracts published were from letters by Edward Turner, Thomas Jones, Sebastian Streeter, Paul Dean, Samuel C. Loveland, David Pickering, James Babbit, Hosea Ballou, 2d, Jonathan Wallace, Robert Bartlett and Russell Streeter.
8. *Universalist Magazine*, IV, 126.
9. *Ibid*.
10. H. Ballou, *Lecture Sermons*, pp. 368ff.
11. *Ibid.*, p. 211.
12. *Ibid.*, pp. 295-96.
13. The three instances enumerated have been pointed out by Eddy, *Universalism in America*, II, 272-73. I believe that Eddy is correct in limiting these to three.
14. *Universalist Magazine*, I, 31.
15. *Ibid.*, pp. 109-10, 113.
16. *Ibid.*, II, 154-55.
17. Whittemore, *Life of Ballou*, II, 161.
18. *Universalist Magazine*, II, 58.
19. Whittemore, *Life of Ballou*, II, 160.

20. *Ibid.*, p. 161.
21. *Universalist Magazine*, II, 207. Whittemore gives conflicting accounts of the reason for Ballou's suspension of his editorial labors. In the *Life of Ballou*, II, 161-62, he attributes it to health; in *Early Days*, p. 310, he says that it was "in consequence of some honorable difference of opinion between him and the publisher." It may have been a combination of both.
22. Whittemore, *Early Days*, p. 311.
23. Letter from "EAR," *Universalist Magazine*, III, 1.
24. *Ibid.*, p. 97.
25. *Ibid.*, p. 125. Identified as Wood by Eddy, *op. cit.*, II, 274.
26. *Universalist Magazine*, III, 131.
27. *Ibid.*, pp. 150-51.
28. *Ibid.* p. 151.
29. *Ibid.*
30. *Ibid.*, p. 154.
31. *Ibid.*, p. 166.
32. *Ibid.*, pp. 170, 179.
33. Whittemore, *Life of Ballou*, II, 193.
34. *Universalist Magazine*, III, 179.
35. *Ibid.*, p. 183.
36. *Ibid.*, p. 191.
37. *Ibid.*
38. *Ibid.*, III, 181, 198; IV, 10, 26, 46, 53, 71, 90.
39. *Ibid.*, IV, 102.
40. Eddy, *op. cit.*, II, 282.
41. Letter from Edward Turner to his daughter, n.d. [but after his removal to Portsmouth in 1824], in Brooks, "Edward Turner," *Universalist Quarterly*, New Series VIII (July 1871), 262.
42. Letter from Charles Hudson to E. G. Brooks, n. d. *ibid.* (April 1871), 179n.
43. Letter from Edward Turner to Russell Streeter, January 21, 1823, in *ibid.*, 180n.
44. Letter from Edward Turner to Russell Streeter, October 24, 1822, quoted in *ibid.*, p. 176n.
45. Letter from Edward Turner to Russell Streeter, January 1823, quoted in *ibid.*
46. Reprinted in Eddy, *op. cit.*, II, 282.
47. *Ibid.*, pp. 283-84.
48. *Ibid.*, p. 287.
49. *Ibid.*, p. 289.
50. *Ibid.*
51. *Ibid.*, p. 290.
52. *Universalist Magazine*, IV, 125.
53. Letter from Edward Turner to his daughter, n.d. [but after his removal to Portsmouth in 1824], quoted by Brooks, *Universalist Quarterly*, New Series VIII (July 1871), 262.
54. Whittemore, *Life of Ballou*, II, 215.
55. Levi Briggs soon disclaimed any concern with the Appeal, as did Barzillai Streeter. See *Universalist Magazine*, IV, 125, 135.
56. *Ibid.*, p. 122.
57. Whittemore, *Life of Ballou*, II, 222n.
58. *Universalist Magazine*, IV, 125-27.
59. *Ibid.*, p 125.
60. *Ibid.*
61. *Ibid.*, p. 126.

62. Whittemore, *Life of Ballou*, II, 222.
63. Signed February 18, 1823. Text given by Brooks, *Universalist Quarterly*, New Series VIII (July 1871), 263n.
64. *Universalist Magazine*, IV, 152.
65. Letter from Edward Turner to his daughter, n.d. [but after his removal to Portsmouth in 1824], quoted by Brooks, *Universalist Quarterly*, New Series VIII (July 1871), 265.
66. Letter from Hosea Ballou to Edward Turner, Boston, May 22, 1827, quoted by Chambré, "Hosea Ballou and Edward Turner—A Contribution to the 'Truth of History,'" *ibid.*, New Series X (January 1873), 46.
67. Letter from Edward Turner to his daughter, n.d. [but after 1824], quoted by Brooks, *ibid.*, New Series VIII (July 1871), 270.
68. Letter from Edward Turner to Hosea Ballou, Charlestown, February 4, 1823, in Chambré, *ibid.*, New Series X (January 1873), 48.
69. Letter from Hosea Ballou to Edward Turner, Boston, February 10, 1823, in *ibid.*, pp. 48-49.
70. Records of the Second Universalist Society of Boston, March 9, 1823, quoted in *ibid.*, p. 43.
71. Letter from Hosea Ballou to Edward Turner, June 11, 1827, quoted in *ibid.*, pp. 44-46.
72. Whittemore, *Life of Ballou*, II, 230-32.
73. *Ibid.*, p. 232. For the text of the settlement see Chambré, *Universalist Quarterly*, New Series X (January 1873), 47. Edward Turner later accused Ballou of holding out for stiffer terms than those presented. Ballou pointed out that, in the committee meeting, "I proposed that each should write his own mind, and then we would all read what was written. And if any one should be acceptable to all, that should be returned as the report of the Committee. All acceeded [*sic*] to mine; and this was all the 'standing out' there was, as to me." Letter from Hosea Ballou to Edward Turner, Boston, May 28, 1827 (included in the Chambré article, p. 48).
74. Whittemore, *Life of Ballou*, II, 235
75. As reported by Whittemore, *ibid.*, p. 259
76. *Ibid.*
77. Quoted by Eddy, *op. cit.*, II, 321
78. *Universalist Magazine*, IV (May 28, 1823), 196.
79. Balfour, *Three Essays*; Hudson, *Reply*; Balfour, *Letters*.
80. Eddy, *op. cit.*, II, 331f.
81. *Ibid.*, pp. 330-32.
82. Brooks, "Charles Turner," *Universalist Quarterly*, New Series VIII (April 1871), 157-58.
83. Whittemore, *Life of Ballou*, III, 87.

CHAPTER XVI. DEATH AND GLORY

1. Whittemore, *Life of Ballou*, II, 407.
2. *Ibid.*
3. *Ibid.*
4. *Ibid.*
5. *Universalist Magazine*, IX, 207.
6. Whittemore, *Life of Ballou*, III, 13.
7. *Ibid.*
8. H. S. Ballou, *Hosea Ballou*, 2d, p. 143.
9. *Universalist Expositor*, I.
10. *Ibid.*
11. *Ibid.*, II.
12. Whittemore, *Life of Ballou*, III, 131.

13. *Ibid.* The original *Universalist Expositor,* edited by the two Ballous, was later considered valuable enough to be reprinted in New York in 1846.
14. Whittemore, *Life of Ballou,* III, 148-49.
15. J. G. Adams, *Fifty Notable Years,* p. 92.
16. Not only as preacher but also as selectman, superintendent of schools, member of the state legislature, member of three constitutional conventions, justice of the peace, town clerk, road commissioner and president of a bank. A. Ballou, *Ballous in America,* p. 326.
17. Whittemore, *Life of Ballou,* III, 122-23.
18. *Ibid.,* pp. 169, 199.
19. H. Ballou, *Nine Sermons.*
20. *Ibid.,* p. iii.
21. *Ibid.,* pp. 119-21.
22. *Ibid.,* p. 134.
23. H. Ballou, *Notes on the Parables* (1832 ed.), pp. 5-7.
24. H. Ballou, *A Treatise on Atonement* (1832 ed.), p. 12.
25. A particularly good example of this can be noted in *ibid.,* pp. 31-32.
26. H. Ballou, *A Treatise on Atonement* (1828 ed.), pp. xv-xvii.
27. *A Treatise on Atonement* (1832 ed.), p. 32.
28. *Ibid.,* p. 33.
29. *Ibid.,* p. 12.
30. Compare the 1805 edition, p. 115, with the 1832 edition, p. 120.
31. *Universalist Magazine,* I, 73-74, 77-78, 81-82, 85.
32. H. Ballou, *Examination of the Doctrine of Future Retribution,* p. 8.
33. *Ibid.,* pp. 9-10.
34. *Ibid.,* p. 11.
35. *Ibid.,* pp. 14-15.
36. *Ibid.,* p. 18.
37. *Ibid.,* p. 19.
38. *Ibid.,* pp. 22-23.
39. *Ibid.,* p. 24.
40. *Ibid.,* p. 28.
41. *Ibid.,* pp. 35-36.
42. *Ibid.,* pp. 36-37.
43. *Ibid.,* p. 37.
44. *Ibid.,* pp. 37-38.
45. *Ibid.,* p. 38.
46. *Ibid.,* pp. 38-39.
47. *Ibid.,* p. 39.
48. *Ibid.,* p. 44.
49. *Ibid.,* pp. 45-46.
50. *Ibid.,* pp. 49ff.
51. *Ibid.,* pp. 47-48.
52. *Ibid.,* pp. 51ff.
53. *Ibid.,* pp. 60-61.
54. *Ibid.,* p. 80.
55. *Ibid.,* pp. 77-79.
56. *Ibid.,* pp. 80-82.
57. *Ibid.,* pp. 86-88.
58. *Ibid.,* pp. 89-91.
59. *Ibid.,* pp. 182-83.
60. J. C. Adams, *Hosea Ballou and the Gospel Renaissance,* p. 18.

CHAPTER XVII. "SALVATION IRRESPECTIVE OF CHARACTER"

1. Whittemore, *Life of Ballou,* II, 90. See the comments of Hosea Ballou, *Universalist Magazine,* II, 18-19.

2. Article in *The Christian Disciple*, 1823, quoted by Whittemore, *Life of Ballou*, II, 237-38.
3. Adin Ballou writing in *The Universalist*, February 4, 1871; quoted by Eddy, *op. cit.*, II, 336-39.
4. A. Ballou, *Autobiography*, p. 218.
5. Professor Alfred S. Cole in a conversation with the present writer.
6. Foster, *New England Theology*, pp. 325-26.
7. Whittemore, *Life of Ballou*, II, 322. See also H. Ballou, "Commendation and Reproof of Unitarians," *Select Sermons*, p. 333, in which he asks, concerning this practice of Unitarians, the prophetic question: "How will this appear in the history of these times, an half a century hence?"
8. *Universalist Magazine*, I (July 10, 1819), 6.
9. H. Ballou, *Select Sermons*, p. 323.
10. *Ibid.*, p. 324.
11. *Ibid.*, pp. 325-26.
12. *Ibid.*, p. 329.
13. *Universalist Magazine*, I (July 17, 1819), 9-10; (July 24, 1819), 13-14.
14. *Ibid.*, p. 9.
15. *Ibid.*, p. 10.
16. *Ibid.*
17. *Ibid.*, p. 14.
18. *Journal of Debates and Proceedings in the Convention to Revise the Constitution of Massachusetts.*
19. Channing, *Religion a Social Principle.*
20. *Ibid.*, pp. 5-6.
21. *Ibid.*, p. 6.
22. *Ibid.*, p. 8.
23. *Ibid.*, p. 15.
24. *Ibid.*, p. 18.
25. See announcement of publication, *Universalist Magazine*, II (December 23, 1820), 103.
26. H. Ballou, *Strictures on a Sermon entitled "Religion a Social Principle."*
27. *Ibid.*, pp. 3ff.
28. *Ibid.*, pp. 5ff.
29. *Ibid.*, pp. 7ff.
30. *Ibid.*, p. 10.
31. *Ibid.*, p. 11.
32. *Ibid.*, p. 13.
33. *Ibid.*, p. 15.
34. Channing, *Works*, pp. 187-88.
35. Channing, *Works*, pp. 347-53.
36. *Ibid.*, p. 350.
37. *Ibid.*
38. *Ibid.*
39. *Ibid.*, p. 351.
40. *Ibid.*, p. 353.
41. H. Ballou, *Candid Examination of Dr. Channing's Discourse on the Evil of Sin.*
42. *Ibid.*, pp. 4-5.
43. *Ibid.*, p. 5.
44. *Ibid.*, pp. 6-7.
45. *Ibid.*, p. 8.
46. *Ibid.*
47. *Ibid.*, p. 9.
48. *Ibid.*, p. 11.
49. Chadwick, *Channing*, p. 254.
50. Chadwick states that Channing's thought "drew nearer and nearer to

Ballou." *Ibid.* This same opinion is expressed in a letter to the present writer from Channing's latest biographer, Professor Arthur W. Brown of Syracuse University, author of *Always Young for Liberty, a Biography of Channing.* Brown, it is interesting to note, takes no notice of Ballou in his book.   .
51. Whittemore, *Life of Ballou*, II, 287-88.
52. *Trumpet*, XXII (August 18, 1849), 37.
53. *Ibid.*
54. *Ibid.*
55. *Ibid.*
56. Quoted by Abel C. Thomas, *Autobiography*, p. 401.

CHAPTER XVIII. "A FATHER IN ISRAEL"

1. Fisher, *op. cit.*, p. 39.
2. M. M. Ballou, *Biography of Ballou*, p. 352.
3. Whittemore, *Life of Ballou*, III, 282.
4. Statistics derived from Guild, *The Universalist's Book of Reference.*
5. The Ballous lived in several houses during their years in Boston. These were on Blossom, Mason, Garden and Myrtle Streets.
6. Among Maturin Murray Ballou's many accomplishments was the founding of *Ballou's Pictorial,* reputed to be the first illustrated newspaper in the United States, and the founding of the *Boston Globe,* of which he was the first editor.
7. The Ballou genealogy may be traced in A. Ballou, *Ballous in America.*
8. Safford, *op. cit.*, p. 224.
9. M. M. Ballou, *Biography of Ballou*, pp. 196-97.
10. Safford, *op. cit.*, p. 268.
11. Quoted by M. M. Ballou, *Biography of Ballou*, p. 216.
12. *Ibid.*, p. 141.
13. Whittemore, *Life of Ballou*, III, 12.
14. M. M. Ballou, *Biography of Ballou*, p. 142.
15. H. Ballou, *Series of Letters in Defence of Divine Revelation.*
16. Whittemore, *Life of Ballou*, III, 38.
17. *Ibid.*, p. 61.
18. *Ibid.*, p. 62.
19. *Ibid.*, p. 274.
20. Quoted by Safford, *op. cit.*, pp. 115-16.
21. Whittemore, *Life of Ballou*, III, 179. I am informed by the Reverend Harry M. Sherman that the statute under which Kneeland was indicted is still on the books of the Commonwealth of Massachusetts.
22. Lalone, *op. cit.*, p. 24.
23. Quoted by Whittemore, *Life of Ballou*, III, 180.
24. *Ibid.*, p. 275.
25. *Ibid.*, p. 275n.
26. *Account of the Celebration of the Seventy-Fifth Anniversary of the Second Society*, p. 24.
27. *Ibid.*, p. 25.
28. *Ibid.*
29. Letter from H. B. Soule to a friend, 1844, quoted by C. A. Soule, *op. cit.*, p. 84.
30. *Ibid.*
31. *Account of the Celebration of the Seventy-Fifth Anniversary of the Second Society*, pp. 24-25.
32. Emerson, *op. cit.*, p. 176.
33. *Account of the Celebration of the Seventy-Fifth Anniversary of the Second Society*, p. 25.

34. Ellis, *op. cit.*, p. 108.
35. *Ibid.*
36. "Order of Exercises, at the Installation of the Rev. E. H. Chapin, as Associate Pastor of the Second Universalist Society, Boston," inserted in the Choir Record Book, January 29, 1843—December 26, 1847, of the Second Universalist Society in Boston.
37. Ellis, *op. cit.*, p. 110.
38. Safford, *op. cit.*, p. 230.
39. *Ibid.*, p. 231.
40. *Ibid.*, p. 230.
41. Chapin Letter of Resignation as Pastor of the Second Universalist Society of Boston, February 5, 1848.
42. H. S. Ballou, *Hosea Ballou, 2d*, p. 237.
43. Letter from Committee of the Fourth Universalist Society of New York to E. H. Chapin. Boston, January 12, 1848.
44. Letter from A. A. Miner to Newton Talbot, Clerk of the Second Universalist Society of Boston. Lowell, April 12, 1848.
45. Whittemore, *Life of Ballou*, IV, 89.
46. Safford, *op. cit.*, p. 232.
47. Emerson, *op. cit.*, p. 181.
48. *Ibid.*, p. 187.
49. *Ibid.*, pp. 187-88.
50. *Ibid.*, p. 177.
51. Sunday School Minute Book, May 31, 1835—July 14, 1839, Second Universalist Society in Boston.
52. *Ibid.*
53. H. Ballou, *Christian Catechism*, p. xiv.
54. Quoted by Whittemore, *Life of Ballou*, III, 305.
55. *Ibid.*
56. *Trumpet*, XXIII (October 26, 1850), 78.
57. *Ibid.*
58. Eddy, *op. cit.*, II, 413.
59. H. Ballou, *Lecture Sermons*, p. 201. See also, *Nine Sermons*, p. 130.
60. Walnut Hill Evangelical Seminary Trustees Record Book, p. 1.
61. *Ibid.*, p. 3.
62. *Ibid.*, p. 4.
63. *Trumpet*, XIV, 29, 57, 61, 84.
64. *Ibid.*, p. 29.
65. *Ibid.*
66. *Ibid.*, p. 72.
67. Not until 1856 did Universalists achieve the founding of their first theological school. Around a nucleus at Canton, New York, was to grow St. Lawrence University. Walnut Hill in Medford, Massachusetts, was to become the site of Tufts College, which opened in 1852 with Hosea Ballou, 2d, as its first president. The Divinity School at Tufts came into existence in 1869.
68. Whittemore, *Life of Ballou*, IV, 78.
69. *Ibid.*, pp. 78-79.
70. *Ibid.*, p. 79.
71. *Ibid.*, pp. 79-80.
72. *Ibid.*, p. 80.
73. *Trumpet*, XX (December 11, 1847), 102.
74. In this statement Ballou made his one known reference to the Winchester Profession of Faith, which he had helped to write in 1803.
75. *Trumpet*, XX (December 11, 1847), 102.
76. *Ibid.*, pp. 102-3.
77. Whittemore, *Life of Ballou*, IV, 110.

78. *Ibid.*, p. 82n.
79. Pratt was paid one hundred dollars for executing this portrait (Treasurer's Account Book, 1884–1869, Second Universalist Society of Boston, p. 78). It now hangs in the Miner Theological Hall of Crane Theological School at Tufts University.
80. Whittemore, *Life of Ballou*, IV, 127.
81. H. Ballou, *Voice of Universalists*, pp. 14-15.
82. *Ibid.*, p. 16.
83. *Ibid.*, pp. 41ff.
84. *Ibid.*, p. 22.
85. *Ibid.*, p. 127.
86. Brooks, "Hosea Ballou," *Universalist Quarterly*, New Series VII (October 1870), 409.
87. Whittemore, *Life of Ballou*, IV, 194.
88. Skinner, "Biographical Sketch of Rev. Hosea Ballou," *Universalist Miscellany*, III (May 1846), 433.
89. H. Ballou, 2d, "Dogmatic and Religious History of Universalism in America," *Universalist Quarterly*, V (January 1848), 80.
90. H. Ballou, *Valedictory Discourse*, p. 51.
91. *Ibid.*, p. 53.
92. Whittemore, *Life of Ballou*, IV, 219.

CHAPTER XIX. THE LAST DAYS

1. Whittemore, *Life of Ballou*, IV, 227.
2. *Ibid.*, pp. 261-62.
3. M. M. Ballou, *Biography of Ballou*, p. 293.
4. *Trumpet*, XXV, 41.
5. Hosea Ballou quoted by Whittemore, *Life of Ballou*, IV, 257.
6. H. Ballou, *Voice to Universalists*, pp. 250-51.
7. The story of this last visit to Richmond, recounted by the Reverend Joshua Britton, Jr., is found in the *Trumpet*, XXV, 41.
8. Whittemore, *Life of Ballou*, IV, 239.
9. *Ibid.*, p. 264n.
10. *Trumpet*, XXIV, 190.
11. Lalone, *op. cit.*, p. 40.
12. Quoted by Whittemore, *Life of Ballou*, IV, 183.
13. *Ibid.*, p. 280.
14. *Ibid.*
15. *Trumpet*, XXV, 6, 22.
16. M. M. Ballou, *Biography of Ballou*, pp. 366-67.
17. *Trumpet*, XXV, 2.
18. *Account of the Celebration of the Seventy-Fifth Anniversary of the Second Society*, p. 30.
19. Whittemore, *Life of Ballou*, IV, 298.
20. 3 P.M., June 9, 1852.
21. *Trumpet*, XXV, 6.
22. Miner, *Discourse at the Funeral of Hosea Ballou*, p. 5.
23. Whittemore, *Life of Ballou*, IV, 304-5.
24. Theodore Parker, "Duties of the Church," delivered at the Melodeon, July 25, 1852, quoted by the *Trumpet*, XXV (July 31, 1852), 30. See also *The Boston Herald* for August 9, 1852.
25. Last Will and Testament of Hosea Ballou.
26. March 1, 1853. Miner, *Choosing Death Rather than Life*.
27. The monument was erected with money collected among Universalists throughout the land. See *Trumpet*, XXV, 6.

CHAPTER XX. EPILOGUE

1. Dialogue quoted from J. G. Adams, *Fifty Notable Years*, pp. 91-92.
2. A good example of this contrast is found in H. Ballou, *Examination of the Doctrine of Future Retribution*, pp. 31-32, where he quotes Channing's sermon *The Evil of Sin*.
3. A. Ballou writing in *The Universalist*, February 4, 1871, quoted by Eddy, *op. cit.*, II, 338.
4. Quoted in *ibid.*, p. 342.
5. J. C. Adams, "The Universalists," *Religious History of New England*, p. 315.

BIBLIOGRAPHY

1. M. M. Ballou, *Biography of Ballou*.
2. Ballou died on June 7, 1852. The publication of his son's biography was advertised in the *Trumpet*, XXV (September 11, 1852), 50.
3. The misunderstanding created by this proposal can be seen in an exchange of letters in *ibid.*, (February 26, 1853), 50.
4. Letter from Hosea Ballou to Thomas Whittemore, November 25, 1829, in Whittemore, *Modern History of Universalism*, p. 433n.
5. M. M. Ballou, *Biography of Ballou*, pp. 352-53.
6. Whittemore, *Life of Ballou*.
7. *Trumpet*, XXV (February 19, 1853), 146.
8. Safford, *op. cit.*,
9. Brooks, "Hosea Ballou," *Universalist Quarterly*, New Series VI (October 1870), 389-420.
10. Chambré, "Hosea Ballou and Edward Turner—A Contribution to the 'Truth of History,'" *ibid.*, New Series X (January 1873), 40-49.
11. In *Pioneers of Religious Liberty in America*.

INDEX TO BIBLICAL REFERENCES

GENERAL INDEX

Adam, T. C., 154

Adams, John Coleman, 170

Aldrich, Artemus, 3, 6

Allen, Ethan, 5; publishes *Reason the Only Oracle of Man*, 22, 194 (n. 1); thought of, 22-27; 28, 30; influence of his thought on Ballou, 54, 194 (n. 6); 57, 67

American Revolution, 5, 10

American Unitarian Association, 141

Andover Seminary, 129

Arianism, 28, 68-69, 134-135. *See also* Trinity

Arlington Street Church, Boston, 141. *See also* Federal Street Church

Arminianism, 28, 148, 170

Arminians, 64, 65

Atonement: Rellyan doctrine of, 18-19; 25, 28, 30, 61-67; nature of, 69-72; 90, 171-172

Babbitt, James, 45, 209 (n. 7)

Baker, Abel, 109

Balch, Jonathan, 37

Balfour, Walter, 129

Ballou, Adin, 129, 170

Ballou, Amey, 2

Ballou, Asahel, 11, 33

Ballou, Benjamin, 2, 11, 16, 33

Ballou, Cassandana (Mrs. Joseph Wing), 40, 152, 166

Ballou, Clementina, 85

Ballou, David, 2, 6, 14, 15, 16, 17, 18

Ballou, Elmina, 47

Ballou, Elmina Ruth, 85

Ballou, Fanny, 34

Ballou, Fiducia, 85

Ballou, Hosea: birth, 4; relationship to father, 4-5; early education, 6-7; love of nature, 7; appearance as youth, 7; talent for leadership, 7; early education in Calvinism, 7-8; theological precocity, 8; doubts concerning Calvinism, 11-12, 13; converted by Baptists, 12; searches Bible for universalism, 13; converted to Universalism, 14; excommunicated by Baptists, 14-15, 193 (n. 29); becomes preacher, 16; attends Quaker school, 16; attends academy, 16-17; early failures at preaching, 17-18; attends General Convention, 18-19; preaches modified Calvinism, 19; impromptu ordination, 20; itinerant preaching, 20-21; influence of thought of Ethan Allen on, 23-26, 194 (n. 6, n. 7); opinion of Deism, 26-27, 90; influence of thought of Charles Chauncy on, 27-28; his determinism, 28-30, 148; influence of thought of F. O. Petitpierre on, 29-30; first preaches unitarianism, 30; settles in Dana, 32; marries Ruth Washburn, 33; family life, 33, 87-88, 114-115, 151-152, 214 (n. 5), 196 (n. 26); controversy with Joel Foster, 34-36; relationship with John Murray, 36-37, 38, 80; views on theological education, 40, 110, 158-159; moves to Vermont, 40; is re-ordained, 44; controversy with Lemuel Haynes, 45-46; publishes *Notes on the Parables*, 48; hymn writing, 50-51, 198 (n. 24); controversy with Hopkinsians, 51-52; publishes *A Treatise on Atonement*, 52; his unitarian views, 67-68; his theory of universal salvation, 72-75; moves to Portsmouth, 77; controversy with Joseph Buckminster, 77-78; controversy with Joseph Walton, 79-80; writes catechisms for children, 81, 157; enlarges *Notes on the Parables*, 81-82; publishes second edition of *A Treatise on Atonement*, 82; controversy with George Forrester, 82; supports War of 1812, 82-85, 203 (n. 59); financial difficulties, 87-88; corresponds with Abner Kneeland on authenticity of Scriptures, 90-91; opposes church establishment,

Brooks, E. G., 161
Brooks, John, 120
Brown, Arthur W., 213-214 (n. 50)
Brown (Baptist Elder), 13-14
Brownson, Orestes A., his account of
  influence of thought of Ethan Al-
  len on Ballon, 194 (n. 6)
Buckminster, Joseph, 77-78, 79, 202
  (n. 16)
Buckminster, Joseph Stevens, 202 (n.
  16)
Bullock, David, 3
Bullock, Mary Ballou (Mrs. David
  Bullock), 2, 3, 4, 6

Callowhill Street Church, Philadelphia, 132
Calvin, John, 102
Calvinism, 3; tenets of, 8, 11-12, 62;
  effect of American Revolution on,
  10; effect of Universalism on, 10-
  11; 26; within Universalist ministry, 30-31; effect of Ballou on, 172
Campbell, Alexander, 43
Celsus, 27
Channing, William Ellery, 102, 141,
  144-145; Ballou's opinion of, 144-
  148; attacks Ballou's theology, 146-
  148; 169
Chapin, Edwin H., 155-156
Chauncy, Charles, 27-28, 30, 34, 35,
  101, 117, 195 (n. 27)
Cheever (Elder of Hartland church),
  41
Christ: penal sufferings of, 8; Rellyan
  doctrine of, 18-19; Ethan Allen's
  view of, 24; subordinate to God,
  24, 37, 68-69; 42, 49; role of, 61;
  in Ballou's thought, 67-69, 134, 201
  (n. 89)
Christianity: effect of Enlightenment
  on, 9; challenged by Deism, 22
Church and state, separation of, 102-
  103, 144-145
Clapp, Theodore, 169
Clarke, Adam, 139
Cobb, Sylvanus, 167
Cole, Alfred S., 213 (n. 5)
Congregationalism: Universalists dissenters from, 41; 44, 141, 142; its
  establishment opposed by Ballou,
  102-103, 144-145

Congregationalists, 9, 45, 51, 77, 78,
  79, 80, 88-89, 142
Constantine, 83

Dana, Massachusetts, 32, 195-196
  (n. 1)
Darling, Seth, 42
Dean, Paul, 94, 96, 111, 120, 122,
  124, 126, 127-128, 129, 209 (n. 7)
Death and glory, 73, 139-140, 146-
  147, 170. See also Restorationist
  Controversy, Ultra-Universalism De
  Benneville, George, 9-10
Deism: its challenge to Christianity,
  22, 26, 90, 170
Deists, 22, 26-27, 90, 154
Democrats, 82-84
Determinism, 28, 29, 35, 57-58, 148,
  170. See also Necessity, Freedom
  of the Will
Devil, 46, 59, 60, 63
Dole, Benjamin, 89
Dunkers, 9

Edwards, Jonathan, 78, 169, 199 (n.
  26)
Election, 8, 10; Rellyan doctrine of,
  18-19; Universalist modification of,
  19; 143. See also Predestination,
  Reprobation
Emerson, Brown, 88-89
Emerson, Ralph Waldo, 32
Emmons, Nathaniel, 169
Enlightenment: effect on Christianity,
  9; 22, 30, 170
Episcopal church, 5
Examination of the Doctrine of Fu-
  ture Retribution, An, 135-140
Everett, L. S., 131
Evil, 29, 56, 147
Federal Street Church, Boston, 141,
  144. See also Arlington Street
  Church
Federalists, 82, 84
Ferris, Walter, 43, 44, 45
Fifth Universalist Society, Boston,
  151
First Universalist Society, Boston, 51,
  94
Flagg, Joshua, 96, 203 (n. 59)
Forrester, George, 82

Sin: origin of, 25, 57-61, 134; use by God, 25-26, 29, 56; 27-28; relation to misery, 28, 91-92; nature of, 54-61; 72, 201 (n. 106), 91-92, 136-139, 146, 172

Skinner, Otis, 162

Society to Propagate the Gospel in Foreign Parts, 5

Soule, H. B., 154-155

Southern Association (of Universalists), 108, 127 128, 153

Stacy, Nathaniel, 29, 39-40, 47

Streeter, Adams, 158

Streeter, Barzillai, 96 122, 127, 128, 210 n55

Streeter, Russell, 105, 130, 209 (n. 7)

Streeter, Sebastian, 17-18, 51, 105, 167, 209 (n. 7)

Streeter, Zebulon, 30, 158

Sutton, Massachusetts, 9

Sweet, Jonathan, 2

Taylor, John, 27

Thayer, Simon, 3, 17

Third Universalist Society, Boston, 110

Thomas, Abel, 132

Thompson, A. R., 166

Thompson, Barnabas, 41

Thoreau, Henry David, 32

Transcendentalism, 159-160

Treatise on Atonement, A: influence of Ethan Allen's *Reason the Only Oracles of Man* seen in, 23, 26; reflects influence of writing of F. O. Petitpierre, 29; 30, 34, 49; first edition published, 52-53; 54-75, 80, 91, 92, 98, 108, 116; revised edition of 1832, 133-135; 171

Trinity, 23; in Scripture and reason, 24; 44, 67-68, 98. See also Arianism, Unitarianism

Trumpet and Universalist Magazine, 129, 130-131

Tufts, Charles, 158

Tufts (College) University, Divinity School, 215 (n. 67); Crane Theological School, 216 (n. 79)

Turner, Edward, 30, 50-51, 76, 77, 80, 86, 87; correspondence with Ballou on future punishment, 91-93; 105, 116, 118, 120, 122 123-124, 125, 126-127, 211 (n. 73), 129, 167, 209 n7

Ultra-Universalism, 146-147, 170. See also Death and glory, Restorationist Controversy

Unitarian Controversy, 141

Unitarian Universalist Association, 141

Unitarianism, 24; preached by Ballou, 30; 67, 68; its rise in New England, 141. See also Arianism, Trinity

Unitarians, 101-102; relationship to Universalists, 141-144; salvation by character, 148; 150, 154, 159, 162, 170, 172

Universal salvation, 9, 72-75

Universalism, 9-10; its rise in America, 10; orthodox opposition to, 10-11, 19, 48; 78, 97, 116, 162, 164, 172-173

Universalist Expositor, The, 131

Universalist General Reform Association. See General Reform Association

Universalist Magazine, The, 118-120, 121-124, 144

Universalists: number of preachers in 1791, 18; relationship to Unitarians, 141-144; increase of, 151; influence of transcendentalism on, 159-160; 170

Universalist Society, Charlestown, 126-127

Universalist Society, Portsmouth, 76-77, 84-85, 86-87

Universalist Society, Salem, 76, 86-88, 94-96, 206 (n. 11, n. 18)

Usher, J. M., 61

Waldron, Isaac, Jr., 84-85

Walker, James, 142

Wallace, Jonathan, 209 (n. 7)

Walnut Hill Evangelical Seminary, 158-159

Walton, Joseph, 79-80

War of 1812, 82-85

Ware, Henry, Jr., 142

Warwick, Massachusetts, 9

Washburn, Ruth. See Ruth Washburn Ballou